COUSTEAU

The Unauthorized Biography
by Axel Madsen

This is the unauthorized biography of the world's most famous living explorer. For four decades he has probed the teeming underwater world he made visible: legions of divers use the aqualung he invented, millions more owe their awareness of the oceans and the sense of nature's beauty and importance to his films and television programs.

Here, for the first time, is the private life of the GREAT JACQUES COUSTEAU.

COUSTEAU
An Unauthorized Biography

AXEL MADSEN

John Curley & Associates, Inc.
South Yarmouth, Ma.

Library of Congress Cataloging-in-Publication Data

Madsen, Axel.
  Cousteau : an unauthorized biography/Axel Madsen.
    p.   cm.
  ISBN 1-55504-430-1 (lg. print)
  ISBN 1-55504-431-X (soft : lg. print)
  1. Cousteau, Jacques Yves.   2. Oceanographers—France—
Biography.
  3. Large type books.   I. Title.
  [GC30.C68M33   1988]
  551.46'0092'4—dc 19
  [B]   87-25275
                                                                    CIP

Published in Large Print by arrangement with Beaufort Books Publishers in the United States and Canada; Along with the Jane Jordan Brown Agency for the U.K. and British Commonwealth territories.

Distributed in the U.K. and Commonwealth by Chivers Press.

Printed in Great Britain

ACKNOWLEDGMENTS

I could not thank all the people who took time to help me prepare this story of the world's most famous living explorer. Let me thank my editor, Susan Suffes, and, in television, Perry Miller Adato, Jacques Leduc, Arnold Orgolini, and Bud Rifkin. In Paris, Toulon, Cagnes-sur-Mer, and Monaco, I owe thanks to Dr. Jean-Pierre Cousteau, Brice Lalonde, Svante and Marie-Louise Loefgren, Dominique Martin, André Portelatine, Lucienne Quevastre, Raymond Vaissière, and Catherine Winter. In London, I am indebted to David Attenborough and Allen Pickhaver; in Los Angeles, to Isabelle Rodoganachi, Pierre Sauvage, and Henri Tusseau. In New York, there are Beth Myers and Susan Schiefelbein; in Washington, Gary Davis, Melvin Payne and the CNN news office; in Manila, William McCabe III; and in Carversville, Gina Smith.

CONTENTS

vii

WHY DR. JOHNSON, THAT IS NOT SO EASY AS YOU THINK, FOR IF YOU WERE TO MAKE LITTLE FISHES TALK, THEY WOULD TALK LIKE WHALES.

—Samuel Goldsmith

INTRODUCTION
TERRA AMATA

Jacques-Yves Cousteau is a man of the coast –
France's other coast, the Côte d'Azur, with its
simmering bays, devotion to gratification,
ancient civilization, and new attempts at
Sunbelt relevance. Cousteau first opened his
goggled eyes to the undersea order in Le
Mourillon Bay in the shadow of the
battleships that for twenty years were his
career. It was in Toulon that he married an
admiral's daughter and saw his two sons born.
He went to war from its naval base and, in
peace, removed live torpedoes from the
ravaged roadstead. It was in suburban Sanary-
sur-Mer that he and his first companions
fashioned masks from inner tubes and
snorkels from garden hoses and went spearfishing to feed an extended family that
included his mother and his imprisoned
brother's children. Fame came two hours'
drive across the red porphyry rocks of the
Esterel Mountains at Cannes. It was in
workaday Antibes across the Baie des Anges

that the *Calypso* was turned into the world's most famous – and most filmed – research vessel. His first underwater habitat was established off Pomegue Island, the first antique treasures lifted from the ocean floor at nearby Grand Congloué. It was off Villefranche and Nice that, to finance real expeditions, he dredged for geological samples, and it was from Monaco's harbor that he sailed on his first open-ended voyage.

In preparing an apartment site on Nice's Rue Carnot, bulldozers stumbled on an ancient habitat. Nice was founded by the Greeks of Marseilles. The Romans added Cimiez and modern-day Niçois named the excavated site Terra Amata, beloved land (in homage to the distant Greek colonizers, the name of the coast's new sci-tech town in the pine woods below Grasse is Sophia-Antipolis). But the bones and artifacts now exhibited under the apartment complex were hundreds of thousands of years older than the Greek and Roman invaders. They belonged to an elephant-hunting people who lived by the azure bay 400,000 years ago.

It is to this beloved coast and fertile foothills of the Alps that Cousteau returns. Here old acquaintances are roused by sonorous phone calls to join yet another adventure or are invited to a festive meal. Cousteau may summon divers, crew members, scientists who have shared both the dangers and thrills of first encounters with strange lifeforms to a restaurant in Juan-les-Pins on the bay overlooking Cannes. Or he may bring Monaco's Prince Rainier or Philippe Tailliez, the first companion of the distant beginnings who now runs a national marine park on the Hyères Islands, an ancient pirates' haven, to a cliffside inn at Eze, all the way up on the Corniche above the Aleppo pines and highrise Monaco. He is naturally at the head of the table, talking, gesticulating, laughing and lifting a glass of Bandol wine from the southern slopes of the Maures mountains, or a glass of Bellet as dry as the knotty uplands of Nice. Up close, Cousteau is surprisingly tall. His nose is beaked like a dolphin's fin, his pale blue eyes behind the spectacles topped by thick semicircles of eyebrows.

Among friends he is a man with a sense of humor, someone who is alternately serious and sardonic. He loves to turn things upside down, to startle, to say exactly the opposite of what people expect. He is a man whose beliefs are very much a part of who he is, a man whose existence is both urgent and detached.

With nervous energy, the world's most famous living exlorer hurtles through a jet-set existence. In his late seventies, he seems at times to be merely hitting his stride. To charm and bully governments, foundations, and corporate entities into getting behind new efforts to safeguard global resources, he whizzes through world capitals sparking off TV series, schemes to help the Third World feed itself, new methods of propelling ships, and, his newest cause – forestalling a superpower nuclear confrontation by exchanging millions of American and Soviet seven- and eight-year-olds who would live for one year in the other country. Children, he says, are members of the human family who have not yet arrived. As adults, we must make sure we pass along the best we've got to the future generations. Better still, it should be our duty to improve life for those who will follow us.

For half a century he has probed the teeming underwater world he virtually discovered. Legions of divers use the aqualung he invented, following his flippers into the sea. Hundreds of millions more owe their knowledge of the oceans and the sense of nature's importance and beauty to his films and television programs.

His ability to inform and to alert, and his media celebrity, allows him to address people over the heads of their governments. His very modern message is that our collective existence has ecological consequences. Most of the time the human factor is harmful; on occasion it is protective of nature. His newest quest is to discover the present and future effects for all life if we ignore our interdependence with what surrounds us.

He has spent the better part of thirty years being what he believes, the rugged individualist who wants to both inspire and shake us up. Celebrity has made him effective, but he thinks of himself as a loner, and in his private moments misses the anonymity of the first heady years. He could be a millionaire, but maintains a lifestyle on the generosity of others. Money holds little fascination. With his wife, Simone, he owns apartments in Paris and Monaco; he is on salary to his nonprofit organization, has a French naval officer's retirement pension, and years ago swapped his aqualung patent for an annuity. If it wasn't for Simone, he has said, he would own nothing and merely keep working and traveling. As it is, he rarely spends more than three days in one place at a time. He has found marriage archaic, a crutch we use to avoid facing our own solitude and decay, but has remained Simone's spouse, if not her exemplary husband, for fifty years. The death in 1979 of their younger son, Philippe, was the tragedy of his life. It brought them closer and their elder son, Jean-Michel, back into their orbit. Simone has been on every voyage of the *Calypso*. She is a self-sufficient woman who has known how to make her own life important.

Possessed by a deep anger with age and its diminished capacities, Jacques Cousteau is a man in a hurry. He is such a public figure surrounded by such a halo that no one will tell him if he is wrong. A banker may tell him of a too large overdraft, but no one in the large polyglot entourage will say no to anything he proposes. Gone are the philosophical joustings with friends and family. He has decided that only the future counts, that the past is without interest. Writing his memoirs holds the terrors of a life coming to an end. He will not set aside the three months it might take even to dictate his life story. He is deliberately booked until 1990, sailing his beloved *Calypso*, helicoptering off to self-imposed assignments, and flying back for his close-ups with new interesting lifeforms.

There is a lot of Jules Verne in Cousteau – the view of the world not yet explored, the boy at heart, inspired, ingenious, quick to laugh – but there is also a practical, nuts-and-bolts side to him, a delight in wrestling with problems and solving them with new technology. And if there are women's men, there also men's men, men who are comfortable among men and with whom men, in turn, are at ease. Cousteau is comfortable in the company of men who thrive on physical effort. Over the years, he has chosen companions who have not found happiness and peace in ordinary existence, men who have often been wounded by life on land and who instead have put their trust in the sea. He is tentacular, reaching out and sucking people and ideas to him.

He hates to analyze himself. People may dissect him, he may examine others, but he has no time for self-analysis. His own idol is the late Bertrand Russell, thinker, mathematician, writer, and, in Cousteau's view, an exemplary man who loved women and life, and had the courage to go to prison for his convictions.

He has himself called JYC – pronounced "zheek" – by intimates and collaborators. The contraction of his name to its initials is a recent affectation, an homage to his late brother, Pierre-Antoine Cousteau. PAC was the much-admired older brother, the one Jacques thought had the brains in the family, the brilliant journalist who by predilection, arrogance, and an obsolete sense of honor chose the losing side in war and was condemned to death. The deep dark secret of

Cousteau's life is the risk he took to invalidate the biblical shrift that no one is his brother's keeper.

Clockwork jet trails, bicontinental commuting, consumer exoticism. The world has never been more accessible; never have so many traveled so much. Yet what do we see, what do we learn? As the romantic specialist in playful natural history, as lead enthusiast of distant horizons, Jacques-Yves Cousteau has impressed upon us the need to cherish our little blue planet, taught us that *Homo technicus* befouls his nest at the risk and peril of all life. His mind tells him the future doesn't look bright. He sees no way of changing people, our leaders, quickly enough to save what must be saved. His heart, however, gives him cause for optimism. Things are not always logical, implacable. A situation will arise that will provoke us, make us understand.

The message was not conceived in stone. It is the result of observed inadvertencies, and of a searching mind. The most remarkable thing about Jacques Cousteau is his evolution, his progression from navy officer to conscience of a fragile planet, from gee-whiz filmmaker to visionary of a global *terra amata*.

JYC is a man in whom are exceptionally joined intelligence and a number of other qualities, a sense of poetry, a sense of humor and a need to exalt and dignify, an abhorrence of what debases society and the planet, psychological as well as physical pollution. He is a man living close to his instincts.

He is a man of the Mediterranean, the first ocean he entered with his man-fish breathing apparatus. He is a man whose work as explorer, inventor, poet, and ringleader of the nascent planetary consciousness has become what the *Odyssey* must have been to successive generations of Greek youths – an awakening to life's multiple promises and to the quickening pulse of discovery.

Cagnes-sur-Mer, Spring 1986

1
SOCIÉTÉ ZIX

Saint-André-de-Cubzac might have the handsomest bridge on the Dordogne and some of the Bordeaux region's savviest wine tradesmen – the family had been wine merchants for generations – but for Daniel Cousteau it wasn't the favored habitat of the men who quickened the pulse of the new century. Daniel's heroes were the men of astounding creations – Edison and his incandescent light bulb, Roentgen and the X-ray tube. His heart was especially with France's men of progress: Gustave Eiffel, who before his tower had built the bridge in Saint-André; Ferdinand de Lesseps and the Suez Canal; the Lumière brothers and their cinematograph; and Louis Blériot, who had just become the first person to cross the Channel in a flying machine. What these men had in common was that they had fled their provinces for the center of gravity of the heady and flamboyant era called La Belle Epoque.

Daniel had felt the irresistible attraction

of Paris, and with way stations in Bordeaux, Rouen, and Marseilles, he, too, made it to the capital. Governments might succeed each other at a dizzy pace and the Boulanger and Dreyfus affairs make tempers flare, but life and opportunities coursed richly along the grand boulevards with their confident architecture, smart shops, celebrated fashions, cosmopolitan denizens, elegant women, and racy nightlife. The Third Republic was politically stable and economically sound. It was optimistic and expansionist, the character traits of Daniel Cousteau himself. Like most middle-class Frenchmen, he had his heart on the left and his pocketbook on the right. He was quick to spring to the defense of Jean Jaurès and his socialists and he was a firm believer in laissez-faire enterprise. Like most of his forty million countrymen, he lived happily with permanent political turmoil, a franc as solid as gold and an unshakable faith in progress.

The handmaiden of progress was commerce, of course, but Saint-André's trade lived on tradition. Lying just north of the Dordogne before it meets the Garonne, the market town had no wine of its own, but it was surrounded by the noble fields and hedgerows where the right soil, the correct amount of sun, the proper amount of rain, the soft angle of slope brought forth the choicest grapes. North and northwest of town were the Blaye and Côtes Bourg hills. A few minutes' drive to the east came Fronsac and Pomerol, the smallest of the fine-wine districts, where Pétrus was grown and the Château d'Yquem produced the world's most expensive wines, and behind Pomerol came St. Emilion, the town itself one of the loveliest medieval burgs in France. To the south there were the Entre Deux Mères whites, and to the west across the river, you saw the Haut Médoc hills and the village of Margaux.

Saint-André was, in essence and significance, far from the excitement of the grand boulevards. In kilometers, it was nearly a day's train ride from Gare d'Austerlitz. As newlyweds, thirty-year-old Daniel and Elizabeth, his eighteen-year-old bride, had boarded the train for Paris, and Daniel, at least, had barely looked back. He was not one of those who made their way to Paris to live as painters or poets, often of tedious preciosity, or colorless folk with mere money. Daniel was a vivacious and outgoing *notaire*, and son of *notaire*, executor of deeds, real estate sales, successions, and marriage contracts, in Third Republic France more lawyer than notary and in a market town of

3,800 a man of substance. He had three brothers, but he alone had gone to law school and the paternal practice would be his if not for his decision to leave the backwater. He wanted to be a fish in a bigger pond.

Elizabeth was different. Also a native of Saint-André-de-Cubzac and one of five sisters, Elizabeth Duranthon was a daughter of Bordeaux's *haute bourgeoisie*. There was some Irish blood in the family and the *z* in her Christian name was not a misspelled Elisabeth but homage to a distant Celtic grandmother. As much as Daniel was a character, Elizabeth was a reserved if not dutiful daughter of provincial rectitude and, when the chips were down, a pillar of strength.

A compact man with a winning smile and prematurely gray temples, Daniel was a director of ephemeral companies, a stock exchange habitué and a man who lighted up at the idea of ferociously complicated financial propositions. He was thirty-one, settled in Paris, and beginning a new career as adviser to an American millionaire in 1906 when Elizabeth had a son. They named him Pierre-Antoine. Elizabeth was soon off to Saint-André-de-Cubzac to show off Pierre – the Antoine was dropped while he was still an infant – to "Aunt Boulaire," "Aunt

4

Yvonnes and Niquette," and the rest of the families.

The American Cousteau worked for as legal adviser, business analyst, factotum, and traveling companion was James Hazen Hyde, the thirty-one-year-old son of the founder of the Equitable Life Assurance Society. Hyde, a passionate Francophile, was first president of Le Cercle Français de l'Université Harvard and organizer of the Alliance Française. In 1905 he had been a director of some forty-eight corporations, including banks, trust companies, and railroads. As vice-president of the Equitable, he had given a ball at Sherry's in New York that he boasted had cost him $200,000. The party had featured a re-creation of the gardens of Versailles and the French actress Réjane emoting in a playlet with the host, dressed in knee breeches, before the guests feasted on ortolans and champagne and danced the night away to several orchestras (there was a full breakfast for those who stayed the course). The extravaganza created suspicion that it had been paid for by Equitable stockholders. In anger, Hyde sold his shares in the huge insurance company at a third of their value to Thomas Fortune Ryan, an Irish immigrant born a penniless orphan who amassed an estate, when he died in 1928, valued at more than J. P. Morgan's. Even with only a third of his former fortune, the much-married Hyde – his first wife was the widowed Countess Louise de Gontaut-Biron, née Martha Leishman – had retained the means of leading an exquisite life in Paris.

When Elizabeth was pregnant again, it was resolved that she should bear the child in Saint-André-de-Cubzac. And indeed, Jacques-Yves Cousteau was born June 11, 1910, in the ancestral home on the right bank of the Dordogne. Soon after, Elizabeth returned with him to Paris. The first baby pictures show him as a cheerful plump infant with a full head of hair and a happy smile. Over the next couple of years, Daniel Cousteau and his family followed the formidable Hyde on his peregrinations through European high society. The earliest memory of the future ocean explorer was of being tossed to sleep on a train.

The guns of August crimped the style of expatriate Americans. As young Frenchmen went off to war in blue hammertail coats and red trousers, and a plunging demand for costly gowns, perfumes, furs, jewels, and splendid motorcars threw many more out of work, Paris began to feel tired, drab, and neglected. Rich Americans contributed to

Edith Wharton's Relief but tended to see the war as a power game and not as a crusade. By the time Woodrow Wilson convinced his country that if the United States did its duty and came into the war the world would somehow be safe for democracy, Hyde and his private secretary had quarreled and Monsieur Cousteau had left his employ.

Peace brought a new generation of Americans to Paris, and Daniel found employment with an athletic middle-aged American bachelor. The Cousteaus spent the new jazz age at sporty resorts and aboard steam yachts. "My parents were moving a lot at a time when it was difficult to move a lot," Jacques Cousteau recalled on his seventy-fifth birthday. He and his brother weren't always along. For them, it was often boarding schools and a yearning to see the world of their parents' travels. In the case of little Jacques – the family never called him Jacques-Yves – it led to an irrepressible curiosity about distant lands and people.

Perhaps as an excuse for not giving their boys a real home, Daniel and Elizabeth were indulgent parents. Pierre was a quick-witted fourteen-year-old strapling with slicked-back hair and Jacques a sickly boy of ten suffering from chronic enteritis and anemia but with an angelical Little Lord Fauntleroy face framed in curly locks when their father's new employer had them all move to New York in 1920.

Eugene Higgins was not only the richest but also the handsomest New Yorker at the turn of the century, a devoted golfer, expert rider, a "good gun," a skillful fisherman, and a yachtsman of no mean seamanship. Sartorially, swooning columnists said, "he is all that can be desired." He owned a townhouse at Fifth Avenue and Thirty-fourth Street, which was the mecca of high society, and a country home in Morristown, New Jersey, but made the headlines with his steam yacht *Varuna,* the most up-to-date vessel of its kind, which went aground on the Madeira islands in 1908. The yacht was a total wreck, but Higgins and a party of his friends from the New York Yacht Club were saved.

Higgins was the only son of a carpet manufacturer whose secret was said to have been in patented laborsaving devices and who left a fortune of $50 million in 1890 dollars. He was engaged to be married a number of times, but to the comfort of society matrons with eligible daughters, all reports proved incorrect until in 1908 his name was linked with that of Emma Calvé, an opera star. The reason for his continued nonmarried state was given as an unhappy youthful love affair. Whatever it was, the same jinx continued to follow him, for he and Miss Calvé were never married.

Not that he was without feminine company. The Cousteau boys were taught to treat Madame Chapelle, his French mistress, with due deference. The sinking franc not only made living in Paris on overvalued dollars possible for American Left Bank literati, it allowed Higgins to acquire a superb townhouse on la Place d'Iéna and to maintain a yacht of imposing dimensions at Deauville for summer cruises. In his sixties, Higgins demanded that his financial adviser match him in tennis, golf, and swimming, which may explain why Cousteau père took up scuba diving when he was in his seventies. Once Higgins blithely entered Daniel in a chess match with a Polish champion.

The athletic Higgins had severe misgivings about doctors' advice to the Cousteaus that their younger son refrain from strenuous physical activity, and during the summer at Deauville, Jacques not only had to exercise, he had to learn to swim.

"I was four or five years old when I became interested in water," he said later. "I loved touching water. Physically.

Sensually. Water fascinated me – first floating ships, then me floating and stones not floating. The touch of water fascinated me all the time."

When the Cousteaus sailed to New York with Higgins and Pierre went to DeWitt HIgh School on the upper West Side, he and Jacques were sent to summer camp at Lake Harvey, Vermont, near the old Scots settlement of Barnet, which in recent times has become noted for a Tibetan Buddhist meditation center. There are pictures of the two brothers in neckties and jackets leaning against a birch tree and one of Jacques in bathing suit grinning toward the camera.

One of the instructors was named Mr. Boetz. Jacques would never quite tell if it was this German teacher who forced him to join the others in daily dives to remove fallen tree limbs from the lake, if the daily branch removal was a personal punishment for mischief, or if young "Jack" himself was the one who suggested the bottom cleaning under a pier so they could dive in every day. "Like all kids, I tried to see how long I could stay underwater," he remembered. "Then at fourteen I tried to go under and breathe through a pipe held above the surface. I found I couldn't, and wondered why." Mr. Boetz would be responsible for the future explorer's aversion to horses. "He forced me to ride horses, and I fell a lot; I still hate horses."

In Manhattan, the brothers learned English, dangled from fire escapes, played stickball in the street, and gained local fame by introducing two-wheeled European roller skates. Pierre was to retain memories of the melting pot at DeWitt, especially the number of Jewish classmates and teachers. There was something comical, he thought, in teachers named Goldbloom and Solomon gravely explaining to boys named Goldberg, Aaron, Rosenbaum, and Oesterreicher that their forebears had given the world liberty in 1776 by revolting against the king of England. It was as absurd, he would write one day, as French classics being taught in colonial schools, and little Senegalese fiercely reciting poems about "our ancestors the Gauls."

Jacques was proud of his big brother. He called him Pedro, thought him the smartest kid in the world, and easily imitated his smart-aleck swagger and too-clever-to-do-homework routines. When the Cousteaus returned to Paris with Higgins and Madame Chapelle in 1922, Pierre begged his father to let him quit school so he could go into business and make money. Daniel was no great disciplinarian, and the boy soon got his way. Later in life, Pierre would say his father should have forced him to continue his studies. "My father," the future journalist wrote with a measure of sarcasm, "was of a deplorable liberalism."

Jacques was no assiduous scholar, no teacher's pet. In fact, he was a bored and listless student. Machines and engineering fascinated him, however. When he was eleven he got hold of the blueprints of a marine crane and built a scale model as tall as himself. Daniel showed the working model to an engineer friend, who after close inspection asked if Cousteau had helped his son. "No, why?" Daniel asked. "The boy has added a movement to this crane which is not on the blueprints, and it is a patentable improvement." Two years later, Jacques built a battery-driven car and discovered the cinema. He secretly saved enough money from his allowance to buy one of the first home movie cameras to be sold in France and, typically, began by taking the Pathé apart to see how it worked. Surviving pieces of home movies show Daniel and Elizabeth at a wharfside – he smiling self-consciously, she holding on to her cloche hat, reaching Higgins's yacht and walking up the gang-plank – and the goateed master of the ship himself, posing with several people.

The France of Pierre's military service, Jacques's schooling, and Higgins's grand style of living was a country where the postwar euphoria was giving way to apprehension and confusion. Politically, France was torn and weakened by waltzing governments succeeding each other in chaotic fashion, none lasting long enough, even if it had the capability, to come to grips with the deep economic difficulties. Since the end of the war, successive governments had shied away from facing the fact that unpopular measures were necessary to restore fiscal sanity. In mid-1926, when billions of short-term treasury loans had come due and the coffers of state were empty, the franc fell to fifty to the dollar and a mob formed outside the Chamber of Deputies, blaming elected offials for the latest crisis. Some of the rioters crossed the Seine to la Place de la Concorde and stoned buses with American tourists, held responsible for plotting the franc's fall. To avoid public panic, the Left caved in to demands for a political truce and a call for a third return of the man it hated most – Raymond Poincaré. "We never see you except in times of trouble," a Communist deputy shouted when Poincaré presented his cabinet to the National Assembly. It was meant as an insult, but contained a large measure of truth.

The climate of 1926 was summed up in this "restoration." Poincaré was a conservative with integrity and an ardent patriot. His government was seen by the Right as a victory for law and order, and after the Poincaré investiture the value of the franc rose. On the far Right, Charles Maurras's Action Française made progress, especially in university and intellectual circles, repeating again and again that the Germans, the Jews, and the Communists were the enemies of France. A splinter group cast nostalgic eyes across the Alps at Benito Mussolini's regime and created a French Fascist party.

At the opposite end of the spectrum, the Communist party, led by an adventurous steelworker, Jacques Doriot, tried to regain looses. Following Lenin's death in 1924, Leon Trotsky had demanded heavy purges in the French party and dispatched hatchet men to Paris to enforce the party line. What Doriot's Communists lacked in numbers they made up for in ingenuity and militancy. In 1926 they drew the surrealists and a great many of the intelligentsia into their ranks.

As much as politics left Daniel indifferent, bored Elizabeth, and was beyond the ken of

Jacques and the other Lycée Stanislas teenagers, it was Pierre's passion. He was a vicarious reader of newspapers and magazines, an argumentative debater, and a young man full of opinions. In the army he felt the clashing currents of the body politic, the yearning for both order and escape, the anti-Semitism and narrow chauvinism, the ardent support on the Left of Joseph Stalin's brave new world in Russia, the envious glances cast across the Alps by the Right toward Benito Mussolini's fascist experiment. Pierre found the army suffused with defeatism, with everybody looking for *la planque*, the easy commission, the cosy assignment. But Pierre was a man of the Left, somebody who argued for fundamental reforms. In no other Western country was the working class so alienated and labor legislation so far behind. Leftists loathed service in the army and agitated for pacifism – why should they die defending such a hostile society again?

Jacques was a movie fan who was fascinated by E. A. Dupont's *Varieties* with its camera swaying from circus rafters to give the sensation of trapeze artists, Léon Perret's opulent *Madame Sans-Gêne* with Gloria Swanson, and any and all the Max Linder, Charlie Chaplin, and Buster Keaton movies.

He was growing into a lanky teenager and, unlike most sixteen-year-old film freaks, he made his own melodramas, shorts filmed with his father's car in suburban streets or at Deauville's waterfront. Like Erich von Sroheim, he put himself in front of the camera, always as the rakish villain. One surviving minifilm shows him, shifty-eyed and with painted-on mustache, take off in a convertible with a pretty lady, only to be pursued by the hero in another car. When the dark-suited villain stops to try and embrace the heroine, the good guy pulls up, drags him out from behind the wheel and over the rumble seat until he lands on the street, and the hero and the lady drive into an iris-out sunset. In another clip, the director-actor plays a swarthy pimp lecherously rolling his eyes at the ingenue; in yet another he begs forgiveness from a heroine but is scornfully pushed back until he splashes, fully clothed, into the harbor.

He couldn't wait to be a grown-up and be taken seriously. He called his production company Société Zix, and never forgot to write out and film end credits: producer, director, and chief cameraman, J. Cousteau. He bought moveable type and printed his first book, *Une adventure au Mexique*, but preferred telling stories with the Pathé, even to make his diaries and logbooks in pictures. Documentary filmmaking intrigued him. He was especially impressed by *Symphonie du monde*, a German montage film on the religions of the world. In school, he remained lazy and a showoff. To punish him for low grades, his parents confiscated his most treasured possession, the Pathé camera, but there was worse to come.

There were to be several versions of why seventeen windows in the *lycée* stairwell were smashed. JYC was either trying to prove that a strongly thrown stone makes only a small hole in glass, or he merely repeated the screen experiment of cowboys shooting small round holes in saloon windows. "I was a misfit," he said later, "like a lot of the men I later mustered for my expeditions."

He was shipped to a rigorous boarding institution in Alsace. The change was instantaneous. Under challenge and discipline, he suddenly began to apply himself to schoolwork, often studying far into the night.

Pedro had gone to America, invited by three Fitzgerald brothers he had met at DeWitt and just escorted through a French summer vacation. He was working at 36 Broadway and writing flippant letters to his kid brother in the Alsation boarding school about his bosses at Crédit Alliance

17

Corporation and what you could do with $25 a week.

Jacques graduated in 1929. He could imagine himself becoming only one of three things – a naval officer so he could see the world, a radiologist, or a film director.

2
WILLPOWER

Navy pilots trained on old single-engine CAMS 37's seaplanes. Midshipman Cousteau had already soloed and taken his camera aloft to film simulated dogfights. There were rumors they'd soon graduate to trimotor Breguet 521's, which were supposed to be a match for the new Caproni Ca-114's Mussolini was using in his campaign in Abyssinia, or Ethiopia, as Emperor Haile Selassie called his country. The Italians had some sharp planes. Jacques and his classmates were taught to identify the newest: the Breda 65's,the Savoia Marchetti SM's, the Fiat BR 120's.

Cousteau had decided to go in for aviation after his return from a world tour. Three years after Charles Lindbergh flew the

Atlantic, French aviators made their mark. Jean Mermoz had linked France with South America by way of West Africa, and there were now regular crossings of the South Atlantic with Latécoère flying boats. Antoine de Saint-Exupéry flew pioneering night flights over the Andes and wrote books about the hidden treasures of experiences under the stars.

Cousteau had entered the Naval Academy at Brest, on the Britanny coast, in 1930 and, as he had hoped, got to see faraway places. Graduating second in his class, he circled the world aboard the training ship *Jeanne d'Arc* in 1932-33. He brought along the trusted Pathé and made a newsreel of the voyage. The footage included a shipboard visit by the Sultan of Oman and, in French Indo-china, a procession in the streets of Hanoi. The feminine charms in exotic ports of call were captured, from the delicate grace of Cambodian dancers at Angkor Wat to Balinese women carrying ornate headgear, to the subtle geishas of Japan. In the South Seas, he leaned on the *Jeanne d'Arc* railing and watched pearl divers, wearing nothing but loincloths and awkward-looking goggles, dive for oysters.

Across the Pacific, the young sailors made landfall in Los Angeles, toured Hollywood studios, and met Claudette Colbert. At a visit to Mary Pickford and Douglas Fairbanks's fabled Bel Air home, JYC had a fellow officer do the cranking so he could have himself filmed accepting a cigarette and light from Fairbanks himself.

As a young gunnery officer, Jacques had been posted to Shanghai and participated in a mapmaking survey along the Indochina coast. In Port Dayot, local fishermen guided a navy launch. At noon, when the tropical waters are dead calm and the heat stifling, one of the Vietnamese fishermen slipped naked into the water. Without goggles or gear, the man disappeared without a ripple. He surfaced a minute later holding wriggling fish in both hands. With a mischievous grin, he explained that at this time of day the fish took naps.

When the tour of duty ended, Cousteau got permission to travel home on his own, and made it the long way through the Soviet Union, with a side trip by car through the Hindu Kush mountains of Afghanistan. His camera captured Afghans dancing and lingered on the frail beauty of a dancing girl. He learned a little Russian aboard the Trans-Siberian Express, as he filmed everything he found interesting. Russia was only a short year away from Joseph Stalin's purges and

Soviet authorities confiscated most of the eager young cameraman's film. It was when he reported back to active duty that he applied to enroll in the naval aviation school.

Pedro had returned also. After a translation job of an American dime-store novel, he had gravitated toward his natural element, journalism. His sharp tongue, wounding sarcasm, and cynical humor, which his kid brother always found glib and smart, made him an ideal talent for the overpoliticized Parisian press of the mid-1930's. Shortening his full name to its initials, PAC started as a general reporter on the daily *Le Journal,* an experience he later said taught him all about the silliness of democracy. He soon drifted toward advocacy journalism, writing sharp little columns on current events. His low regard for democracy and his insidious anti-Semitism contracted, he stated, in New York and in the army, made him shift to the political right.

Rancorous and intolerant, French conservatives generally resented the antics in parliament and demanded a forceful leadership. The Right had at its disposal a vigorous, if overheated press. Its voices ranged from *L'Action Française,* the organ of diehard royalists who were roused daily by inflammatory articles by Charles

Maurras, the poet who railed against Germans, Jews, and romanticism as the enemies of France, and by Léon Daudet, who wrote with the most vituperative pen in Paris, to the weekles *Candide* and *Gringoire,* which inveighed against democracy, the "corruption" of the parliamentary system, and the British. Fascist Italy was the two magazines' idol, and both journals were the favorite reading material of a large number of army and navy officers. Also popular with military brass was the weekly *Je Suis Partout* (literally, "I Am Everywhere"), founded in 1930 and bankrolled by the wealthy perfumer René Coty and publisher Arthème Fayard. Like the rest of the ultra-right press, *Je Suis Partout* was obsessed by decadence and driven toward authoritarian solutions. It was edited by Pierre Gaxotte, an erudite and adroit historian turned polemicist who once a week gave dinners at his favorite restaurant for young journalists. It was Gaxotte who spotted PAC's talent, invited him to one of his dinners, and told him he absolutely must write something for *Je Suis Partout.* His first contribution was a piece on the Scottsboro case, seen in Europe as dramatic evidence of the oppression of American blacks.

On the theory that one way for a debutant

journalist to be noticed is to interview a famous journalist, Pierre had seen the celebrated Tatiana. He didn't quite have enough for a splashy piece and made an appointment with Tatiana's secretary to get the details that made the difference. Fernande Semaille was a petite Parisienne with a caustic wit not unlike PAC's own – her friends called her Paprika. The attraction was mutual; it was love at first sight. When Jacques was introduced he thought his brother's girl was the cleverest female he had ever met.

The only inconvenience was that she was married. Her husband was Maurice Toesca, a novelist of PAC's age, who wrote about happiness based on amorous harmony. At least the Toescas had no children. Pierre and Fernande became inseparable. Her divorce was quickly followed by their marriage.

The generals that *Je Suis Partout* openly courted included Jacques's supreme commander. Admiral Jean Darlan, Chief of Naval Staff, was a magnetic figure from his chiseled handsome face and flattish bald head to his impeccable polished shoes, a man with the eye of an amused gambler and an able, ruthless personality. No great lover of France's World War I ally, Great Britain, Darlan wasn't sure that in a rematch of the

Great War France would come out any worse if she sided with Nazi Germany. This sentiment did not prevent him from having developed a close personal relationship with Lord Chatfield, the chief of the British Admiralty.

Rightists considered Darlan too loyal to republican ideals and instead put their hopes in Marshal Henri Philippe Pétain. It was known in upper military circles that the hero of Verdun, a man in his seventies, was losing faith in the democratic process. As *La Victoire* asked in bold type on page one, January 10, 1934, "How can we get rid of this weak and rotten regime? Who is the leader who will emerge in France, as he emerged in Italy and Germany?" The intellectual revolt of the Right was spreading to large sections of the officer corps.

Pierre became a father that year when Fernande gave birth to a girl. They named her Françoise and moved into a lovely huge apartment at 48 Avenue de la Motte-Picquet at the Champs de Mars and the Eiffel Tower. The apartment was really his parents'. Elizabeth enjoyed being a grandmother, but Daniel was usually off with Higgins. Now in his late seventies, Higgins maintained a yacht of battleship proportions in Deauville and, with his ever-faithful

Madame Chapelle, sailed in season. He loved to cross the Channel and sail along the English coast to Torquay, the holiday resort in Devonshire which surpassed Deauville in the beauty of its bay setting and its mild, almost Mediterranean weather.

Paprika shared her husband's passion for politics. She helped him any way she could and as a couple they mingled freely with the heavyweight intellectuals of the far Right. The stentorian voices of the Left, André Malraux, Ernest Hemingway, and the International Brigades might be fighting for the Spanish Republic – Malraux cut a fashionable figure in Madrid as chief of his own air squadron – *Je Suis Partout* covered the civil war from the fascist side. THe correspondent with General Franco's armies was Robert Brasillach, a gifted novelist, commentator, and critic three years younger than PAC and a pallid, owlish caricature of the bookish egghead. With his brother-in-law Maurice Bardèche, he was writing a quick volume on the heroism of Franco's forces. PAC, Brasillach, and Fernand de Brinon, a former newspaper editor and expert on Franco-German relations, attended the Nazi party meetings in Nuremberg in 1937 and 1938. Brasillach was especially overwhelmed by the hypnotic mass rallies and longed for a totalitarian regime in France. Lucien Rebatet was another writer seduced by muscular and racist solutions. Perhaps the most talented among them, he had written for *Je Suis Partout* since its inception and with his wife, Véronique, was a frequent dinner guest of Pierre and Paprika.

Hothouse politics was not the passion Jacques and his fellow ensigns lived for at the navy's aviation school at Hourtin, an Atlantic coastal town west of Bordeaux (and twenty minutes' flying time from Saint-André-de-Cubzac). Young career officers competing for their aviators "wings" lived in their own world. Cars, girls, practical jokes, and airplane performances were what they concentrated on. The cinema and tinkering with mechanical devices were what excited Jacques.

A few weeks before graduation, he borrowed his father's Salmson car to go to a friend's wedding in the Vosges mountains. Daniel's S4C had a 1.5 liter twin cam engine, a three-bearing crank, gravity feed, and four speeds. Jacques loved to drive it. Salmson exported a lot of S4Cs to Britain. The English had an affection for small luxury machines.

Jacques was still climbing hairpin curves in the mountains when it got dark. He switched on the headlights and gunned the engine. As he rounded another uphill curve, the headlights suddenly went out. He slammed on the brakes too late. The car flew through the blackness and crashed.

"I will always remember the accident, when I was alone at night, bleeding on a country road, with nobody coming," he said later. "It was two o'clock in the morning, and I thought I was going to die. I was losing my blood. I was in a terrible state with twelve bones broken. Turning to the sky, trying to lie down on my back, which hurt a lot, looking at the sky and the stars, I said, my god how lucky I was to have seen so many things in my life."

When he came to in the hospital, a glance at the attending physician told him it was serious. His left arm was broken in five places; his right arm was paralyzed.

Drifting back from unconsciousness a couple of days later, he was told the right arm was infected and would have to be amputated. Shaking his fevered head, Ensign Cousteau refused. When he was told he would never recover use of both arms, he thought himself lucky again. At least he would be able to move around. Sitting in a wheelchair for the rest of his life would be infinitely worse.

The infection was eventually cured, but the right arm remained lame. A career in aviation was a dream gone into tailspin. He sulked in frustration and refused to see anybody. Pedro, his parents, his aunts from Saint-André-de-Cubzac came anyway. He knew he looked pitiful, hobbling around the yard in his oversized bathrobe, chest and arms in plaster. He had been slim before; he was positively haggard now.

Through sheer willpower and excruciating exercises, he would win. He knew that. The physical therapy was indeed agonizing, and achingly slow. It took eight months to move a single finger, another two months before he could bent two fingers and the wrist.

All he was interested in was his recovery, but the spring and summer of 1936 were eventful. Emperor Selassie fled Ethiopia and the Italians entered Addis Ababa, putting an end to the post-war era of the League of Nations. Naked aggression paid off. Mussolini was so resentful at France for having failed to back his aggression that he denounced French-Italian accords. French conservatives and Catholics, who in the name of "Latin civilization" were ready to condone Il Duce's African land grab, blamed Great

Britain for the fiascos of the League of Nations and for driving Italy into the arms of Adolf Hitler's restless Germany. During the Ethiopian crisis, the French government of Pierre Laval had asked London for definite guarantees that England would come to France's aid if Hitler moved into the demilitarized Rhineland or tried to attack France. The British refused, and on March 7, Hitler had reoccupied the Rhineland. His excuse was the much-delayed French ratification of a French-Soviet pact negotiated by Laval and Stalin.

On April 26, France went to the polls in heavy rain and elected a leftist coalition. The advent of the Popular Front was welcomed by the masses as a thrilling victory promising overdue social and economic reforms. The head of the coalition government was socialist Léon Blum, a man prey to self-doubt and self-criticism, and given to airing his soul-searching in public. Blum and his party had spent their entire lives in the opposition. Now, just turned sixty-four and without cabinet experience, the socialist leader formed a government and the experiment of the Popular Front was launched.

But the great event of the summer of 1936 happened in none of the predictable hot spots, but in Spain. On July 18, a full-scale

29

military rebellion took place. As in France, Spanish general elections had given power to the Popular Front, a coalition of radicals, socialists, and Communists. Its program was more anticlerical and democratic than socialist, but it was enough to provoke monarchists, fascists, the Church, and the armed forces. The rebels, under General Francisco Franco, as well as most observers, expected a quick victory. Instead, the republic rallied the workers of Madrid, beat off the military conspirators – of the armed forces' 200 generals 195 joined the rebellion – and asserted its hold over most of the country.

The Spanish Civil War was instantly the dominating topic of international affairs and, in France and England, the theme of passionate domestic controversy. The great issue of democracy versus fascism seemed to be at stake in the elected Republican government's attempt to fight back the armed forces' coup.

Admiral Darlan, who had only contempt for Blum's socialist "school-teachers," nevertheless agreed with the new Prime Minister that a fascist Spain was not in the interest of France and Britain. Since Darlan was a friend of Lord Chatfield, Blum sent him to London to sound out the British naval chief. Darlan came back empty-handed. The British Admiralty thought Franco was a good Spanish patriot "who would know how to defend himself against the encroachments of Mussolini and Hitler" and Britain was certainly not going to do anything against him and his putsch. Blum felt himself boxed in. His personal desire to help the Spanish Republic was opposed by Britain, his own country was deeply divided, and there was a fear of a larger war. While Blum announced an embargo on arms shipments to Spain and the German embassy in London assured the British government that "no war material had been sent from Germany and none will," the American consul in Seville was watching the arrival of pilots and Savoia bombers from Italy and Junkers and antiaircraft guns from Germany for Franco's forces.

Jacques Cousteau had not been able to present himself for the pilot's exams. His right arm remained slightly twisted, but the accident, as it was, probably saved his life. With one exception, all his classmates at the aviation school were killed in the opening weeks of the war that was only three short years away.

When Jacques returned to active duty – and more therapy – he was assigned to

Toulon. France's second naval port lies behind its anchorage, one of the safest and most beautiful harbors of the Mediterranean, surrounded by tall hills crowned by forts. Suburbs lie along the shore and form terraces on the slopes of the surrounding hills, to the west toward Sanary-sur-Mer where Cousteau was to build a villa, and to the east above Le Mourillon Bay and its beaches. In Roman times Toulon was celebrated for the manufacture of the imperial purple. The dye was obtained from the color glands of the pointed conches that abound the coast by steeping them in salt and boiling them for ten days in leaden vats. The sumptuous color was used to dye silk and wool and, in classical Rome, it was reserved for emperors. During the seventeenth and eighteenth centuries, tourists with a taste for spicier folklore visited the galley ships in the Old Port. Each ship had twenty-six oars per side, each manned by four men, each with one foot bound on the deck and one wrist chained to the oar. Slaves were allowed to go ashore when chained together in pairs. Players of musical instruments were much in demand at Toulon Weddings. Young Napoleon nearly razed the city in anger in 1793 when royalists handed over the port to a British-Spanish fleet.

The French fleet in the Mediterranean was considerable. Toulon was home port to more than sixty warships, and in the North African colonies France had battleships in Mers-el-Kébir in Algeria and smaller units in Bizerte, Tunisia. Yet it was only toward the end of 1936, when Hitler and Mussolini signed an agreement on Austria, that efforts were begun to modernize the armed forces. The nation that during the Great War had best understood the importance of aviation as an instrument of war and that had been one of the strongest in air power, finally formed an Armée de l'Air and nationalized 70 percent of the aeronautical industry.

Jacques Cousteau was assigned to navy artillery, ammunitions, and gunnery equipment, and almost immediately met a lieutenant a little older than himself named Philippe Tailliez. Very much a navy officer in bearing and manner, Tailliez stuttered and therefore spoke very slowly. He loved the beach, whether at Sanary or Le Mourillon, and once he had heard Cousteau's story of the accident, suggested Jacques take up swimming as a means of strengthening his arm.

On the beach, Cousteau met a civilian who was in many ways the opposite of Tailliez, an easygoing bohemian with an affection for children, animals, and making toys. Frédéric Dumas was something of an artist, living without any visible means of support, mostly on the beach and on a tiny boat he possessed. He was a champion spear fisherman who soon showed the two navy types how to catch groupers and how to grill them over a campfire of seaweed and driftwood.

Posterity would fail to ascertain who of the three new friends first brought goggles to the beach that summer. While Cousteau taught artillery to enlisted men aboard the battle ship *Condorcet,* one of his students told him about an uncle of his who went diving with Tahitian goggles off Cannes and with bow and arrow fished groupers, dorados, and leerfish. Tailliez and Dumas knew Guy Gilpatric, an American writer living in Cap d'Antibes who for years had practiced underwater hunting with a harpoon and aviator goggles. Cousteau got to know the author and would one day quote his stories about octopuses. An octopus brought to shore would cross a fire to get back into the sea, Gilpatric maintained. Dumas confirmed this when he dived with an underwater rocket one day and waved it in front of an octopus. He stopped when he saw signs that the animal had been burned. Gilpatric also told of bringing an octopus home and putting

34

it in an aquarium covered with a heavy lid. A short time later, the aquarium was empty and Gilpatric found the octopus going through his library, book by book, turnng the pages with its arms.

To be able to really *see* underwater, whether with South Sea pearl divers' spectacles or aviator's goggles, left an indelible impression on the twenty-six-year-old Cousteau. "Sometimes we are lucky enough to know that our lives have been changed," he observed later in life. "It happened to me that summer's day when my eyes opened to the world beneath the surface of the sea."

Soon, the three friends began experimenting with diving. To see more, dive deeper, stay longer, and above all, have fun, they fashioned masks from inner tubes and snorkels from garden hoses. They talked of nothing but exploring the magical new world. Cousteau the tinkerer was determined to find a way of diving that would give them complete freedom. He began a series of trial and error experiments with mechanical breathing devices, including oxygen tanks with which he nearly killed himself twice. Together with Tailliez and Dumas, he went to see the navy's pioneer in the field, Yves de Corlieu, the future inventor of divers' flippers, and was told of the fatal flaw of oxygen; below 10 meters it becomes toxic.

The problem had badgered divers as far back as 5000 B.C., when the Sumerians spun the tale of a swimmer who sought the weed of eternal life beneath the waves. Vegetius, a Latin writer of the fourth century, has a drawing representing a diver wearing a tight-fitted helmet to which is attached a leather pipe leading to the surface where its open end is kept afloat by means of a bladder. Medieval woodcuts show submerged men sucking on bags full of air or puffing on tubes reaching the surface. Cousteau plunged into studies of John Scott Haldane, the British scientist who had just died after a lifetime devoted to elucidating the exchange of gases during respiration. He also tried out an oxygen lung developed by the British in 1878.

He was determined to take his Beaulieu camera snorkeling with him, and fashioned a waterproof housing complete with clothes-pin lever to change the focus. The black-and-white negative was made of still photo rolls spliced together. Shooting time was limited to 30 seconds, after which he had to surface to rewind the camera. The first subject; Dumas the spear fisherman.

Man has fished since the dawn of time and over the millennia has developed a mixture of healthy respect and dread for life in the deep. Dolphins and porpoises have a mythical affinity with humans and, the Greeks believed, would save a drowning man. Octopuses were monsters sometimes reaching up to seize a man or an entire ship, whales were terrors of biblical proportions.

"At the very beginning, we sometimes felt a sense of revulsion when we touched the sticky surface of a rock covered with an unfamiliar form of animal life," Cousteau remembered. Over the years, he and his divers would be bitten, stung, and burned by all kinds of marine life, but their encounters – and the filmed and written reports they brought back – were not confirmations of devil fish and man-eating monsters. The lifeforms they met they endowed with intelligence, and their descriptions were often of species easy to tame. Certainly there would be a tendency to "Disneyize" the deep, especially in the big television specials of the 1970's – to show divers petting and cuddling strange-looking lifeforms, inspecting the gaping maws of killer whales or being towed by turtles – but there was never to be any transference to the undersea world of atavistic hunting instincts, no exaltation of the spear gun or other deadly paraphernalia.

Gentle curiosity is not obvious in men choosing careers in a country's armed forces, but this gift was united in Cousteau, Tailliez, and to a lesser degree, Dumas. When Dumas was ten he found octopuses off Port Issol and brought them back to the beach to show them to the young daughter of friends of his parents. The girl let the octopuses crawl up and down her arm. The display became the intense focus of attention, especially by the girl's horrified parents. But when Dumas – "Didi" to his friends – got to dive and met his first sizable octopus, he didn't spear it but was struck by its yellow eyes with their black pupils. He thought he saw a spark directed at him, an expression of interest. He held the octopus in his hand for a moment, then let it go and followed it. When it got tired of fleeing, of squirting ink at him and pretending it wasn't there at all by sitting on the ocean floor and taking on the color of the sand, it let itself be stroked. Slowly, its rhythms became peaceful until Dumas played with it as with a cat.

The idea that little-known animals are worth understanding, that they have *some* inherent value and therefore may not be treated any way we please is not what one might expect from a pair of navy officers and a beach bum. What was remarkable in those first primitive dives in Le Mourillon Bay was that Cousteau, Tailliez, and Dumas didn't follow man's ancestral instinct of killing first and asking questions later. The consequences for the future of ocean exploration were to be momentous.

3
LOVE AND WAR

He met her at a party in Paris that year, a slim tawny-haired girl with big green eyes and a large mouth that easily creased into a captivating, almost sad, demure smile. Friends introduced them and suddenly they were talking about boats. He had his camera with him that evening and got a snippet of her, sitting with friends and turning toward the camera buff calling out her name.

She was Simone Melchior. She was seventeen, still a *lycée* student, but she had matured out of the hectic flush of adolescence into a reserved, very young woman. She came from three generations of admirals. Her only regret, she said gravely,

39

was not having been born a boy so she could go to sea herself.

The courtship was assiduous, carried out long-distance and lasting one year. Until she finished school, Jacques spent every furlough commuting from Toulon to his parents' and Pedro and Fernande's apartment on Avenue de la Motte-Picquet to see her. When it came to career enhancement, he could hardly have done better. The Melchiors belonged to the *haute bourgeoisie*. Her father was a former naval officer, now an executive with Air Liquide, France's principal producer of industrial gases with plants around the world. In fact, Simone had spent part of her childhood in Japan when her father was stationed there. For her, he was a natural selection. Sure of her character and of her person, she knew she would marry a naval officer. He was outgoing, eager, passably irreverent and given to bursts of laughter. And how he could talk about boats. His navy career, as the Melchiors made a point of finding out, looked promising. His background was entirely acceptable and his brother was a journalist whose byline was beginning to be recognized.

The July 12, 1937, wedding came three weeks after the fall of the Popular Front and two months before France and Great

Britain permitted Germany to dismember Czechoslovakia. A friend caught bride and groom with the Cousteau camera, she a wisp of white organdy, he in gala uniform, advancing under the unsheathed swords of his fellow officers.

The newlyweds began looking for a modest house at Sanary, ten kilometers from the Toulon base where officers, from Admiral Darlan down the pecking order, lived. Jacques and Simone were so pleased with each other and with life, Dumas would remember, that their pride and fervor were almost tangible. Simone joined the boys goggle-diving. Jacques filmed her fishing underwater with spears, arbalests, and spring guns.

Pierre and Fernande came visiting with little Françoise. The two sisters-in-law liked each other and found out they were both pregnant. The husbands talked politics and engineering, Pierre explaining that Léon Blum's successor, Edouard Daladier, might have led his Radical-Socialists into the Popular Front coalition in 1936, but he was now moving to the right as fast as he could. Nobody was in the mood to go to war to prevent the Sudeten Germans from becoming Germans again. The French and Czech armies might outnumber Hitler's forces two to one, but even the Left backed a hands-off policy. They saw the CFT, the Confederation of Labor, issue a manifesto against "an imperialist war" in support of "a country arbitrarily created" less than eighteen years ago out of defeated Germany and Austria. Jacques wondered if Pedro knew that a diver's air supply must have a pressure equal to the depth he's at, that Haldane had discovered you need 1.5 cubic feet of air per minute to keep carbon dioxide at a safe level.

As Hitler invaded a cheering Austria and made it part of *Gross Deutschland*, Jean-Michel was born in Toulon. Six months later while Pierre was in Munich covering the meeting of Hitler and Neville Chamberlain, Fernande gave birth to a boy they named Jean-Pierre. Baby Jean-Michel got photographed with his father's navy cap and with his mother holding him tight. When he could sit up on the floor, Papa Jacques filmed him playing with his alphabet blocks.

Off duty, Jacques continued to dive with Dumas and Tailliez. Rain or shine, winter or summer, the three friends were to be found wading into the water at Le Mourillon Bay or below the Sanary cliffs. Jacques learned to perform the expert's surface dive, descending 15 to 20 meters in a few seconds. What frustrated him were the limitations imposed by a single lungful of air.

They built two homemade tanks filled with oxygen and tried them out. "But the more we studied our problem, the more convinced we became that a better answer lay in the use of compressed air," Jacques recalled. "We knew there would be no particular difficulty in getting compressed air cylinders to take below and in devising tubes to conduct the air to the diver's mouth. The task that confronted us, however, was to get a regulator valve which would automatically feed the compressed air to the mouthpiece in the ratio to the diver's depth." He talked to his father-in-law. Air Liquide made oxygen, nitrogen, carbon dioxide, fuel gases such as acetylene, and high purity gases such as krypton and xenon. Since humans breathe both in and out, the difficulty was finding a way of *not* exhaling the spent air back into the oxygen. Melchior said he would ask around about some kind of valve that would allow inhaling and exhaling through the same mouthpiece.

The gathering clouds of 1939 – the fall of Barcelona to Franco's troops in January, Italy's invasion of Albania, and Hitler's renunciation of a nonaggression agreement with Poland – became ominous by summer. The volte-face nonaggression pact that Hitler and Stalin suddenly signed in August had Foreign Minister Georges Bonnet summon General Maurice Gamelin and Admiral Darlan to the Elysée. Without the assurance of Russian help, a war against Germany to sustain Poland was an enterprise full of unknowns and perils, he believed. What he needed to know was whether the armed forces were ready. With a lot of qualifications, Gamelin and Darlan told him they were.

There was a possibility that Lieutenant Cousteau would be posted to the French embassy in Lisbon as a junior naval attaché. Before the assignment could become a reality, however, war broke out.

The war that France and England reluctantly declared on Germany September 3 quickly settled into the *drôle de guerre*, which the British called the phony war. In eighteen days Hitler's brand-new armor overran Poland and in the fall – the loveliest autumn Paris had known in decades – the Fuehrer was making peace overtures. France had eighty-five divisions facing an enemy with little more than a covering force, but did little in the West to keep its commitment to

Warsaw. Britain did no more. Its small contingent of two divisions didn't reach the "front" until the end of September. After a perfunctory "Saar offensive" by nine French divisions, all was quiet on the Western front. By loudspeakers and large signs the Germans chided the front-line French about the absurdity of "dying for Danzig" and blamed the English for the whole thing. "Don't shoot. We won't if you don't." Often French troops would hoist a crude sign of their own signifying their agreement. Sometimes Wehrmacht troops across the Rhine would cheer soccer games played by Frenchmen on their riverbank.

In Paris, not only *Je Suis Partout* partisans but a majority of public opinion felt there was no need for sacrifice. So long as the Germans didn't attack, why indeed shed French blood for Danzig? At night Paris was blacked out as protection against air attack. Gas masks were distributed, but the air raids never came, and life returned to near-normal. The theaters, music halls, operas, and movie houses that had closed during the first days of the war reopened. At the Casino de Paris, Maurice Chevalier and Josephine Baker played to packed houses.

The Cousteaus regrouped. Jacques was made a gunnery officer aboard the cruiser

Dupleix, Pierre was called up. There was one missing person. Daniel had been caught with Higgins in Torquay. Joseph P. Kennedy, President Franklin D. Roosevelt's ambassador to the Court of St. James, had suggested strongly that Higgins not sail, that the Royal Navy might intercept the yacht if Higgins tried to leave British waters. Communications between Britain and the continent were difficult, but it was understood Higgins and Daniel were at the Imperial Hotel in Torquay.

If the army under Gamelin was an ossified command structure of old men, the navy under Darlan was also riding at anchor. Gunnery officer Cousteau's *Dupleix,* commanded by a Captain Hameury, was one of four medium-tonnage cruisers in Toulon. With them were three full battleships, the *Strasbourg, Provence* and *Dunkerque,* plus fifty smaller warships. The navy also had units in Bizerte, Tunisia; Mers-el-Kébir, Algeria; and an Allied task force was stationed in Alexandria, in British Egypt. But the Germans were not in the Mediterranean and Hitler's ally Benito Mussolini prudently stayed out of the war. There were drills and more drills aboard the *Dupleix,* but the boilers weren't fired up. Rotation shore leaves were quietly organized. Jacques was home with Simone and little Jean-Michel at Christmastime. In February 1940 the country offered itself the luxury of a government crisis. Three hundred representatives abstained when Daladier asked for a vote of confidence on the way he conducted the war. His unexpected loss of a majority brought Paul Reynaud, Daladier's energetic finance minister to power. Reynaud agreed with his friend Colonel Charles de Gaulle that the war should be prosecuted more vigorously, and he had established close contacts with Britain's Admiralty chief Winston Churchill, whose ideas he shared and whose energies and imagination he admired. Reynaud, who lived with the slightly mad, excitable, and meddlesome Hélène de Portes, was thought to be too "Anglophile" by many. Now, he had his chance to fight the war with vigor and imagination. In Toulon, shore leaves were shortened. Simone was pregnant.

Suddenly in April the lull was over. After Hitler's surprise attack and occupation of Denmark and Norway, the Luftwaffe struck airfields in northern France. German armor crossed the borders of Holland and Belgium. In two days seven German panzer divisions pierced the "impenetrable" Ardennes and began rolling toward the Meuse and Sedan rivers. By May 16, the Allies had suffered their first disaster, causing panic in the high command and consternation in Paris. Three weeks later, General Erwin Rommel's armor swept across northern France to the Channel. The Luftwaffe hammered the ragged remnants of Allied armies standing at Dunkirk. In London, Chamberlain resigned and Churchill, promising "nothing but blood, toil, tears and sweat," became Prime Minister. Desperately, more than 300,000 men were ferried across to England from the beaches of Dunkirk.

The outskirts of Paris were bombed on June 4. Six days later the Reynaud government abandoned Paris and in a convoy of ministerial limousines fled south to Tours on the Loire River. On the 10th, Italy declared war. The next night, Italian bombers, responding to a Royal Air Force strike on Turin, carried out a series of raids on Toulon, two Riviera towns, and across the Mediterranean, on Bizerte, Tunisia. The damage to the Toulon arsenal was minimal. At the first opportunity, Cousteau phoned home. No one had been hurt in Sanary, Simone told him.

On the 12th, Churchill and members of his high command flew to Tours. Hastily, he was put up at the Château de Muguet, as

48

less than 160 kilometers to the north, the first German forces crossed the Seine below Paris and pressed forward along the Marne River. Going into a strategy session that night, Reynaud was gloomy, Churchill cheerful. The situation was desperate, Churchill was told, but he imagined Parisians fighting, block by block, house by house, a burning city collapsing on a garrison that refused to accept defeat. Coldly, a French general told him reducing Paris to ashes would in no way affect the final outcome. Churchill suggested that if coordinated warfare became impossible, the French could carry on in guerrilla fashion until the Americans came into the war. This time the eighty-four-year-old Marshal Pétain objected that by the time the United States made up its mind, guerrilla warfare would have reduced the entire country to ashes. Churchill replied that the alternative was no less appalling. Over coffee and cognac, Pétain told Churchill what he was too ashamed to tell Reynaud – France would have to seek an armistice with Nazi Germany.

The next morning, Churchill took Admiral Darlan aside. "Darlan," he said, "I hope you will never surrender the fleet." Darlan replied, "We shall never hand [it] over to Germany or Italy. Orders to

49

scuttle will be given in the event of danger."

As Churchill flew back to England and the French army defending Paris was ordered to fall back toward the Loire, Cousteau went to war.

With Captain Hameury on the bridge and Lieutenant Cousteau with his men at his battle station, the *Dupleix* slid out of Toulon during the evening of the 13th and turned east toward Salins to await further orders. In the morning Toulon had been hit by the Italian air force, and to prevent a sitting duck situation should there be renewed attacks, the fleet moved out. The radio crackled with coded messages. A counterattack on Genoa, Italy's biggest seaport 200 kilometers east of Cannes, would be attempted.

The weather was propitious for a stealth attack. The moon disappeared behind clouds as they steamed east and were split into two strike forces. The first group would shell the fuel depots at Vado; the second the Ansaldo and other industrial complexes at Sestri on the western outskirts of the city. *Dupleix*'s mission: shelling the coastal batteries of Erzelli and Pegli Sestri and the Stopponi Works.

The armada arrived off Genoa shortly

before dawn on the 14th. As part of group 2, *Dupleix* raised her guns toward the coastline, 15 kilometers away and, at 0428 hours, fired her first shot at the western suburb of Sestri Penente. The shore batteries in turn opened fire on the assailants.

The heavy naval and air strike lasted nearly two hours. *Dupleix* mistook the empty Lerona Valley for the industrial Polcevera Valley, but scored direct hits at the Stopponi Works. A small destroyer hit the Ansaldo-Fossati Company bull's-eye, destroying offices, a boiler room, and railway cars. Total casualties, postwar records revealed, were four dead and thirty-four wounded. The Erzelli coastal batteries hit the light cruiser *Albatros,* damaging the vessel but causing no casualties.

At 0610 hours, the fleet pulled back and began evasive zigzagging back toward Toulon. At the same time, the German Eighteenth Army entered Paris and marched down the Champs Elysées. By evening, the Reynaud government fled south to Bordeaux. At the Hôtel Splendide, General de Gaulle ate a hasty meal with his aide. Marshal Pétain sat a few tables away. De Gaulle walked silently over to pay his respect to his supreme commander. Pétain shook hands without uttering a word. A few

51

moments later, de Gaulle got into his car and headed for Rennes, on his way to London. In a famous radio appeal four days later, he denounced Pétain for suing for peace and vowed to fight on.

The *Dupleix* and the rest of the Mediterranean flotilla sailing back to Toulon received an ominous radio message from Darlan: Fight on until a true French government, independent of the enemy, gives orders to the contrary. Disobey any other government and never surrender your ship.

Senators and representatives in chaotic Bordeaux were split in two camps – one in favor of the government leaving for North Africa, the other advocating its remaining in France. Marshal Pétain said he would never leave France and while the *Dupleix* reached Toulon and German armies hurtled south toward Marseilles and the Italians attacked from the east, negotiations for a French surrender began in Compiègne in the railway car where the Allies had dictated their armistice terms to the Germans in 1918. Article 8 of the German terms stipulated that the French fleet would be demobilized, disarmed, and laid up under the control of Germany or Italy.

When the British ambassador in Bordeaux

got wind of the terms and forwarded an unauthorized copy to London, Churchill advised him to tell Darlan that if the French fleet could not be surrendered to Britain or the United States, it should be scuttled. During the afternoon of the 23rd, Darlan radioed all ships warning that the British were trying "to get their hands on the French fleet and the French colonies." The same evening, the government signed the capitulation agreement. Pierre Cousteau was among the 100,000 French soldiers who were now prisoners of war. For Jacques and the rest of the *Dupleix* crew it wasn't over yet.

Churchill reasoned that if his armed forces could take, or put out of action, the French fleet, they could keep the lifelines in the Mediterranean and the Atlantic open and defend the island against the inferior naval forces of Germany and Italy. If, on the other hand,the French fleet were to be added to the Axis navies, Britain's prospects for survival were bleak. On July 3, Churchill launched Operation Catapult to seize, or effectively disable or destroy all French warships. Within an hour all French ships in British ports were taken, and by day's end their crews were interned and given the choice of rallying to de Gaulle's Free French forces or being sent home. Very few chose to join de Gaulle.

In Algeria, the French fleet in Mers-el-Kébir refused the British ultimatum to sink their own ships or be sunk. The Royal Navy bombed and torpedoed the French warships as they tried to escape the harbor. A total of 1,300 French sailors died. The battleship *Strasbourg*, although crippled, escaped.

On August 10, *Dupleix* sailed out of Toulon against a new enemy. A major British force, including three cruisers and ten destroyers, atacked the French naval base at Oran, Algeria. The French destroyer *Mogador* managed to escape and was heading across the Mediterranean with the *Provence*. *Dupleix* was sent out for a nighttime rendezvous with *Mogador* and *Provence*, and to provide escort back to Toulon. All three arrived back without incident. In Vichy, the spa city near Lyons where the provisional government was setting up, Darlan was ready to declare war on England. He told a closed cabinet meeting he had instructed the *Strasbourg* to launch a surprise attack on a British squadron returning to Gibralter. In London, de Gaulle called it a terrible blow and correctly foresaw a drop-off in the recruitment of Free French. For Churchill, who announced the action in the House of

Commons, it was a boost. The British people were facing the enemy alone now, and by striking ruthlessly at an ex-ally, the government had shown it feared nothing and would stop at nothing.

In Toulon, the mood was one of anger and resentment. Such British ruthlessness would have been welcome had it been struck against the Germans before the fall of France.

Pierre was one of tens of thousands of prisoners of war in makeshift camps near Sens, 200 kilometers east of Paris. They were a demoralized, hungry, and dysentery-ridden mass of men who had only two obsessions; when would the Germans let them go home and what would they eat next. Women began to appear outside the barbed wire, looking for husbands and throwing food and scraps of news over the fence. The Germans were only occupying Paris and three-fifths of the country, leaving an unoccupied zone in the south and southeast under Marshal Pétain.

Jacques kept his rank as gunnery officer and was assigned to one of the hillside forts protecting Toulon. Below him in the glistening harbor and roadstead the battleships *Strasbourg, Provence,* and *Dunkerque* lay at anchor next to seven cruisers including his *Dupleix* ninety ships in all. The fleet was disarmed and, in accordance with the armistice terms, in *gardiennage*, or caretaking by the Pétain government. Hitler had decided against occupying all of France. To humiliate Mussolini, he forbade an Italian occupation of Toulon.

In December, Simone gave birth to a son. They named him Philippe – after Tailliez, who had also come through unscathed. Simone and Jacques were in contact with their families in Paris. Fernande was sure Pierre would be allowed to come home soon. Whether they would ever see Daniel was another question. He was still in England with Higgins.

The hours at the fort up on Mont Faron were short. There was not much to watch for. On off-duty hours, he made home movies with Simone, Jean-Michel, and the baby. He also went diving. Compared with the activities of man, the undersea world seemed serene, fecund and life-affirming, even with the eat-and-be-eaten laws that governed marine biology.

4
THE AQUALUNG

In his broadcasts from London, Charles de Gaulle kept reminding his countrymen that "overseas France" – nearly half of Africa and the smattering of far-flung territories in the Caribbean and Pacific – was not in enemy hands, that part of the navy was safe in Algerian and Moroccan ports – seventeen ships actually – that whole divisions had made it across the Channel from the Dunkirk beaches, and that the British were fighting on. But Jacques Cousteau had a hard time imagining Germany's defeat, as fascism was triumphant everywhere: Nazi Germany ruled Europe from Norway to the Mediterranean, from the Atlantic to the Black Sea; Italy invaded Greece and in Africa plunged into British Somaliland and Libya; and Japan, the third member of the Axis, occupied French Indochina. The Soviet Union, the hope and focal point of so many progressive passions, occupied the Baltic states while in the United States, Franklin Roosevelt began his unprecedented third term by only cautiously leading his country away from traditional isolationism toward alignment with Great Britain.

Cousteau and the artillery specialists under his command were busy booby-trapping the whole fleet. Against whom they weren't quite sure. But bombs were placed aboard every ship in the Arsenal anchorage and the roadstead. And once they had wired together the strategically placed explosives aboard the three battleships, seven cruisers, twenty-nine torpedo boats, twelve submarines, and assorted other warships, they went through endless rehearsals should the order ever come to scuttle the fleet. Cousteau didn't mind being overprepared. They had placed enough explosives to sink the most modern half of the French navy.

At Vichy, the cheerless health resort that was the capital of Jacques's unoccupied France, Pétain and his Premier, Pierre Laval, not only resigned themselves to knuckling under, but by emulating Hitler's regime tried to curry enough favor with the dictator to have him go easy on the defeated nation. At the same time, the eighty-five-year-old Pétain and his Vichy regime managed to frustrate the Fuehrer. Under the original armistice terms, Vichy France was supposedly free to govern itself, but Hitler kept adding new conditions and continued to pressure Vichy to work with Germany toward Europe's New Order. By adamantly adhering to the armistice terms, Pétain refused to do the one thing Hitler wanted most: hand over the fleet. Hitler could force the issue militarily, but that would mean occupying all of France.

Collaborators – they liked to call themselves realists – were out in the open and part of everyday life. The Germans let hundreds of thousands of prisoners of war go. From the clear-cut rules, the rejection of compromise and complicity that the POW's imposed on themselves in the camps, the returning soldiers discovered the improvised ingenuity, the artful dodging and liquid idealogies of the home front, of people living in an occupied land. As Alfred Fabre-Luce would write about the convulsions of conquered France, "Those who have no leverage whatsoever and have nothing to barter with must learn to be humble in the extreme. When you have to spend several hours in line, filling out forms, getting the paperwork together, signing that you are not Jewish, you don't recover your self-respect too quickly."

Pierre Cousteau spent one year as a POW, but when he got home his fortunes changed overnight. He not only found Fernande, the children, and his mother unscathed, although undernourished in a freezing apartment, he also found a top job as editor in chief of *Paris-Soir*, the afternoon tabloid that Otto Abetz, the Reich ambassador and virtual ruler of occupied France, wanted started up. Together with *Le Figaro*, *Le Temps*, and *L'Action Française*, *Paris-Soir* had fled south and started printing in the Vichy "free zone," although with diminished influence and press runs. The prewar editorial staff published a *Paris-Soir* in Lyons; the *Paris-Soir* PAC edited was the "new" tabloid that the Propagandastaffel on the Champs Elysées encouraged, the *Paris-Soir* that was distributed in both zones.

Finding food absorbed the waking hours of Parisians and carefully weighted their day-to-day conduct. With restaurant meals nearly nonexistent, Elizabeth and her daughter-in-law took to scouring city and suburbs for edibles. Elizabeth had her ways with butchers to sometimes get extra meat, and in the chilly apartment managed a certain art of living at the frugal dinner table that her grandchildren would remember.

In Sanary, Jacques and Simone had an easier time even though it was fish nearly every day. Cousteau, Tailliez, and Dumas continued their diving. They also brought home the evening meal. Big groupers were a favorite, served baked, fried, grilled, and disguised in ingenious ways. Jacques learned to kill fish with a spear, a crossbow, a cartridge-propelled harpoon, and even – in a bet with a skeptical friend – a knitting needle. Dumas also caught a variety of seafoods, but Jacques never developed a taste for squid, whether baked, fried, grilled, or otherwise.

In Paris, Pierre found his friends in the highest places. Fernand de Brinon, with whom he and Robert Brasillach had attended the Nazi rallies in Nuremberg, had interviewed Hitler when France fell and found the Fuehrer's terms for a defeated nation generous. De Brinon was a friend of Abetz and became a kind of middleman between Abetz and Pétain, or as the Marshal put it, "the faithful interpreter of my thoughts to the German authorities." His office could issue travel permits to the Vichy zone and, if people were arested, could intervene with the Wehrmacht and the Gestapo. He was in daily teletype contact with Vichy where Admiral Darlan was called Pétain's "crown prince." The offices of Jacques Doriot and his Parti Populaire Français (PPF), France's Nazi party, in the Rue des Pyramides around the corner from the headquarters of Paris' military commander, General Dietrich von Choltitz, were where the most ardent collaborators met and where influence was transacted. It was at the PPF that *Je Suis Partout* found a new cartoonist, Ralph Soupault, whose artwork had a violent anti-Semitism all of its own, even by the standards of *Der Stürmer*.

Brasillach, who had also been a POW, assumed the editorship of *Je Suis Partout*. He, PAC, Lucien Rebatet, and Pierre Villette wrote shrill, violent racist editorials, polemics, and denunciations in the weekly. Brasillach was literary enough to publish a playwright like Jean Anouilh and the popular satirist Marcel Aymé, and the paper swung behind it a considerable part of educated public opinion. Its circulation rose from 100,000 to 300,000, astonishing Propagandastaffel Chief Gerhard Heller, a less than fanatical bureaucrat who found the Nazi apologies all the more valuable because they were written by talented Frenchmen.

In June 1941, Hitler's attack on the Soviet Union, the largest enemy he could find, not only had French Communists breathe more easily again, it had them begin the first resistance. For the collaborators, the opening of the Eastern front allowed them to portray themselves as defenders of Western civilization against the Bolshevik hordes. In May, when Jews were forbidden to engage in practically all business and professional activities, Darlan became Pétain's number two man. Darlan immediately went to Berlin to try and convince the Fuehrer to modify the armistice statutes so France could join in the defense of the West. Hitler refused. A month later, Darlan sounded out the American ambassador to Vichy, William Leahy, about an eventual surrender of the fleet to the Allies.

German retaliation to resistance fighting was merciless. For each member of the Reichwehr killed, the Gestapo shot a number of French hostages. In November grenades were tossed into restaurants and hotels occupied by Germans, and when railway sabotage began on the Paris-Britanny main line, three men picked up at random were shot. In Bordeaux, the ratio was fifty to one when a German major was found dead in the street.

Jacques joined the underground and began looking for ways to be effective. His motives were not idealogical but reflected a sense of career rectitude. When one is an officer, even of a defeated force, one tries to *do* something.

The Germans were not on the Mediterranean coast; the Italians were. And the Free

French were on the other side in Algiers and the other North African bases. Admiral Jean Laborde, the commander of the disarmed fleet in Toulon, was in contact with "dissident" commanders in Algiers, and down through the ranks everybody more or less knew where everybody else stood.

December 1941 brought the United States into the war. The summer of 1942 saw the Germans drive deep into the Ukraine, the Japanese take the Philippines, and for French Resistance fighters unlucky enough to be caught or informed against, deportation to concentration camps. The fall brought the first Allied victory when the British stopped General Erwin Rommel's Afrika Korps in Libya. It didn't take Cousteau and his men long to realize that diving could be a clever front for espionage, that he and Tailliez, for example, could go diving off Sète and while in the water have a good look at the Italian shore installations. If they were picked up, what were they if not a pair of harmless eccentrics?

Of course if they had breathing devices they could swim underwater into the harbor and, at dawn or dusk, surface enough to make more detailed reconnaissance. Carefully, word went through secure channels to Algiers: What would the Allies consider crucial intelligence about the Italian navy?

Cousteau's considerable energy was devoted to his compelling interest – the firsthand exploration of the ocean deep. Dredges and nets could snatch specimens of life to the surface, but that was like examining animals at a taxidermist's. The key to on-the-spot observation of marine life in its own environment without cables, steel helmets, and heavy armor was to strap tanks on your back and, through hoses to a mouthpiece, deliver compressed air to your lungs in amounts regulated to equalize the pressure within your body to the pressure of the surrounding water. The key to that was to find a regulating valve delicate enough to respond to the human breath. The fall in pressure produced by your inhalation should somehow displace the diaphragm in the valve to admit air from the tanks. At exhalation the diaphragm should close and allow the breathed-out air to escape into the water in the form of bubbles.

Melchior had not forgotten his son-in-law's request to sound out Air Liquide engineers in Paris. The company was involved in developing a substitute for the scarcest of commodities, gasoline, and was experimenting with natural gas as an ersatz auto fuel. The man to see was Emile Gagnan.

Whether Jacques and Simone were going to get their *laissez-passer* through Pedro's influential friends, or, like thousands of others, pay a farmer on the "border" to take them across became immaterial when, on November 27, Hitler abrogated the armistice terms and occupied all of France.

The Fuehrer also had his spies, and after he learned that Darlan was in Algiers making overtures to the Allies he lost whatever faith he had in the Vichy military chiefs. Having first used his submarines to secretly sow underwater mines in the Toulon roadstead so no ship could escape, he launched Operation Lila during the night of November 27. Two crack divisions led the sneak attack.

The SS Reich division occupied the Saint-Mandrier peninsular overlooking the anchorage and the 7th Panzer pushed into the Arsenal and, at 4:30, burst into the marine prefect's office and pinned the officer on duty to the wall. The surprise was total.

A junior officer, however, managed to alert the bridge of the battleship *Strasbourg*. Admiral Laborde, in turn, was alerted and ordered a general alarm. Despite incendiary Luftwaffe bombs dropped over the harbor to illuminate the way for the armored divisions, elements of the 7th Panzer got lost in the maze of Arsenal buildings and alleyways, and only reached the first gangplank at 6:00. SS troops also found themselves at Le Mourillon instead of the Old Port.

The delays allowed Laborde to give the one order they had never stopped rehearsing since 1940: Scuttle the fleet! As planned, one explosion set off the next, illuminating the predawn sky and wakening greater Toulon's 300,000 inhabitants.

Cousteau was at Saint-Mandrier shortly after dawn with his camera. SS troops stood around, grinning. Shattered by explosions and devastated by fire, the warships were sinking or keeling over on their side. The *Strasbourg, Dunkerque,* and *Provence* were going down in billowing clouds of black smoke, as were seven cruisers including the *Dupleix,* seventeen destroyers, sixteen torpedo boats, six transport ships, tankers, minesweepers, and tugs. One destroyer, one torpedo boat, and five tankers were not scuttled and were seized by the Germans, but five submarines managed to sail the gauntlet of mines and Luftwaffe dive bombings. Their fate would reveal the confusion and ambivalence among their commanders. While three of them reached Algeria, the fourth went to neutral Franco Spain to be interned until war's end, and the understaffed crew of the fifth sank it in deep waters and rowed back in dories. The first BBC broadcasts told how Moscow, Washington, and London hailed the valiant French sailors. Rumors circulated in town how the Fritzes had got lost and arrived too late.

Observing the grinning SS men watch the ships burn and sink, Cousteau was sure they hadn't bungled their commando action, that the sinking was so sly coup against the *Schleus.* If anything, the scuttling lifted a potentially heavy mortgage from the Germans' future war effort. The postwar discovery of Hitler's archives would prove Cousteau right. The two armored divisions had not been trained to board and seize the ninety warships; their mission had been to provoke a suicide. After the loss of the battleship *Bismarck,* Hitler had lost faith in large surface fleets, fired Admiral Erich Raeder as commander of the Kriegsmarine, and redoubled the submarine warfare effort.

Cousteau felt impotent. He was a naval officer without a navy. He also felt it was prudent to move Simone and the boys out of harm's way before the next turn in the war. He would be a better Reisstance fighter if he knew they were safe. He knew that the point of resistance fighting was to be effective, not to be heroic, and he naturally tended to see the war's outcome as a question of who had the edge in technology – who could build the most modern ships and armaments out of reach of the enemy's bombs. In the meantime, there was the appointment with Emile Gagnan.

Jacques and Simone were in Paris in December.

Wartime living favored improvisation, the short view of things, getting by, finding a bicycle tire, tomorrow's dinner. No doubt to cover the ignominy that would befall his brother, Jacques Cousteau was to remain very discreet about his wartime activities. But however apolitical he was, he and Pedro must have discussed the turns of events, if not the likely end of the war. PAC was in his salad days and in 1942 his side was going from victory to victory, steamrolling into the Ukraine, island-hopping in the Pacific while subjecting England to the relentless blitz. Jacques, who loved his brother and believed him to be the cleverer of the two, was joining the anonymous armies of the night and trying to weigh risks in proportion to what could be achieved. He wasn't particularly proud of what he was told would be his mission – espionage, he would say after the war, was somehow unfair. Françoise and Jean-Pierre Cousteau remembered their uncle and aunt at Avenue de la Motte-Picquet, but no stormy arguments *en famille,* no fights between their father and uncle.

Editions de France was publishing PAC's first book, *L'Amérique juive* (literally, "Jewish America"), 120 pages in which he recalled his family's sojourn in New York and his own school year at DeWitt High in 1921. Dedicated to "my friends at *Je Suis Partout,*" the book's thesis echoed the Nazi proposition that Germany's Jews had brought anti-Semitism upon themselves by taking over more and more of the Weimar Republic's wealth and by worming themselves into positions of power. In the United States, Jews had succeeded in perpetrating a giant expropriation of the economy and reducing business interests to cowering silence.

And Americans were ruled by a crypto-Jew. Roosevelt was really Rosenvelt. Quoting a P. Alamoritz of the *Detroit Jewish Chronicle,* PAC traced the Roosevelts back to a Rossocampo family of Sephardic Jews who were chased out of Spain in 1520 and settled

70

in Holland under the name Rosenvelt. The first Rosenvelt in America in 1649 had married a Jewish woman named Heyltje Kunst.

There was a defiance, a knowledge that they were gambling with their own lives, in the behavior of prominent intellectual Nazi collaborators, a number of postwar observers noted. These collaborators dramatized themselves with the belief that their victory would be absolute. There was an almost sexual edge to their kow-towing to Abetz, Heller, and the rest of the occupiers. As Brasillach later wrote, "Whatever their outlook, during these years the French have all more or less been to bed with Germany, and whatever quarrels there were the memory was sweet."

The anarchic Louis-Fernand Céline, Brasillach, and Rebatet were to be more infamous than Pierre Cousteau – Céline for his repellent pessimism and jaundiced alienation (that the 1968 student rebellion would find chic), Brasillach as the most enthusiastic fellow traveler who could shock Abetz by complaining that Jewish children were not always deported with their parents, and Rebatet for *Les Décombres* ("Ruins"), one of the most repulsive novels written and published during the Occupation. PAC was the journalist, nervy and cynical with an

71

unerring finger on the weekly pulse and the slangy, devastatingly seductive style that sold papers.

One thing the brothers agreed upon was to protect their children from the follies of their own generation. Jacques would send Simone with Jean-Michel and little Philippe to Mégève, an Alpine station high in the Savoie mountains near the Italian-Swiss border. Pierre agreed that their mother, Françoise, and Jean-Pierre should join Simone and the boys in Mégève. Fernande was to stay in Paris; much of Pierre's inside information was gathered at mundane affairs that Abetz, Heller, and other Propagandastaffel higher-ups laid on at the Reich embassy and the Hotel Majestic for their tonier French friends and their wives.

Jacques met Gagnan in his cluttered Air Liquide laboratory. Word reached Paris that Admiral Darlan had been assassinated in Algiers, where, in the last about-face, he had aligned himself with the Allies. A young Gaullist was accused of the murder.

Cousteau explained what he was looking for, and Gagnan, a pipe-smoking be-spectacled man a few years older than Jacques with a little Charlie Chaplin mustache, reached to a shelf behind his desk and brought down a small object. "Something like this?"

While Cousteau had a look, Gagnan explained it was an automatic shutoff valve he had made for those "infernal natural gas tanks we've had to put on our cars. Same kind of problem, you know."

After Cousteau persuaded Air Liquide to fund the prototype – Jacques was persuasive but it didn't hurt that his father-in-law sat on the board of directors – they went to work. In three weeks they had designed and built a "lung" that fitted an adaptation of Gagnan's automatic regulator to Cousteau's hoses and mouthpiece and a pair of oxygen tanks. The valve was the size of an alarm clock and, according to their calculations, it should let highly compressed air escape from the tanks until it balanced the water pressure, then feed air to the diver through the mouthpiece. In the early spring of 1943 they took their prototype to the Marne River outside Paris.

There was no friend filming the event this time, only a snapshot of the skinny Cousteau in his black bathing suit standing knee-deep in water. "As long as I lay horizontally in the water, the lung worked beautifully. When I stood up, however, air escaped with loud bubbles, wasting great quantities of my

73

supply. And when I lay head down in the water, I had trouble getting air out of the regulator. Disconsolate, I crawled out of the water. We got back in the car and drove sadly to Paris." Still, it was the world's first attempt at a weightless, face-first-like-a-fish dive.

They were closer to a solution than they thought. They had arranged the intake and exhaust tubes on the lung in such a way that one was 15 centimeters higher than the other. Back in Gagnan's lab they put the two tubes at the same level and after one more tryout had a device practical enough to submit for a patent. In their joint patent office application they called their breathing apparatus the "Aqualung."

In Algiers, General Henri Giraud, Darlan's successor, agreed to cooperate, if not consolidate, with de Gaulle's Free French forces, an act termed treasonable in Vichy. Admiral André Lemonnier became de Gaulle's naval chief and began reorganizing a French contingent for the Allied combat fleet. In the spring, the Russians defeated the Germans at Stalingrad and in North Africa American and British armies linked up to drive Rommel's German and Italian divisions toward the coast of Tunisia. Cousteau's group got the order from

Lemonnier to try to get a copy of the Italian navy's code book. Posing as an Italian officer, Jacques led a party into the Italian headquarters at Sète and spent four tense hours photographing top-secret papers, including the naval signals code. On May 12 the Germans and Italians were routed in North Africa. Transmitted to the Allies, the code book helped detect the crumbling Italian navy's intentions as General Dwight Eisenhower's forces swept from Bizerte, Tunis, and Malta across to Sicily.

Jacques made periodic visits to Mégève, but spent the summer trying out the Aqualung in the Mediterranean. Posting Dumas as a lifeguard, he donned the 50-pound Aqualung and realized his dream. "I experimented with all possible maneuvers – loops, somersaults, and barrel rolls. I stood upside down on one finger and burst out laughing, a shrill distorted laugh. Nothing I did altered the automatic rhythm of the air. Delivered from gravity and buoyancy, I flew around in space." With Dumas and Tailliez, he took the Aqualung to greater and greater depths. The three of them made more than five hundred separate dives. It was October when Dumas, in one carefully planned plunge, reached 72 metres.

The effects of increased pressure on

human functions were both exhilarating and critical. With each dive they learned more. Swimming too long in cold water, they discovered, can subtly bleed off body heat until a diver finds himself suddenly exhausted. Holding the breath during the last 10 meters of ascent can rupture lungs as they expand during the rapidly decreasing pressure; deep descents can cripple with hard-hat divers' old disease, the bends, unless the freestyle diver also decompresses the nitrogen bubbles in his bloodstream by lingering at successive stages on the way up.

Below 45 meters, they encountered a treacherous condition that Cousteau called the "rapture of the depths" and doctors called nitrogen narcosis. The buildup of nitrogen in the diver's body somehow drugs or anesthetizes his senses. Magnificently drunk, he becomes an underwater god. He may offer his mouthpiece to a passing fish. Cousteau's scariest brush with the rapture would be in the Red Sea in 1951. Strange lifeforms, half real and half nightmare, surrounded him as he sank into a world of dreams. Stretching temptingly below him was what seemed to be the infinite sweetness and quiet of a blackness that would yield up the secrets of the universe if only he were to go a little deeper.

Inhaling oxygen concentrations above 65 percent at one atmosphere pressure was dangerous. Underwater the pressure increased by 1 atmosphere with each 10 meters, or 33 feet. The deeper they went the more oddly the gases in their tanks and lungs behaved.

Cousteau brought his waterproof camera along. He, Tailliez, and Dumas filmed each other donning aqualungs and diving in. Cousteau also filmed his friends under water, short black-and-white takes of divers propelling themselves forward like marine animals, scenes with schools of fish in the foreground and, behind them, men-fish shooting diagonally across the field of vision.

Getting negative film was the biggest difficulty. Although released for the duration of the Occupation, Cousteau was a navy officer still on active duty. As such he had no reason to want motion picture negative. Indeed, to apply for a ration of raw stock from the Germans might set in motion a Gestapo investigation. "I went to all the photo shops in Marseilles and Toulon, buying from them as many rolls of thirty-six exposure Isopan F black-and-white 35 millimeter film for still cameras," he remembered. "And at night, with Simone under our blankets because we had no

77

darkroom, I spliced these rolls together into 15-meter strips. We loaded 15 meters like this because my camera took only 15 meters. I don't think anybody with common sense would do it. It was absolutely crazy."

The payoff was in the water. To see – and capture on camera – the living fish was a thrill. It changed perceptions and attitudes. Swimming among the fish made killing them a totally new moral dilemma. Jacques got a shot of Dumas *feeding* fish.

The first short was called *Par dix-huit mètres de fond* ("At a Depth of Eighteen Meters"), but there was another subject that presented itself – sunken ships. People had never really seen shipwrecks at the bottom of the sea. Diving to 20 meters, Cousteau, Dumas, and Tailliez discovered the sunken British steamer the *Dalton*. Like children finding a new playground, they swam in and out of portholes, flippered behind fish on the bridge. Jacques filmed his friends gliding over barnacled railings, through holds to discover the ship's encrusted wheel, the captain's bathtub. The resulting 1943 short was *Epaves* ("Wrecks"), followed in 1944 by a poetic short called *Paysages du silence* ("Landscapes of Silence").

The new year saw the turning of the tide for the Allied forces everywhere. Investigating the *Dalton* made Cousteau realize the military potential of the Aqualung. To the occasional German patrol drawn to the assembled rubbernecks on the beach, Cousteau played the harmless eccentric. But he could imagine especially trained Aqualung commandos penetrating enemy harbors, attaching explosives to the hulls of enemy ships, and destroying coastal defenses. The thing was to get the invention to the Allies.

In the Pacific, U.S. ships dealt a series of crippling blows to the Japanese fleet, and soldiers and marines started leapfrogging from one Japanese-held island to another to force the enemy out of his conquered domains. The Germans were also on the defensive. Soviet armies launched massive counterattacks against Nazi-held territory and were gathering momentum all along the Eastern front. The Italians had lost their African empire, and the Americans and the British were slogging up the Italian boot. By May, an invasion of France was rumored to be the next big Allied offensive.

It happened at dawn on June 6, 1944. On a 120-kilometer stretch of the Normandy coast, wave after wave of soldiers waded through the surf and the German bullets to scramble up the beaches. By nightfall in one sector alone, they held 15 kilometers of the once fashionable beaches from Trouville to Deauville. Five months later, Cousteau was in London to introduce the Aqualung to the Allied navies. And to see his father. Daniel and Higgins had never left Torquay and had spent the war at the Imperial Hotel.

At the same time, Pierre and Fernande were fleeing through bombed-out Nazi Germany ahead of the retreating Wehrmacht.

The last hours in Paris had been both painful and miraculous. The capital was without gas, electricity, and public transportation. The Americans were in Chartres, an hour's drive away, and the Free French fighting the last Germans at the Préfecture de Police on August 17, when PAC and Fernande reached the PPF headquarters in the Rue des Pyramides, where a column of Wehrmacht trucks were to evacuate top collaborators. The evening had been hysterical. Lucien and Véronique Rebatet had phoned the apartment begging not to be left behind – Céline who had heard his own death sentence announced on the BBC had already fled with his wife Lucette and their cat Bébert – and as desperation spread, PAC's telephone had become the nerve center directing everybody to the Rue des Pyramides. The cartoonist Soupault and his wife piled in under the truck canvas after the

Cousteaus, but the column didn't move. For three hours they waited, each moment fearing partisan machine guns would salute their departure.

Militia members, PPF diehards, numbering 20,000, similarly piled into Wehrmacht trucks or military trains, only to find themselves caught up in the retreat eastward, exposed to Allied bombing raids and Free French sabotage attacks. In Vichy, Pétain, claiming he was a prisoner, was being driven away under armed guard. The destination of Pétain, Laval, and the remnants of Vichy, and the ultras alike, was the former Hohenzollern castle of Sigmaringen on the Danube, an hour's drive south of Stuttgart. The fiction of a French government-in-exile fighting de Gaulle and his foreign paymasters was maintained until the end of the war – Céline would write *D'Un Château à l'Autre* ("Castle to Castle"), an apocalyptic farce of the Vichy twilight at Sigmaringen.

PAC would also write a book about his *danse macabre* through Nazi Germany's ultimate disasters, "sealed under a permanent avalanche of incendiary bombs and steel and the incoherence of animal panic." With a vague notion of reaching safety in Milan, a group of them, including the Cousteaus, set out from Konstanz to cross

81

the Alps through Austria. Barely inside Italy, they heard of the Fuehrer's suicide in his bunker, Mussolini's murder, and Field Marshal Albert Kesselring's capitulation in Italy. They also heard that Italian resistance fighters were marching on the Austrian border.

In London, meanwhile, Jacques was cooling his heels. He spent days trying to convince British and American navy commanders that aqualunged "frogmen" could become human torpedo-layers. The Anglo-Saxons, as de Gaulle called his English-speaking allies with some hauteur, dubbed Cousteau's invention Self-Contained Underwater Breathing Apparatus – soon shortened to Scuba – but they had a war to win and saw this gangly Frenchman's invention as coming too late in the war to make a difference. Cousteau persisted and talked to anybody he could find. One was James Dugan, an American reporter he met at the lively nightspot called Le Petit Club Français on St. James Place. He couldn't help sell the Scuba invention to Ike, but he listened. Dugan would be Cousteau's first translator and lifetime friend.

Fearing the onrushing Italian partisans and fearing returning to the crumbling Third Reich, Pierre, Fernande, four other men, two other women, and a ten-year-old orphan whose parents had been killed in U.S. bombing raids split off from the others and turned west, hoping against hope they might reach safety in Switzerland. Stumbling across the Alps in the snow at 2,600 meters altitude they reached a Swiss village and gave themselves up. After conferring with Berne, the local police escorted the five refugees back into Austria where they became U.S. Army prisoners in Landeck.

At war's end, Jacques rushed back to France. The apartment on Avenue de la Motte-Picquet was intact. It was Daniel's and he followed, although for only a short visit – Higgins needed him. Elizabeth came to Paris. Before reporting to active duty under Admiral Lemonnier in Toulon, Jacques made his way to Mégève. It was out of the question to let eleven-year-old Françoise and seven-year-old Jean-Pierre go to Paris. The *épuration,* the purges that were a mixture of popular wrath and private settling of scores, was in full swing and the children of a noted collaborationist – "collabo" in the current slang – could expect the worst humiliations. Quietly, Jacques and Simone took his brother's children with their own two sons to Toulon.

Mines and bombs were lying in the

roadstead and along France's coasts, and if the Aqualung couldn't be used for war, it could be used for peace. Frogmen wearing scuba gear and using his diving technique, Cousteau told Lemonnier and the top brass, could safely locate and defuse underwater charges.

Croix de guerre and other decorations for his work in the resistance would be forthcoming, but more immediately Jacques was allowed to move into a requisitioned house in Sanary. It was none other than Darlan's villa, high on a hill overlooking the Mediterranean.

The American commander of the prison camp in Landeck was no great Francophile. What he had seen of de Gaulle's prickly forces – asking GI's to hang back so they could march into Paris first, and talking about the honor of having won the war – had left him scornful of Frenchmen in uniform. And now he had to guard this Frog who had lived Stateside and had played stickball on the corner of Ninety second and Broadway.

The camp was full of people running out of hope. Hungarians who had fought in the SS, Poles who to survive had become kapos in concentration camps. Ukrainians who knew that being turned over to the Soviet army meant death.

Pierre had little difficulty communicating with the commander and obtaining Fernande's release. He also managed to get word to his parents that Fernande and he were alive and to tell them where he was. The commander warned him when the visit of French army officers was announced, and PAC stood in the Polish lineup while the officers looked over the prisoners and tried to trip up French-looking men with sudden questions in French. Eventually, the commander told Pierre he could go visit his wife in the village if he gave his word of honor he wouldn't try to escape. Dutifully, PAC returned to the camp at night.

One day Jacques drove into Landeck. Fernande was the first to know. Jacques had arranged everything, false ID's for both Pedro and her, fake passports and transit visas to Spain as the first "drop" on the escape route to South America. The brothers embraced. Tears flowed. Jacques told them about Françoise and Jean-Pierre. The news about PAC's friends was not so good. Brasillach had been executed by firing squad. Céline had found refuge in Denmark, Rebatet had been arrested in Sigmaringen. But Pedro wouldn't escape. He had given his word to the commander of the camp. Jacques tried everything to convince his brother, but Pedro remained firm. He kept saying he had given his word.

Hours later, Jacques left.

French officers showed up again to comb the camp. This time PAC was turned over to them. He was taken to Fresnes, the infamous penitentiary outside Paris, which had been the transfer point of so many thousands deported to concentration camps. Tapped messages from cell to cell told him Rebatet was there, too.

5
SANARY

For us kids it was a fabulous time," Jean-Pierre Cousteau remembered. "We were my sister, my two cousins and me, with my uncle and aunt and my grandmother. It was marvelous because we didn't go to school. My grandmother took care of my sister and me; Simone looked after Jean-Michel and Philippe. My grandmother made me work a little; she taught me to write. Jacques came home every evening. We saw him with

86

Dumas and Tailliez. The house was the meeting place for all these people. Friends were there constantly. It never stopped. We had fish almost every day because they went fishing for groupers.

"My sister was twelve. As the only girl and older than us boys, she was off on her own a bit. Jean-Michel was eight, Philippe was six, and I was in the middle, seven-and-a-half. We were allowed to take turns going out with my uncle, Tailliez, and Dumas. They fished for groupers, dived, and filmed, and one of us boys was in the boat while they tried out their gear. Tailliez impressed us a lot because he was very reserved and because he stammered. We were scared of him. Dumas, who was married by now, took us swimming and fishing and carved toy boats out of driftwood for us. We were three beach urchins."

The reason Françoise and Jean-Pierre didn't go to school was that no school would take the children of a notorious "collabo" whose trial for treason was coming up in November 1946. Fiercely loyal to PAC, Paprika stayed in Paris to organize his defense. To shield the children – the prosecution wanted the death penalty – she agreed to let them stay in Sanary. Simone was very good to Françoise and Jean-Pierre.

To minimize the difference between them and her own boys, she kept Jean-Michel out of school.

The first flush of wrath against collaborationists was giving way to indifference or unease over the purges. Not only had intellectuals stood in court and accused others who now strutted around with fresh Legion of Honor decorations in their lapels, but writers and artists with impeccable records were beginning to wonder aloud why collaborationist authors and journalists who had put their bylines on their wartime writings were prosecuted with such vigor while clemency, if not outright pardon, was accorded to lawyers who had been informers and industrialists who had actually strengthened the German war machine. Françoise Mauriac and Albert Camus had petitioned de Gaulle to spare Brasillach's life. Unable to forget Brasillach's 1944 exhortations to French volunteers to keep fighting alongside the German army, the general had refused. Friends were trying to assure Céline's discreet return and a letter campaign in favor of Rebatet was under way.

Jacques, who had proved he would do almost anything for his brother, wanted to testify at the trial. His superiors told him not to. If he had to, they advised him, he should do so as a civilian. He testified in his navy officer's uniform and with his Resistance medal on the breast pocket to little effect. On November 23, Pierre-Antoine Cousteau was condemned to death.

The sun still shimmered in the ocean below Sanary. The kids, tanned little savages, still went out with Tailliez and Dumas. Back from the trial, Jacques set in motion a petition to have PAC's sentence commuted. His parents took the burden of Françoise and Jean-Pierre's education off his and Simone's shoulders. The two children would have to go to school somehow and since French schools didn't want them, their grandmother left with them to join Daniel and the ninety-year-old Higgins in England. Françoise entered a fifth-grade and Jean-Pierre a first-grade class in Torquay. As often as it was allowed, Elizabeth went to France to see her son on death row.

Jacques needed to turn his back to the past and look to the future. Air Liquide was putting the Aqualung into commercial production and Admiral Lemonnier, for one, was quick to grasp the advantages of scuba diving. Civilians, too, showed up at Sanary, mostly journalists and would-be divers. *Par dix-huit mètres de fond* and *Epaves* were given prizes in the short and documentary category at the new Cannes Film Festival. Dumas was eager to establish new diving records. Jacques was thirty-six and knew he had a whole new world just ahead of him.

Testifying, in uniform, for the defense of a Nazi collaborator sentenced to death would severely constrain Jacques's career as a navy officer, but Toulon harbor and huge stretches of France's coasts were full of mines. And his argument for training a team of scuba divers was persuasive. His enthusiasm was contagious, but it was his two short movies that convinced the brass.

The navy commissioned Tailliez – JYC's superior in rank – and Cousteau to form the *Group d'Etudes et de Recherches Sous-Marines* (GERS) to study the physiology of freestyle diving and to try minesweeping with humans going down to locate mines rather than surface ships locating mines with sonar, hooks, and paravanes. Quickly, Tailliez and Cousteau enrolled a group of young naval officers and seamen, and hired beachcomber civilian Frédéric Dumas, who became known as "Didi" to everybody.

Cousteau, Tailliez, and Dumas conducted daily underwater classes. To rid their men of any fear of the deep, to train them for emergencies and build up their confidence, the instructors had them swim down 10 meters and there pass mouthpieces and backpack tanks to each other. For their minesweeping, they were assigned a former German motor sloop rechristened the *Elie Monnier*.

They went to work in the Toulon and Sète roadsteads. In Toulon, they removed live torpedoes from a sunken German U-boat and aboard a sunken German barge found enough magnetic mines to virtually wipe out the entire city. The area was "fenced off" and marked on all navigational charts because no one knew how to disarm these mines sensitive to everything from magnetic fields and pressure to sound and heat. West of Sète, they found German mines hidden under a shelf 12 meters down. Surface minesweepers using hooks and paravanes would never have located these "Katy" mines. Working in half-hour shifts, four teams spent five weeks locating and exploding fourteen mines, a job the navy acknowledged could never have been done by conventional hard-hat diving. In 1948 the government would declare the Sète roadstead clear, which didn't prevent one ship from being blown up two years later.

Besides the work with the GERS unit, Cousteau had a lot of time to himself. Many things remained unorganized during the first postwar years and most evenings he was home.

Simone was probably the world's first woman scuba diver. Jean-Michel and Philippe made their first dives when they were eight and five, fitted with miniature Aqualungs. Their father had one of his friends film the family underwater: Mom, Dad, and the boys descending hand in hand in a trail of bubbles. "I've been doing it so many years that the experiences are all mixed up," Philippe recalled in the mid-1970's of his earliest diving recollections. Jean-Michel remembered his father as a philosopher, who took the boys out under the stars to tell them what life was about.

The Cousteaus loved Sanary. They couldn't afford to buy the Darlan villa when it was auctioned off by the government, but Daniel was able to buy them a tiny but spectacular cliffside plot across the road. The property faced the sea. Jacques threw himself into the building with passion and enthusiasm. The design had to be his. He was in his classical period, admiring Spartan frugality, Platonic geometry, and Socratic irony. They were three adults and four children, which meant many rooms, but a bed and four walls were all a person needed, so the rooms became monk's cells devoid of furniture. By contrariness, Jacques named the finished house Villa Baobab after the biggest tree in Africa.

Tailliez and Cousteau requested permission for their unit to film submarine maneuvers. The result was *Une plongée du "Rubis,"* a short documentary giving a whole new point of view of underwater activities. Had anyone ever seen a torpedo shoot out from a submarine and glide through the water toward its target, a sub actually laying mines? The *Rubis* offered the team a chance to test emergency evacuation of a sub by aqualung. Dumas squeezed into the *Rubis*'s air lock and, breathing air compressed to almost five atmospheres, waited until the inner hatch was clamped shut. Then, with Jacques filming, the outside hatch was opened and Didi shot up in a cloud of bubbles. Jacques and Didi also used themselves as guinea pigs in a navy experiment of the effects of explosives on the submerged human body.

The team constantly flirted with the outer limits. They established that the practical limit of scuba diving was 50 meters. Below that depth they were confined, not by equipment, but by the complex temporary changes taking place in the body chemistry.

93

Breathing air under high pressure increased the nitrogen in the bloodstream, provoking the narcotic effect that Cousteau called the rapture of the depths. In addition to these treacherous narcotic effects, there was the need to allow the body to desaturate from the excess nitrogen before returning to the surface. Lieutenant Jean Alinat's major contribution to the GERS unit was establishing graphs of how long a diver should halt on his way up from a day's first dive (four minutes) and how long on his second dive (two halts of sixteen minutes each). Adding helium to the air in the tanks prevented the buildup of nitrogen in the body, but lengthened the decompression on the way up to an hour-and-a-half.

Slowly, painfully, and on occasion at mortal risk to themselves, they established tables for the best air mixes and for the permissible rates of ascent. They made 80 meters the practical limit of diving in clear warm water. Helium mixed with oxygen allowed a diver to go beyond 80 meters; but the cold, the silence, the overwhelming sense of isolation, even in the midst of fellow divers, and the knowledge that if things went wrong the pressure at these depths could crush life, limited such saturation dives to an experimental few.

The Fontaine de Vaucluse, immortalized by the exiled Florentine poet Petrarch in the fourteenth century, is the wellspring of the Sorgue River, a pool in a crater under a limestone cliff in the Alpine foothills east of Avignon. A trickle flows until March, when the water cave erupts in a rage that floods the Sorgue for five weeks. Then it subsides. The phenomenon has occurred every year of recorded history.

Generations of hydrologists had leaned over the fountain and evolved dozens of theories, the best being that Vaucluse is an underground siphon, or a system of inner caverns lying higher than the water level of the surface pool, that the spring runoff seeped into these subterranean caves and caused the annual spillover. A retired army officer who had settled nearby suggested the Undersea Research Group dive into the fountain to learn its secret. The navy gave its permission to try and on a Saturday in August when the spring was quiet, Jacques, Simone, Tailliez, Dumas, and a truckload of navy officers and sailors drove into Vaucluse.

The mayor and half the town dropped whatever they were doing and eagerly helped carry tanks, aqualungs, a portable decompression chamber, hundreds of meters of mountain climbers rope, ice axes, and a new air compressor to fill the tanks, up the wooded trail to the fountain. Simone didn't like the venture at all. She stood with the locals in the limestone lip overlooking the water crater and watched Jacques in long johns get into a dry suit and Dumas into an Italian frogman outfit. Lieutenant Maurice Fargues, the unit's resourceful equipment officer, threw in almost a hundred meters of rope weighed down by pig iron. He would always have a hand on the rope. One tug by Cousteau or Dumas meant Fargues should tighten the rope to clear snags. Three tugs meant paying out more line and six tugs was the emergency signal for him to haul them up as fast as possible.

Weighed down with tanks, flippers, axes, and waterproof flashlights, Cousteau and Dumas plopped in. After staying motionless in the pool for a minute to test their ballast and buoyancy, Jacques shot down head first, followed by Didi. Thirty meters down Jacques found the pig iron standing on a ledge. He shoved it down the slope without noticing he had lost the line coiled on his arm and continued down a tunnel that made him think of the Paris Métro. His ears and head ached. The beam of his flashlight revealed

96

no ceiling on the inner cavern but picked out the rope. At the end of it he saw Didi, his frogman suit filled with water, holding his light like a ridiculous glowworm.

They had the rapture of the depths, Cousteau realized, but instead of the familiar lightheaded drunkenness, he felt heavy and anxious. His brain managed to register the danger. He swam down to the nearly unconscious Dumas, who grabbed his wrist with sudden strength. Jacques twisted free and played his flashlight on Didi's face mask. Didi's protruding eyes were rolling inside the mask and a minute later he lost control of his jaws and his mouthpiece slipped from his teeth. He swallowed water but somehow got the grip back into his mouth.

Cousteau realized he was in a state of idiotic exhaustion from some mysterious effect of the cave. He knew he could not swim to the surface carrying the inert Dumas in his heavy waterlogged suit. But he did get his hands on the rope. Dragging Didi with him, he made the first three pulls on the line when suddenly it slackened. The more he went hand over hand the more the rope fell through his hands. Fargues was paying out rope; over a hundred meters curled into the cavern. Cousteau dropped the rope and, feeling himself near fainting, began to claw his way up the rock. He found a good ledge but was dragged down by the weight of Dumas. The shock of falling down again turned his mind to the rope. He remembered what the six tugs meant and jerked the rope, confident he could count to six. He was ready to cut the rope to Dumas, thinking Didi was dead already, but instead kept repeating the distress signal.

Above, when the bubbles stopped, Simone couldn't stand it anymore and left the hill. She dashed down to a cafe and ordered a stiff cognac.

In the cave, Jacques felt the rope tighten. Dumas's tanks clanged against the rock and they were being hauled up. In less than a minute Fargues pulled them to the surface and leaped into the water. Tailliez and several pairs of strong hands got hold of Cousteau. Fargues and a doctor worked over Dumas's vomiting stomach, while Cousteau warmed himself at a flaming cauldron of gasoline.

Someone raced down the hill and into the care, yellilng one of the divers had drowned. Simone cried, "Which one? What color was his mask?" The one with the red mask, the harbinger said. Jacques's mask was blue.

Five minutes later, Dumas was on his feet, standing by the fire. Cousteau handed him a bottle of brandy. He took a drink and announced he was ready to go down again. Jacques wondered where Simone was. When she came back up, she saw Didi standing by the fire.

With a modified work plan, Tailliez and Guy Morandière went down in the afternoon. Forty meters down, Tailliez felt the inviting throbs of nitrogen narcosis. He knew that was impossible at a mere 130 feet. Morandière realized Tailliez's breathing was disorderly and before they could make the six-pull signal to be hauled up spent confusing minutes, each thinking the other was in trouble. When Tailliez surfaced and found footing, he was wild-eyed. In his right hand he held his dagger and blood flowed from his fingers. He did not feel it.

Driving back to Toulon that evening, Jacques, Simone, and Didi talked about nitrogen narcosis and subjective fears. Dumas wondered if it couldn't have been the air they breathed. The next day they ran a lab test on the air left in the cylinders. The analysis showed 1/2000 of carbon monoxide. The pressure at the depth they had been increased the effect sixfold. They started the new diesel compressor and saw it sucking in its own exhaust. They had breathed enough carbon monoxide to kill anyone in twenty minutes. "It's extraordinary that we didn't all stay in that cave," Dumas would say in 1985, remembering the episode.

In February 1947, Alex Ancel, a former colleague of Pierre, obtained a prosecuting judge's permission to interview PAC and another convicted journalist in his chambers. He was there, Ancel told them when they were alone, to do a favorable piece on their ludicrous case. Was there anything he could do in the meantime, call somebody, transmit a message? While Ancel commiserated about their unjust fate, his photographer snapped pictures of the agreeably surprised and smiling pair. The headline of the resulting reportage read, "THESE MEN HAVE ONLY 100 DAYS TO LIVE. PAC's and Lucien Rebatet's execution by firing squad was set for April 6. The last hour came and went, and three days later the sentences were commuted to life imprisonment.

Jacques's team had its first fatal accident the same year. In a routine dive to discover what fouled the dragline of a minesweeper, Dumas set a record of 100 meters – the height of a 22-story building. A few weeks later Fargues went down along a rope hung with slates, wrote his name on one 130 meters down (30 stories), tried to go farther, lost consciousness, and drowned.

As much as Cousteau thrilled in the new discoveries, he hated daredevil stunts. "I hate danger," he would say on a number of occasions, "but once we have taken all the precautions there always remains a certain dose of danger that we have to deal with. Over the years, exploring the sea has meant taking chances, running risks."

Cousteau was eager to get thousands of meters below the practical limit of scuba diving and was to have descended that summer in Swiss physicist Auguste Piccard's diving saucer, a craft based on ballooning principles, after the GERS unit assisted in the preparation. Although the bathyscaph – Greek for "light boat" – had survived an unmanned test dive, it was damaged beyond repair on its ascent.

The Piccards were a family of scientists. The sixty-three-year-old Auguste had, at different times, held the world's altitude record and with his twin brother Jean and the Belgian physicist Dr. Max Cosyns made balloon flights to the edge of the stratosphere in pressurized cabins. From 1937, Auguste and his son Jacques had designed, built, and tested successive bathyscaphs named FNRS 1 and FNRS 2 for the Belgian Fonds

National de la Recherche Scientifique (National Scientific Research Group) that partially financed the project. Cousteau got to take part in the test of FNRS 2 off West Africa and became technical adviser with Piccard and Cosyns to FNRS 3. Dumas contributed vital ideas for the design and both went down nearly a mile in a canyon off Toulon. Powerful lights were mounted on FNRS 3, and Cousteau compared looking and filming through the craft's porthole with gazing at the Milky Way on a beautiful summer night. The big surprise was to see huge sharks – and a spread-out newspaper – on the ocean floor.

While most of the GERS unit worked on the bathyscaph project, Jean Alinat and two other team members, this time assisted by the Army Corps of Engineers, went back to the problem of cave diving, not in the Vaucluse fountain, but in the subterranean Vitarelles spring in the Massif Central. On a tenth dive, Alinat reached the entrance to a siphon 130 meters below the surface, swam into a narrow tunnel, passed up through 12 meters of turbid water that blurred his face mask like a windshield in rain, and realized his head was in air. He was in a sealed clay vault. He removed his mouthpiece and mask and breathed natural air. Flowing water brought oxygen to the vault. Making the first human footprints on the slippery rim, he explored further and found a new labyrinth of caves under the clear water, before he returned through the siphon to the surface.

The Undersea Research Group experimented with underwater television and, another first, color film. Cousteau had assumed pigmentation to be pallid and uninteresting, and was astonished to see incrustations of algae that seemed a dull gray 15 to 30 meters down glow with violent reds and oranges near the surface.

To overcome seawater's natural filtering of colors, he brought artificial light 50 meters below the surface and filmed a first deepsea sequence in brilliant hues. The team went on an archeological expedition off the coast of Tunisia during the summer of 1948 and recovered treasures from a Roman galley believed to have sunk in 80 B.C. Lying in 42 meters of water, the ship had been built by the general and dictator Lucius Sulla to transport his plunder from Athens. From its deck, Cousteau brought up three marble columns and two Ionic capitals, part of a temple that apparently had struck the future emperor's fancy. Diving and filming would remain a lifelong passion.

Eugene Higgins died in Torquay that July. *The New York Times* couldn't say exactly how old that city's once wealthiest bachelor was but assured its obituary readers that he died a bachelor, leaving only a nephew in Palm Beach, Florida, and two nieces in Aiken, South Carolina, and New York City. Higgins left a legacy to Daniel, his adviser and companion for nearly thirty years.

Although other family members used the apartment on Avenue de la Motte-Picquet, it belonged to Daniel and Elizabeth. They were finally free to return permanently to Paris. They stayed in Torquay, however, to see fourteen-year-old Françoise and ten-year-old Jean-Pierre through school. Fernande was ill and there was no end in sight to PAC's prison term despite appeals, regular parole hearings, and a very changing political climate. The Berlin blockade by the Soviets in June and the opposing Western airlift was putting a final nail into the coffin of the grand alliance that had defeated Hitler's army. The Americans, British, and French were busy fusing their occupation zones into an allied Federal Republic and the Russians were establishing a rival German Democratic Republic in their Eastern zone. The cold war was making "good Germans" out of the arch enemy of three years ago.

Newly released political prisoners wrote back to PAC that Parisians were astonished to hear there were still "collabos" in jail.

Jacques was not interested politically or personally. Pedro was angry with him for not visiting him enough in Clairvaux, the prison 225 kilometers east of Paris he had been transferred to after the death sentence had been commuted. PAC kept a diary and during a particularly depressing time bitterly noted that his brother should not have interceded but let him face the firing squad. At other times, when PAC had recovered his sarcastic, superior self, he jotted down observations about Jean-Paul Sartre and his tony Left Bank existentialism and remembered attending the premiere of *No Exit* in 1944 together with distinguished SS officers, and how Pablo Picasso, the new darling of the Riviera, had cleaned out his backlog of paintings, selling them to cultivated Germans.

Jacques's mind was on totally different matters. Throughout 1948 he was on the lookout for a boat of his own. What he wanted was a floating laboratory and diving platform that would be closer to his and his divers' needs and aspirations than the *Elie Monnier* and various other navy tenders and tugs they had turned into makeshift work stations. He wanted to leave active duty for a while and spend more time with his family. Being the master of his own boat would allow him to have his wife sail with him. Of course, it meant Jean-Michel and Philippe would have to go to boarding school, but it also meant a family life during school holidays because the boys could join their parents on board.

Cousteau's interests – and reputation – were spreading like the circles a stone plunked into a pond leaves behind. He was eager to apply the aqualung and all its potentials to nonmilitary objectives. The Piccards and Cosyns had introduced him to Claude-Francis Boeuf, a brilliant ocean-ographer with the La Rochelle Laboratory on the Atlantic coast, and to Jacques Bourcart, who had surveyed the offshore Toulon trench, and they in turn had brought him in contact with other scientists. Sea-floor discoveries posed new evolutionary questions. Indeed, the whole undersea world was so entirely new that each plunge brought up ever more questions about biology and intelligence in the sea which would take decades of research to answer. There were reasons to believe that biological factors made the sea into a vast network of paths and highways. Every species apparently had its route, and there were routes for every season. This meant that a true research vessel wouldn't go out at random, but could perhaps follow great underwater webs.

And there were the widening rings of his filmmaking that spread in other directions. Since *Par dix-huit mètres de fond*, he had made five other shorts, all well received, all shown at film festivals. He couldn't wait to make an underwater film in color. People had never seen anything like it, Maurice Bessy, one of the young people connected with the Cannes Film Festival, told him. And more interesting was the fact that, nobody knew better than he, Tailliez, and Dumas how to film under the sea.

Perry Miller was a very young and pretty American who in far-off New York kept hearing about Jacques Cousteau. A recent divorcée with the looks and aspirations to become an actress, Miller was working at the United Nations Department of Social Affairs. Her job was to inventory shorts, arts and science films, documentaries, and other nonfiction films that belonged in a very elastic social sciences category. This cataloguing led her to the screening of all sorts of interesting European films that no one in America had ever seen and, with her own money, to Europe in 1949 in search of a selection that might be part of a U.S. theater's playbill of newsreel, short, and main features. In Brussels, Rome and at the new United Nations Educational and Scientific Organization (UNESCO) in Paris, people gave her lists of their suggestions. The films of Jacques Cousteau were almost always on top.

When she phoned the number she was given, a Daniel Cousteau answered. Yes, he was taking care of his son's affairs. Yes, a screening of his films could be arranged, a meeting as well. On the appointed day, Miller went to Avenue de la Motte-Picquet and, as she entered the elevator, saw a tall thin man rush after her. She held the door and they went up together. Getting off on the same floor, they guessed they were each other's appointment. I think that from the very beginning we really hit it off," she would remember. "He had made all these films and none of them had been seen in America. His feeling was, What do I have to lose? Here is this crazy American girl spending her own money. I also think he was intrigued by the fact that a very young woman would be doing this."

She was captivated too. She found him to have a wonderful sense of humor, to be alternately very serious and sardonic, to say exactly the opposite of what people would expect him to say. She returned to New York and, to drum up support and find a distributor for her selection of unusual films, set up a committee of influential film and media people.

Robert Flaherty, the nature filmmaker who had just finished *Louisiana Story,* paid for a screening of her European selection. An editor from *Life* who attended was especially enthusiastic about the Cousteau underwater shorts. Perry arranged further screenings for Time-Life people, and on November 27, 1950, *Life* ran seven pages of photos and text about the scuba-diving inventor-filmmaker and his work. When distribution executives at Universal Pictures saw the *Life* spread, they made an $11,000 bid for *Par dis-huit mètres de fond, Epaves, Paysages du silence,* and *Une plongée du "Rubis".* "Nobody else made an offer, and it was still a steal," Perry would say. "But that began Cousteau's career in America. Universal distributed them as theatrical shorts and as a result people got interested."

Making underwater films was already a reality. Now Cousteau's dream of a boat of his own and a furlough became true in 1949 when he found the *Calypso* and Admiral

Lemonnier arranged a leave from active duty.

Cousteau knew perfectly well what kind of ship would make the best research vessel: a minesweeper. In the course of its duties, a minesweeper is expected to be subject to occasional underwater explosions, so minesweepers are generally well built. They are usually easy to handle and they have a shallow draft that is ideal for maneuvering in and out of waterways or bobbing above knife-sharp coral reefs. Cousteau's search led him to André Auniac, the head of the naval shipyard in Antibes, the seaside resort halfway between Cannes and Nice. Auniac in turn put him in touch with Thomas Loël Guinness, a wealthy Englishman, a former member of Parliament, and an old salt.

Guinness pointed Cousteau toward Malta, the British Island bastion between Sicily and North Africa which had played such a strategic role during the war. Valletta harbor was full of surplus ships.

The *Calypso* was both surplus minesweeper and working car ferry. She was not big – 46 meters long (a "150-footer," the English said) and 8.2 meters across the beam – but she was sturdy, constructed with double planking and very narrow spaced timbers. She had two engines and propellers giving her a ponderous if stately 10.5 knots top speed. she was in excellent condition and very maneuverable.

She was built in Seattle in 1942 during President Roosevelt's lend-lease program to help beleaguered Great Britain. She had gone to war as the Royal Navy's mine-sweeper J-826, and in recent years had worked as a ferry, carrying eleven cars and up to four hundred passengers between Victoria on Gozo Island and Valletta. It was as a ferry that she had been named the *Calypso,* for the nymph-daughter of Atlas and Tethys who, according to Greek mythology, reigned over the isle of Ortygia in the Ionian Sea. When a storm threw Odysseus on her shores, she welcomed him with hospitality and kept him with her for seven years. To retain him forever she offered him immortality, but Zeus ordered her to release him.

Legend would have it that Cousteau named the minesweeper-ferry after the goddess and that he got her by promising never to reveal the identity of the British philanthropist who financed the purchase and never again ask for money. The benefactor was Guinness and the sales contract was signed July 19, 1950, five weeks after Cousteau's fortieth birthday.

6
"IL FAUT ALLER VOIR"

People who knew Jacques Cousteau in the 1950's called him a "fabulous producer," a sobriquet that not only referred to his movie success but also to his sonorous verbosity, confident civility, soaring aspirations, and craggy charm. His captain's sway and swagger blended provocatively with his enthusiasm, easy camaraderie, and contagious curiosity. Tall, skinny, and superbly tanned, he wanted to understand what no one else had been able to see, to extend himself by pushing the human reach into the earth's briny mantle. He knew how to handle men and surrounded himself with people who wanted to live more fully and find meaning in adventure. And his wonderful inquisitiveness spread naturally to his crew members. *"Il faut aller voir,"* meaning, "we must go and see for ourselves," became a collective credo, an almost fanatical insistence that human beings belong in the sea, that to understand our watery planet we must dive into it.

112

The fifties were to remain Cousteau's most thrilling decade, the intoxicating years when his ocean discoveries were so many "firsts." He knew he was good copy and could be prodded to say almost anything that would help his reputation. When on land, he was always ready to meet journalists, film people, and industrialists who might be interested in the commercial potentials of free diving. If businessmen couldn't immediately think of industrial applications for scuba diving, he was brimming with ideas of his own. How about marine design, salvage, and shorefront construction? How about mining the seafloor, laying pipelines, or surveying for that brand-new technology, offshore oil drilling? One commercial area that didn't immediately occur to him was diving gear for amateurs. By the end of the decade there would be one million dedicated skin divers in the United States alone, the majority discovering their fascinating new playground wearing suits, masks, and aqualungs manufactured under a Cousteau license by an Air Liquide subsidiary.

What Cousteau was learning fast in 1950 were the twin arts of organizing enthusiasm and raising money. Being a shipowner in and of itself taxed his financial acumen to its limits. The generosity of Loël Guinness gave him a superbly seaworthy minesweeper-ferryboat. The real fun began when the *Calypso* was brought to Antibes for conversion to research vessel.

André Auniac finagled a permission to put the *Calypso* in the navy's dry dock while he began scavenging the shipyard for surplus parts. Simone sold some of her jewelry while her father and father-in-law began approaching Air Liquide and other manufacturers for outright gifts of equipment. Claude-Francis Boeuf, who with his assistant, Jacqueline Zang, had become good friends of Jacques and Simone, contributed the idea of a nonprofit organization. The suggestion quickly translated into the Compagnies Océanographiques Françaises (COF), responsible for commissioning, managing, and administering the finances of the *Calypso*'s future expeditions. In turn, earnings from privately sponsored research, as well as grants and royalties from possible movies, books and magazine stories, would be plowed back into the Oceanographic Company.

To do something with himself and make some money for COF while *Calypso* was reborn, Jacques and Didi went out in a chartered boat to test color photography more thoroughly. Color film was quite new, and no one knew what happened to definition and color shifts when exposed in the ocean twilight. Cousteau and Dumas tried combinations of emulsions, flash and natural daylight, and even dipped flashbulbs in tinted varnish of various hues before they managed to get satisfactory color pictures. To allow their cameras to "breathe," they attached a mini-aqualung feeding compressed air to the camera housing, thereby allowing for an adjustment of the air intake to compensate for the increase of pressure as divers and cameramen descended. Lighting underwater scenes proved a more difficult challenge. On land, a powerful flashbulb exploded in pitch darkness can illuminate a circumference of 18 meters. In the sea, dense with its zillions of microscopic organisms and suspended minerals, a similar flash would barely light up a two-meter radius. It would take years for the Cousteau teams to blueprint, systems engineer, manufacture, and train themselves to use reliable underwater lighting equipment.

The removeling of the *Calypso* was extensive. The ship was virtually stripped down to hull and engines. the interior was altered, a flying bridge, masts, and aluminum crow's nest were added, together with a diving platform off the stern. New navigational aids, including sonar, were purchased and a "false nose" was built. This was a metal well constructed around the prow and ending with a bulbous observation chamber three meters below the waterline. Here, two or three crew members could see and film through six portholes.

If remodeling was expensive, running a research vessel and recruiting and maintaining a crew were prohibitive. "*Calypso* was my very first challenge so in the very beginning we were obliged, Simone and I, to devote all we had," JYC was to remember. Simone sold more of her jewelry, and a timely government contract that made the *Calypse* a scientists' excursion boat for a few trips saved them for another couple of months. Packages of color stills were sent "on spec" to magazines and scientific journals the world over, while wealthy friends kicked in lump sums. The manifest of the *Calypso*'s maiden voyage as a research vessel in June 1951 showed to whom the Cousteaus were beholden. Besides the captain, Simone, Dumas, the engineer Octave ("Titi") Léandri – the first man actually hired – and thirteen-year-old Jean-Michel and eleven-year-old Philippe, both registered as cabin boys, the list included Roger Gary,

116

a Marseillais industrialist, and Edmond Mauric, an architect; Pierre Malville, an Antibes restaurateur and yachtsman; a young photographer, Jacques Ertaud; and a sailor nicknamed Malaga on loan from Gary's yacht. The *Calypso* was not yet equipped with lifeboats so Malville lent Cousteau a dinghy.

Elizabeth died that year. On one of her regular trips from Torquay to visit Pierre in prison, she suffered a fatal stroke while staying in the apartment on Avenue de la Motte-Picquet. Life had not been easy for her. She had remained the pillar in Daniel's unconventional life, through the wandering years in America and England, their wartime separation, and her elder son's disgrace. At an age when she should have enjoyed distracted grandmotherhood, she had taken on the responsibility of bringing up PAC's children.

Daniel had been in Torquay twelve years. Had it not been for Elizabeth's death, Jean-Pierre later speculated, he probably would have stayed. Now distraught and suddenly restless, Daniel wanted to return permanently to France, Jacques and Simone would have to make room for him.

The elder Cousteau was a vivacious

seventy-five-year-old. People who met him for the first time thought he looked almost shockingly youthful. As the years dulled the memory of Elizabeth, he thrived in his widowerhood and in Jacques's growing fame. He remained something of a character, persuasive, charming, politically innocent yet capable of dealing masterfully with bureaucrats. Marine biologist Raymond Vaissière remembered him as a sprightly presence in the administrative background of expedition planning, government contracting, and organizing. Indeed, to give him something to do, JYC suggested his father get involved with COF, and from 1951 on, "Daddy," as everybody affectionately called him in deference to his mastery of English and years among "Anglo-Saxons," worked at home base in all manner of functions from government liaison to escorting visiting scientists through French customs. His pride was his multi-volume scrapbook of newspaper clippings about his son.

The *Calypso* left Toulon on its first expedition November 24, 1951. The destination was the Red Sea and its coral reefs. Three days out the *Calypso* ran into a storm that, JYC would remember, saw "the prow leap out of the water, sometimes even to the bilge keels, before plunging deeply into the

118

following wave." Shaken up in the drums, the fuel oil picked up dirt and gradually clogged fuel lines and filters. First one, then both engines conked out.

Because COF didn't quite have the money to fund a full-blown expedition and the captain and Simone had exhausted their personal resources, fully paid crew members were kept to a minimum. Titi Léandri was there, with first engineer René Montupet, boatswain Jean Beltran, and the blue-eyed Alsation cook, Fernand Hanen. Simone served as nurse, secretary, and assistant to Hanen, while La Rochelle Laboratory hydrologist Jacqueline Zang, the expedition's only other woman, and her boss, Claude-Francis Boeuf, doubled as galley helpers.

Captain François Saôut, Jacques's former commanding officer and a skilled sailboat racer who was to become the *Calypso*'s alternate skipper until his retirement in 1960, shared the deck watch with the expedition's doctor, Jean-Loup Nivelleau de la Brunière. The physician had so much wanted to be part of the expedition that he had embellished his résumé with ticked off participation in all sorts of fictitious voyages. By the time he admitted the truth, he had proved himself so competent JYC forgave him.

"The captain has a way of making you feel important," diver André Portelatine would remember. "He always had a special comment for each person. Everybody was a specialist, of course, but your particular line of study or work had nothing to do with your assigned job on the ship. We all stood watch, either on the bridge or in the engine room, and a photographer could be teamed up with a Sorbonne professor, a geophysicist would get galley duty with an engineer."

Pitching in and sharing cramped living space were to be permanent features of life aboard *Calypso*. Captain and Mrs. Cousteau had their own midship living quarters – office, eventually with their own shower, sink and toilet, but everybody else doubled or tripled up in crew and passenger cabins. By the time of the lush television contracts, accommodations would be vastly improved. But the *Calypso* remained a small wooden ship, and her master always had a knack for making her crew and visiting scientists work on enthusiasm, joshing comradeship, and a certain manly grace under pressure. "The meals were always elaborate, leisurely affairs with many courses from crudités down through cognac," Portelatine said. "In the early days everybody smoked cigars, pipes, or cigarettes, and by the end of the evening

120

the mess hall, or *carré*, reeked of smoke. By eleven, however, if you weren't on watch you were asleep."

To be young and French in the late 1940's and 50's was to have been hemmed in by the war and to be eager to go abroad. The postwar pop culture cultivated studied nihilism, Françoise Sagan, Côte d'Azur living, and the romance of faraway places. Cousteau's crews would always be badly paid, work themselves to the limit, endure ice and heat, mosquitoes, stingrays, prolonged if collective loneliness on sea, and when expeditions were land-based, live three or four per hotel room among folding chairs and pinned-up navigation charts, but Cousteau never had any difficulty recruiting hardworking, dedicated people. Eager young men came to him in droves, some like Nivelleau ready to say anything to get on board, some with psychic troubles they still had to work out, but all welcoming physical efforts, difficulties, and risks. "Many of those who come to us are sensitive young men who have not found happiness or peace in leading an ordinary life," Cousteau would say two decades later. "And that is what makes them valuable to us. I cannot help thinking that the men of the *Calypso* resemble, in many ways, those of Jules Verne's *Nautilus* – men who had been wounded by life on land, and who thereafter put their trust in the sea."

What got a young man hired was competence and companionship. Over the years Cousteau would come to insist on new crewmembers having at least two specialties. "One of them can be diving, but diving alone is not enough," he said. "You have to be a good diver and something else. People who come are either rejected or accepted by the rest of the crew. We lose about one person a year, but people who are accepted and cherished by their friends will stay, maybe, twenty or twenty-five years. It's like a transplant, an organ transplant. It is rejected or accepted. That's the way we make our team."

In return for unquestioned loyalty, Cousteau treated his teams with utmost regard for their survival. Major and very costly projects would be delayed while critical equipment was tested again and again. Cousteau would install every possible safety device imaginable, from early television monitors and shark cages to decompression chambers and elaborate escape hatches and insist on constant training, especially in diving techniques. The first law aboard the *Calypso* would always remain: Never take unnecessary risks. In dives, JYC enforced the rule that everybody must know what he's supposed to do and must have achieved mastery at it.

This unflinching insistence on safety was to pay off over the next thirty-five years. In November 1952 off Marseilles, Jean-Pierre Serventi, one of Cousteau's more experienced divers, descended 80 meters to retrieve a buoy chain only to be brought up unconscious and to die while the *Calypso* raced to port. In Antarctica in 1972, first mate Michel Laval went to meet an incoming helicopter on Deception Island when he tripped or slipped on ice and was struck and instantly killed by the chopper's tail propeller. During a seemingly routine dive in Lake Ontario in 1980, Remy Galliano, a member of the *Calypso* team for more than a year, apparently misjudged his depth in muddy waters and died of air embolism. They were to remain the only fatalities in fifty-five expeditions and over 30,000 dives.

However desolate or antipodean their work stations, crews and divers were flown home for rest and recreation every six months. Cousteau adhered to the French maritime law mandating such rotations on ships that do not return to home port once a year. Approaching rotation time, the *Calypso* would head for some anchorage or harbor with airline connections, send off one team and, while awaiting the next crew, undergo various repairs. At such downtimes, Jacques and Simone were usually the only ones on board.

Remarkably perhaps for a naval commander, Cousteau was to remain extremely relaxed about dress codes, hairstyles, leisure activities, and mess hall humor. Crews have gone through phases of turn-of-the-century mustaches and sideburns, full beards and Yul Brynner skinheads. JYC and Simone have seen rotations where crews collected comic books, shark teeth, red coral, and marmoset monkeys, and others where everybody made audio tape diaries and cooked and ate elaborate seafood dinners. Stretching the breadth of the main aft deck, the mess hall was the biggest and busiest room on the ship. With passable irreverence, General Pierre Cambronne, who at the battle of Waterloo answered Anglo-Prussian summonses for his surrender with *"merde,"* looks down from his framed portrait on much chewing and diversion, much retelling and debating of a day's events, much stroking of nodding beards, Scrabble playing, puffing on pipes, and plotting of practical jokes.

Gustave Cherbonnier, a Sorbonne professor specializing in mollusks, became the object of the first prank as the *Calypso* rode out a storm. Montupet got the engines restarted (it was the oil filters) and, near Port Said, the first flying fish landed on the deck. While the biologist finished his watch, the flying fish was carried below deck and put in his bunk. Everybody waited for the primal scream that followed his sliding under the covers. A note on his pillow innocently called the fish the initial specimen for his collection.

Cherbonnier loved animals. Stuffing dead specimens in formaldehyde jars in the Red Sea, he once exclaimed, "What an irony that I must kill them in order to study them."

The *Calypso* sailed through the Suez Canal December 5, and ten days later had taken on fresh water and supplies in Jidda, the Saudi port through which most pilgrims came to Mecca in those pre-jet days, and one rosy morning, with Jacques himself in the crow's nest, reached the Farasan islands and their stunning coral reefs.

Second only to Australia's Great Barrier Reef in size, the Farasan islands reefs were, in 1952, a largely uncharted archipelago of reefs, both barrier and fringing shoals, and deep but nonnavigable channels 75 kilometers off the most desolate stretch of the Saudi-Yemini coast. Edging past these

125

razor-sharp reefs that could cut open the bottom of the *Calypso* in a second, they anchored at Abu Latt, an old, uplifted reef made entirely of fossil coral. A base camp was established, and for the next five weeks geophysicist Haroun Tazieff, biologists Claude Mercier and Vladimir Nesteroff, Cherbonnier, Zang, and JYC himself lived by a shallow lagoon, while Saôut took the *Calypso* on reconnaissance and sounding excursions that established huge undersea basins of volcanic origin in the surrounding sea.

The group on Abu Latt were there to dive and Cousteau's nudging *"il faut aller voir"* insistence on direct observation was a wonderful stimulus for the scientists. The first two weeks' diving was limited to snorkling as the brand-new compressor needed to fill the aqualung air tanks refused to start, but the sparkling blue waters were so rich in flora and fauna that Cherbonnier and Mercier found unknown species and gallantly named several of them *Calypseus, Saôuti,* and *Cousteaui.* On January 3, 1952, when Montupet discovered the compressor's exhaust pipes were too small and with a roar that deafened everybody got the 50-horsepower engine going, Captain Cousteau ordered champagne broken out.

Cousteau, Dumas, and still photographer Ertaud were the first to strap on aqualungs and head for the deep. The living coral itself, with its myriad forms and hues, was pulsating with life, predators and prey, ranging up and down the evolutionary scale. The three men encountered hump-headed parrotfish, powerful jacks, shoals of blue bonitos, silver sardines, small gray, purple and black coral fish, fleeting damselfish, and innumerable dabs of colors of hydrozoans, ascidians and sponges, many of them flocking to have a look at the masked and finned divers, a species they had never seen before. Triggerfish, electric blue or iridescent green and yellow, mingled further down with schools of big yellow-spotted groupers. Moray eels tucked into crevices stuck out their heads for a look. Deeper still tigerfish with their venomous dorsal fins swam unafraid above celery-shaped alcyonarians, hairy crabs, giant clams, and sea snails. The trio drifted over clumps of coral that resembled mauve petrified heather, over organ-pipe coral and graceful *Acropora* coral spreading filigrees like parasols.

The reef ended with a ledge overhanging a blue abyss. Dumas was examining a small opening in the cliff when Cousteau saw a shark, four meters long, swim toward Didi.

Jacques hooted through his mouthpiece. Didi gave no sign of hearing and a minute later the huge shark turned and slid away. "It occurred to me then, and our later experiences seemed to confirm, that we were actually safer at this great depth than nearer the surface," Cousteau was to write in his first *National Geographic* magazine piece later that year.

There was only one frustration. The working limit for a trained aqualung diver was 70 meters, with 100 meters the absolute frontier for one minute thrusts. Yet they saw the rich wall of teeming unexplored life beckon below their reach.

The scientist and photographers, however, were happy with the rich zone of life accessible to them. Cherbonnier and Mercier happily surfaced with flora and fauna, catalogued their finds, and dropped them into formaldehyde. While Zang took innumerable water samples, Jean Dupas, an army parachutist on detached duty, and Nesteroff hunted elusive specimens such as hump-headed parrotfish with spear and cartridge-propelled harpoons without ever catching one. Dumas tried with dynamite to no better avail.

Ertaud and Jean de Wouters d'Oplinter, a Belgian engineer who was to invent an

128

amphibious camera, took pictures while Cousteau and Dumas kept extensive logs. The underwater photo sessions were cumbersome affairs, demanding three divers, one to snap the picture, two to hold the lights.

It was neither Dupas nor Nesteroff with their weapons, nor Dumas with his dynamite charges, but d'Oplinter and JYC who stumbled on a striking pair of parrotfish in a lagoon during one of the last dives. The two men cautiously turned toward the big fish, which for once didn't flee, but allowed the intruders to float with them through the shallows. Now and then the fish would charge against the coral and, with a crunch, bite off a chunk. To obtain a tiny amount of assimilable nutrients, Cousteau later calculated, they would have to swallow enormous amounts of corall, 10 tons of it every year. Now and then the fish would defecate a big cloud that muddied the water. JYC swam near one of these clouds. It was sand, the same kind that covered the bottom of the entire lagoon. The trio had found one of nature's reef-building machines at work. Eons of coral-munching parrotfish, along with sea currents and winds, had built the hundreds of low sand islets.

After dropping off several of the scientists on the Ethiopian shore for flights from Addis

129

Ababa back to France, the *Calypso* sailed home through the Suez Canal and the Mediterranean. Her master was determined to come back and *film* it all. Spirits were dampened when they reached Toulon and learned Claude-Francis Boeuf and Jacqueline Zang had died in an accident at Addis Ababa airport.

The news from America was more positive. Perry Miller thought she might be able to get Jacques a television deal. In a letter, James Dugan wondered if there wasn't a book in the *Calypso*'s Red Sea logs.

To keep men and ship afloat until a new expedition could be organized and funded, COF went into the sunken treasure business. Jacques and Didi put their notes and logs together. Dugan's idea was worth a try. Next, Cousteau flew to Washington, his first visit to the United States since passing through Los Angeles in 1932.

With a briefcase full of Ertaud's Ektochrome transparencies, Didi's and his own Red Sea pictures, and an outline for an article on undersea exploration, Jacques leaped up the steps to the National Geographics headquarters on 17th and M streets. The society, which since its foundation in 1888 had sponsored and supported the arctic explorations of both Robert Peary and Richard Byrd and published firsthand accounts of other explorers, was the world's largest and wealthiest institution of its kind, with an international membership of three million, all of whom received the society's monthly magazine with its distinctive canary-color bordered cover.

Gilbert Grosvenor, president, editor, and son of the founding geographer-writer, immediately agreed to publish the Red Sea account and accompanying photos, and asked about Cousteau's future plans. Jacques was eloquent, lyrical, and to the point. The *next* mission would have to be a three-, perhaps four-year term, an early, almost preliminary stocktaking of the world's oceans. For the first time we were discovering the third dimension, the depth, of the seas – and the extent of our ignorance. Incredible as it may sound, we know practically nothing about life below 180 meters. We don't even know how many creatures inhabit the deep. We know next to nothing about the intelligence in the sea, even the intelligence among marine mammals. Would the National Geographic help finance this next, indispensable thrust into the unknown?

Grosvenor was impressed by the lanky

Frenchman and promised an early decision. Grosvenor wanted Cousteau to meet members of the board, the staff, and a fellow JYC might find very interesting, a professor of electrical measurements at the Massachusetts Institute of Technology and co-inventor of a high-speed electronic flash capable of exposures as brief as a millionth of a second. Harold E. Edgerton had filmed what the human eye cannot see, freezing the motion of a drop of water, stopping the humming-bird's whirring wings. Maybe Edgerton could be persuaded to put his mind to the problem of deep-sea photography.

In New York, Cousteau met Edgerton, Jim Dugan, and the lovely Perry. She was involved in her own career, which instead of acting was beginning to parallel Jacques's. Nonfiction filmmaking was her passion and her wide industry contacts led her toward television and, at CBS-TV, a job as film coordinator searching out documentaries. New York was on the eve of a revolutionary new wave called *Cinéma-vérité*, a whole new thrust toward heightened reality and intimacy that technical innovations and perfections in film stock, camera construction, and magnetic tape recording made possible, and Perry was in the middle of it.

While Perry made appointments for

Jacques to see various network executives, he and Dugan started translating the Cousteau-Dumas notes and logs and work up a presentation. A publishing contract was signed with Harper and Brothers. Dugan would be more than a translator. He would organize and help write out in English the logs and notes in book form. At CBS, meanwhile, Perry managed to get Cousteau a deal with *Omnibus,* a ninety-minute program set up by a Ford Foundation grant but carried under commercial sponsorship. "Cousteau made three films for *Omnibus,*" she recalled, "and that was really his first consciousness of an American public."

The Grand Congloué is a rock sticking out of the surf 20 kilometers southeast of Marseilles's harbor off the Cape Croisette. Marseilles was founded by Greek mariners from Phocaea in Asia Minor about 600 B.C., and probably settled by Phoenicians before that. Over the millennia, the Grand Congloué has been the bane of countless ships, and the bottom around the arid, uninhabited rock is littered with shipwrecks. It was off the southern rock face of Grand Congloué that Cousteau and his team discovered a 1,000-ton Roman freighter owned by one Marcus Sestius which sank

133

around 230 B.C. In 1952 this argosy was the oldest seagoing vessel ever found.

Through the summer the *Calypso* served as diving board and shuttle between Marseilles harbor and Grand Congloué. Once the magnitude of the discovery was realized, new equipment and divers were added. For fear that winter storms might make a wreck of the *Calypso* if she stayed moored to the rock, a platform accommodating a shack with generators, equipment, and living space for six was attached to the rockside, mostly with mountain climbers' pitons, and steel cables.

A pair of sixteen-year-olds who were to become lifelong team members joined that summer: Albert ("Bebert") Falco, a husky, quiet diver with an instinct for what to do underwater and how to deal with marine life; and Raymond Coll, a Spaniard of few words who was to be the first human to hitch a ride on the back of a whale shark. Together with Dumas, they and newcomers Raymond ("Canoë") Kientzy, Henri Goiran, the smallest diver, and Serventi formed the core of the diving team. JYC's decision to go for a novelty – closed-circuit television – to help locate Sestius's cargo brought twenty-three-year-old engineer André Laban into the charmed circle.

134

Lying below 50 meters of water and twenty centuries of silt, the argosy's cargo proved to be thousands of wine amphoras, or two-handed storage jars, and as many ceramic tiles and sets of dinnerware. To free the goods from the sediment and debris, the divers used a novel and sometimes capricious underwater vacuum cleaner, a flexible pipe and air hose capable of sucking everything up to a kind of huge prospector's pan and sievelike strainer on the *Calypso*'s deck. Here, archeologist Fernand Benoit of Marseilles's Musée Borely and his assistants picked out the thousands of shards, ceramics, pots, and tools, and other artifacts and kept an inventory of everything. Broken amphoras were homes to thousands of octopuses and a standard joke was to stick an octopus into the intake pipe and have it regurgitated topside. The horrified archeologists usually threw the surprised animal back into the sea. A more elaborate hoax Falco tried was to send modern coins up in an amphora and to surface hearing the whoops of archeologists who at first glance thought they had discovered antique treasures. A number of amphoras were found to be intact. Never a man to miss a photo opportunity, Cousteau called television and press reporters to witness the opening of one jar and to taste with him and crew the twenty-one-century-old vintage.

He had plenty to toast. In September, National Geographic agreed to help fund the next mission. As is often the case in instances of multiple underwriting, the sponsorship of the prestigious American society made the backing of the French navy, Ministry of Education, and Academy of Science fall into place.

Cousteau was obsessed with diving into the virgin depths below the aqualung threshold and, while in the Red Sea, had toyed with the idea of a one- or two-man craft. In the *Calypso* mess one day, he had picked up two soup plates and placed them rim against rim. The ideal shape would probably be a kind of diving saucer, looking like a horseshoe crab perhaps, resistant to pressure, easily maneuverable, and small enough to be carried aboard the *Calypso*. Inside, one or two men would lie flat on their stomachs and see through a pair of frontal portholes. Pumps delivering seawater to strategically placed jets would deliver the power, and by turning these nozzles on and off it should be possible to steer the minisub.

Since no such craft existed, Cousteau added the OFRS, the Office Français des Recherches Sous-Marines, to COF. The Red

Sea and Grand Congloué activities had shown it would be logical to assume that other tailor-made gear would be needed. The OFRS, in which a group of Marseilles officials and industrialists agreed to invest, would not only develop a prototype of the diving saucer but would also eventually manufacture, patent, and sell it and any other underwater equipment the *Calypso* team might dream up. André Laban became the director of the new organization, and Jean Mollard, a young electrical engineer, the first diving saucer builder.

Cousteau was back in the United States in early 1953 to see Perry, give lectures, visit Edgerton's lab and invite the MIT professor to be part of the upcoming voyage, and complete plans with *National Geographic*. He was charmed by her beauty, her independence and self-confidence. She found him to be a man who was not handsome in the usual sense but had an enormous attraction for women. She sensed that he appreciated women, that he was married to one who understood him, that whatever happened he would never divorce Simone.

Pery had a wonderful apartment on East Thirty-sixth Street, and many of the meetings with Jim Dugan that resulted in the book *The Silent World* were held there. The

137

book was culled from the logs that JYC and Dumas had kept for the past fifteen years. Translated by Cousteau and smoothed into sometimes poetic prose by Dugan, *The Silent World* gave its readers a sense of personal participation, of what a diver sees, feels, and thinks as he descends into the ocean twilight. It covered the Cousteau experiences from the 1943 dip in the Marne through the postwar aqualung mine-sweeping, the Fontaine de Vaucluse and undersea archeology discoveries, and the depth record trials to the Red Sea coral reef expedition.

Harper and Brothers brought out the 266-page illustrated book in February. *The New York Times* reviewer was Rachel Carson, who found *The Silent World* a fascinating distillation of Cousteau's pioneering undersea explorations. "Beyond its ability to stir our imagination and hold us fascinated, this is an important book," she concluded. "As Capt. Cousteau points out, in the future we must look to the sea, more and more, for food, minerals, petroleum. The aqualung is one vital step in the development of means to explore and utilize the sea's resources." Carson was still a short decade away from publishing *The Silent Spring*, which was to cause the first stirring of ecological awakening in America. In 1953 the oceans were, both author and reviewer agreed, for man to exploit.

Daniel Cousteau met the balding Edgerton and his son and assistant Bill at Cannes to help them and their half-ton of equipment through customs. Politely, the agent opened just one box. It contained six jars of peanut butter. An official eyebrow shot up and a crate was ordered opened. It revealed a cache of paper hats that Edgerton had brought along for an occasional *Calypso* party. Next came a sonic transmitter that ticked like a time bomb and looked like nothing a Cannes customs agent had ever seen. After that officialdom set to work and, the MIT professor would remember, "It took Cousteau senior another six hours of steady debate to extricate us and our belongings."

Work was still going on at Grand Congloué, but after a diversionary descent aboard the navy bathyscaph FNRS 4, the Edgertons and their equipment were installed aboard the *Calypso* and a tiny darkroom rigged out. The language barrier proved to be nearly hermetic. Conversations with the crew were carried out in sign language and in the polyglot jargon of electricians and photographers. In no time the Edgertons were nicknamed Papa Flash and Petit Flash.

The elder Edgerton was cautiously optimistic. Shooting pictures with his strobe light in the vast darkness of the ocean deep, he said, was like photographing birds by blindly lowering a camera from a balloon on a dark foggy night into an unknown forest. And there was the problem of knowing if and when the camera touched the sea bottom. After you had winched out a mile of cable, you had no idea whether your camera at the end of the line had reached the ocean floor. Topside, all you would feel was the dead weight of the cable itself.

In August, however, Jacques was ready to give it a try. With Simone, fourteen-year-old Philippe, Edgerton père and fils, Jim Dugan, and a party of marine biologists, JYC took *Calypso* on a three-week cruise between Sicily and Tunisia to dredge for possible life on the seafloor. The piles of bottom mud that the dredge brought to the deck were enthusiastically greeted by the biologists, who carefully sifted through the goo for starfish and sea cucumbers. Only Captain Saôut was unhappy and in sorrow remarked, "Once I had a clean ship." Papa Flash would remember Philippe and Scaphe, the

Cousteaus' dachshund, pawing through the smelly stuff.

To overcome the problem of knowing if and when a camera touched the seafloor, Edgerton had invented a "bottom detector," an underwater sound transmitter attachable to one end of a cable. Casually one day, Jacques asked if Edgerton would mind losing a camera. "No more than my right arm," Papa Flash answered. "What do you have in mind?"

Cousteau had in mind to fashion some sort of sled and attach to it one of Edgerton's strobe lights and cameras and drag it along the seafloor. The professor agreed, and an aluminum contraption was assembled. Saôut insisted on inserting a plank crosswise, as a hydrofoil to help the sled plane in the water. Someone else loaded it down with chains for a lower center of gravity. Simone appended the National Geographic Society pennant, Dugan attached a *Requiescat in Pace* sign and Dumas gave a brief funeral speech for Edgerton's camera. Its owner set it to take some eight hundred intermittent exposures and at the end of a very long line the device was lowered over the side.

To everyone's surprise when they hauled in the line an hour later, sled, camera, bottom detector and flash came up intact. After being developed, the first strip of negative was nothing to write home about, as Edgerton would say. But the thousands of photos they took during the ensuing months from the little sled brought from the pockmarked lunar landscape of perpetual darkness the first startling images of sea fans, starlike creatures, and even an elusive shark.

After the tour of the Tyrrhenian Sea and the waters between Corsica and Sardinia, it was back to Grand Congloué for *Calypso*. Archeological vacuum cleaning paid the bills and kept the team together, but *Calypso* was supposed to be an oceangoing research vessel and there was something painful in seeing her serve as work barge and coastal lighter. Then, one of oil's fabled seven sisters came up with a proposition that made distant horizons a reality again.

7
WORK AND WHALES

An executive of British Petroleum showed up at the Marseilles dry dock where the *Calypso* was undergoing her first overhaul in three years. Literary fame was at the origin of the visit, the Englishman told Cousteau. BP's chief geologist had read *The Silent World* and wondered whether men diving in aqualungs couldn't be used in oil prospecting. Jacques grinned and said all he had to know was *where* BP wanted to go prospecting.

Oilmen were used to quick decisions and in no time the *Calypso,* her master and crew were chartered to D'Arcy Exploration Company, BP's exploration subsidiary named after William Knox D'Arcy, who in 1888 had staked two brothers with the Australian equivalent of $100, seen them make the biggest gold strike in Down Under history, and later bankrolled the wildcatters who found oil in Iran.

Oceanography would have to wait. The D'Arcy agreement was the first big contract. Cousteau wasted little time doubling COF's fleet, buying a stout 20-meter converted fishing trawler named *Espadon* (swordfish) to finish the Grand Congloué job. He invited André Laban and Raymond Kientzy to come along to the Persian Gulf and recruited as a cameraman a well-to-do young man ready to run off to sea.

Louis Malle was twenty, restless, fresh out of the Institut des Hautes Etudes Cinématographiques (IDHEC), and knew how to scubadive. The would-be filmmaker had no intention of joining his four elder brothers in the family business in northern France and regarded himself lucky to be considered as undersea cameraman.

The fall of 1953 had seen family pressures come to bear on Cousteau. The last of the "collabo" journalists to be released – Lucien Rebatet had been set free a year and a half earlier – Pierre was paroled and ill with cancer. He was bitter toward society and angry at his brother for not having cared enough to do more for him, for being wrapped up in his own career. Counting his year as a prisoner of war, the forty-seven-year-old PAC had spent over ten years behind bars. Free, his name was taboo, his voice on the telephone met with pained silence. He was offended by the semi-official blacklistings and the ostracism with which publishers met him. Well-meaning people who, as he said, had been Pétainists in 1940 and cleverly Gaullists in 1944 told him not to make waves. You're not going to stir up sordid ancient history? they asked.

PAC had written a book on Marcel Proust in prison, but no one would publish it. The heirs might not like it, he was told. He began writing the story of his and Paprika's flight through the collapsing Third Reich. He had lost none of his corrosive wit and planned a picaresque saga on human folly, his own included. He was told such a memoir would not see print until after his death.

Fernande had been his best support, writing him every day during his eight and a half years in prison and traveling once a week to Clairvaux to see him. She was not well, suffering from what would be diagnosed as a brain tumor. The children were back with her. Françoise was nineteen and practically living her own life, but fifteen-year-old Jean-Pierre was happy to be with his mother. They had been separated during his formative years and he needed her emotionally.

Jacques and Simone were eager to sail. Malle was hired as a cameraman and on January 7, 1954, the *Calypso* left Marseilles in a freak snowstorm.

The first half of the voyage was by now familiar, through the Suez Canal and the Red Sea, where Cousteau and Dumas wanted to show Laban, Kientzy, and Malle the wonders of the coral reefs. Impressed by the blue coves framed in bright coral ledges and lilac mountains, the new team members came up yelling, "Incredible!" Among the new recruits was Bonnard, a Portuguese water dog. Almost unknown outside Portugal and

145

the Azores, where fishermen have bred these strong black dogs as water retrievers, Bonnard would dive three meters for objects and loved rough weather. The more the ship heaved and waves crashed over the deck, the happier he was.

After Aden, where they picked up a pair of D'Arcy geologists, it was all new sailing along the coast of Yemen, where they encountered a stupendous school of porpoises, thousands of mammals advancing abreast in frenzied leaps. Crouched in the nose chamber, Malle managed to film the playful mammals making a game of riding the ship's swells. In the Gulf of Oman, they made landfall in Muscat. Because of quarantine laws Bonnard was not allowed to go on shore leave, so when a party of *Calypso* crew members spotted the unmistakable hairy shape of a Portuguese water dog in the middle of the Muscat *souk,* they shouted "Bonnard!" and rushed forward to take him back on board before he was clapped into six months' quarantine. The dog backed off, snarling at them. A crowd gathered and a big frowning man waded in. The dog was his. Muscat, it seemed, had been a Portuguese possession three hundred years earlier and only their dogs and the fort overlooking the southern approaches to the Strait of Hormuz were left. After passing through the strait, an inlet carved through limestone that has the reputation of being the hottest place on earth, it was on to British Petroleum's 12,000-square-mile mining concession off Abu Dhabi.

The next two months were the toughest yet for aqualung work. It was the season of the fiercely burning *khamsin* sandstorms that sprang up without warning. The Trucial Coast might be one of the hottest stretches of land on earth, but the water was cold and teeming with sea snakes and sharks so that shark cages had to be lowered to the work stations; in case of danger, divers could scuttle inside and close the cage behind them. In all, the *Calypso* dropped anchor four hundred times to prospect and take geological samples. The prospecting was done with a gravimeter, a huge bell-like machine swung over the side and lowered to the bottom. If a slight anomaly in the earth's gravity was registered it indicated a possible oil dome under the seafloor. Divers were then sent down to get a sample of the rock floor.

The D'Arcy geologists knew of test drills that had gone down hundreds of meters in the rock, but off Abu Dhabi steel bits crumpled like paper napkins. The first solution was to send down a pair of divers, one with a chisel, the other with a huge maul. It took nearly superhuman strength to swing the hammer through the water, but short of blasting, it was the only way. Then Dumas got the idea of using a jackhammer. The *Calypso* had compressors for filling diving tanks and a kind of pneumatic chisel was rigged together with a compressed air pipe. When Dumas went down and applied his chisel to the granite, he was bounced three meters off the bottom. He surfaced and added weights to his belt and managed to obtain a few chips. It was back to chisel and maul.

A total of 150 rock samples were brought to the *Calypso*'s deck, to be bagged, dated, and labeled with the exact position of the ship and flown to London for analysis. The Sheik of Abu Dhabi offered Cousteau and crew a feast aboard his dhow, where, as usual, Simone was the only woman present. The ruler conversed with the Cousteaus through a Lebanese interpreter, had himself photographed leafing through the pictures of *The Silent World,* and thanked the undersea prospectors – as well he might. Cousteau would remain convinced the *Calypso* crew did all the hard work in finding the offshore oil that in a few short decades would make the 900,000 inhabitants of the United Arab Emirates the richest people on earth.

Emaciated and exhausted but having earned their keep, the *Calypso* team left Abu Dhabi. At a fueling stop at Doha, on the Qatar Peninsula, Cousteau received news from his father that the French Ministry of National Education had agreed to underwrite a major part of future explorations and that the *Calypso* was now the official oceanographic ship of France. In Paris the Centre National de la Recherche Scientifique (CNRS) had chosen the first marine scientists and were flying them out to join the *Calypso*.

The CNRS-selected scientists were none other than Gustave Cherbonnier and two of his biologists. After they and Jim Dugan had been picked up, the *Calypso* left the gulf for the Indian Ocean and veered off the shipping lanes toward Africa. It was exhilarating for the Abu Dhabi work gang and for the newcomers. They met hosts of flying fish, came upon a huge sea turtle basking on the surface and a mysterious scarlet blanket of eggs floating in the ocean. A thousand kilometers east of Kenya, they met their first whales, a large family of sperm whale cows, infants, and a huge black bull.

They gave chase. The leviathans soon proved more powerful than any reconditioned minesweeper and the pursuit turned into a guessing game. Where would the whales spout next? Luck would have it that after several passes, three adults surfaced directly ahead. One of them turned across the *Calypso*'s bow. Cousteau was nearly knocked off his feet as ship and whale collided. Loose gear clattered and a pane fell out of the chartroom window.

The whales turned off the *Calypso*'s course. The animal in the middle was hurt and winded and apparently unable to dive. Moving shoulder to shoulder, the two animals on the flanks seemed to help the injured comrade along. Pursuing whales staying on the surface was easy and JYC listened to the whales underwater with earphones plugged into the echo sounder. He thought he heard the injured animal shriek repeatedly. On the bridge, crew members pointed in all directions. Whales rose in pairs and converged on the accident scene. "I believe they answered the shrieks of distress," Cousteau wrote in a 1955 *National Geographic* article. "Perhaps zoologists won't agree, but I am convinced these noble creatures have a sense of solidarity. In 15 minutes there were 27 whales around the ship. Two babies were seen swimming crazily alongside big cows."

Before the fate of the injured whale was decided, there was a second collision. They all felt the port screw tearing into flesh. A second later they saw four deep gashes in the back of a baby whale.

The infant, which was five meters long and probably no more than three months old, tried to rejoin his family. Whales fell back to surround the wounded. The bull rose out of the water to three-quarters of his length in an act of superb defiance before falling back on his tail. Apparently, the bull gave the order to retreat because the family disappeared, not to be seen again.

Sharks appeared. Saôut and two crew members managed to get a line around the infant whale in its spreading patch of blood and to secure it against the ship. Dumas got out his shotgun and with one well-aimed bullet gave the coup de grace. Antishark cages were lowered, divers suited up and, with JYC, Laban, and Malle leading with cameras, went down to film the chilling frenzy.

Sharks turned up toward the whale with their mouths open and sniffed along the flanks before setting their teeth in the flesh and shaking their bodies like terriers to tear off lumps. With his rifle, Dumas shot a four-meter-long blue shark. It was hauled on deck where Cherbonnier cut it up for study. Somebody got a piece of whale from the shark's stomach and baited a shark hook. The deck was soon covered with writhing sharks, as barefooted men hopped away from jaws and tails.

North of the Seychelles, they enacted the ancient mariners' rites of equatorial passage with a party that saw dressed-up cannibals dunk and feather the fourteen crew members who had not yet crossed the equator. Captain Saôut played Neptune, complete with trident, crown, robes, and a beard made of yarn. One by one, the fourteen novices were placed in a barber chair on the edge of an improvised canvas pool. They were lathered, shaved, and dumped into the water before they had their faces smeared in flour and were given a sweet bun to mark their membership in Neptune's watery kingdom.

When it was all over, somebody shouted that Bonnard had not been initiated. Electrician Paul Martin placed the dog in the barber chair. Bonnard wagged his tail as he was lathered. The cannibals ducked him three times and the cook gave him his sweet bun before Bonnard dived into the pool again. When they let the water out, he was still there, wagging his tail.

Filming sharks occupied part of the voyage home. It wasn't easy. Beyond the difficulty of all underwater filming, there was the difficulty and expense of making it safe. Filming below 10 meters requires artificial light, meaning lamps and cables and divers to man floodlights, .plus cables linking "grips" and cameramen. Shark cages offer protection but they are unwieldy, and most footage was filmed with the cage door open since seeing the steel rods in the foreground of a shot of a cruising big white takes away some of the authenticity.

In the Gulf of Suez, Malle led Laban, Kientzy, and boatswain Albert Raud down a reef to film sharks. At 30 meters, Laban lost sight of Malle and swam deeper, looking for telltale bubbles. Malle was nowhere to be seen. With grunts and gestures, Laban, Kientzy, and Raud decided to look for sharks on their own. They hooked their cables together when Raud saw a pair of sharks below and Kientzy spotted three sharks gliding above.

Raud darted down and came to the end of the cable linking his lights to Laban's camera and Kientzy's lights. At the same time, Kientzy shot upward, coming to the end of his tether. The opposite pulls left Laban, who hadn't seen any danger, strapped in a fearful center. The trio surfaced, fuming at each other. Malle popped up, demanding to know where everybody had been. "I found some lovely sharks," he complained.

The incident told Cousteau how exhausted everybody was after six months of hard diving. They had all made at least three, and often up to five, dives a day. The draining fatigue hit the moment a diver emerged from the buoyant water and climbed up the diving ladder. Suddenly, the triple-steel tanks on his back and the lead-weighted belt seemed to weigh a ton. On deck, he managed to shrug off the backpack and usually just sank to the hot planking, grateful to lie sprawled out in the sun.

JYC decided it was time to ease up. No more work except routine watches. A continuous game of cards was started in the mess and played through the Gulf of Suez, the Great Bitter Lake, the canal, and the dash across the Mediterranean.

Before reaching home, they ran into the worst gale Cousteau had ever known in the Mediterranean. Off Corsica, somebody alerted the bridge that what looked like

Bonnard was in the roiling sea behind them. Raud dashed to the mess where Bonnard was supposed to be locked up with the card players. The animal was nowhere to be found. The *Calypso* turned back and crew members hurled life preservers into the frothing waves, telling themselves Bonnard must have slipped out and gone to the open aft deck to enjoy his kind of weather.

They circled twice. They couldn't even see the life floats they had tossed into the seven-meter waves. The water was cold, and Bonnard couldn't have suffered long. Wrote Cousteau, "There were tears among us."

8
FAME

Calypso and crew reached Marseilles November 1, 1954, both exhausted and ready for winter repairs, the ship going into dry dock until the following March, the men disbanding until after New Year's. For Jacques and Simone there were personal affairs to attend to.

Fernande died quietly. PAC had been released, it seemed, just to see his wife fade away. His own cancer was not getting better, and he barely understood his children. When he had gained his release, he had not seen Françoise and Jean-Pierre since they were nine and six. Françoise was on her own now, and Fernande's death was felt most cruelly by sixteen-year-old Jean-Pierre. Quietly, Simone told him, "Nobody can replace a mother, but I will be your second mother." Like Jean-Michel and Philippe, he would remain in boarding school but henceforth spend his vacations at Sanary.

Then, in quick succession, Pierre remarried and became the father of a second daughter. He asked Françoise and Jean-Pierre for their permission to marry Françoise Ganzmann, a woman of Alsation origin. Both said yes, but Jean-Pierre was to wonder later in life what would have happened had they said no.

PAC found an outlet for his polemic talents in the marginal *Rivarol* magazine, writing mordant, acidulous weekly columns on current events. The relations between the two brothers were cool and distant. "Some people talked of an estrangement between my father and my uncle," Jean-Pierre said. "During my father's years in prison their relationship had been tense because my

156

father blamed my uncle for not visiting him enough."

Jean-Pierre was impressed by his uncle's life as explorer, inventor, moviemaker, and master of his own ship. What the adolescent would never forget was his uncle telling him on more than one occasion. "Your father is much smarter than I; he's the real intelligent one." The kindred affection Jean-Pierre and Simone had for each other was without the mother-son strains that affected her relationships with Jean-Michel and, especially, Philippe. Philippe's adolescence and youthful years were filled with rebellious defiance. "If Jacques said something was white, Philippe would immediately say it was black," was the way Jean-Pierre described his cousin's oedipal confrontations with his father. "The relations between Philippe and his mother were often tense, affectionate but high-strung. He could be aggressive toward her, but she'd come right back at him." Jean-Michel and Philippe attended the École des Roches boarding school in Normandy. During holidays they were in Paris or Sanary with Daddy Daniel, or if the *Calypso* was within reach, aboard the research vessel with their parents.

Jacques was becoming famous as an author and was eager to transfer his renown

157

to the screen. In the United States *The Silent World* had sold more than 486,000 copies by the end of 1953 (worldwide sales would eventually top five million), and he plowed the royalties into the full-length documentary he was sure he could make from the footage Malle and he had shot. They needed more exciting visuals, and he was sure they could get them the next time out.

He was also ready to test the diving saucer Jean Mollard and the OFRS people had built. Many engineering groups had joined to shrink the necessary electric motors, pumps, and instruments into saucer space. The outer shell was made of bright yellow fiberglass. The interior was cramped with a tank holding water ballast for attaining zero weight in the sea, pumps to shift mercury ballast fore or aft to cant the saucer down or up, and a series of batteries to power everything. JYC gave the okay to build a full-fledged prototype, as well as a crane along the lines of the British Petroleum boom that had lifted the gravimeter in and out of the Persian Gulf. The hydraulic crane would have to be able to clamp onto the saucer when it surfaced in rough waters, to ensure the craft wouldn't be lost in the sea.

The dry dock overhaul was extensive.

Alexis Sivirine, a Russian-born captain's son and engineer with the Compagnie Générale d'Entreprises Electriques in Marseilles, volunteered his time and enthusiasm as supervisor of the *Calypso* repairs. For the next thirty years, Sivirine would make scrupulous notes of all modifications, and keep sketches and data of all remodeling and equipment. Meanwhile, Dumas and Malle were busy purchasing film stock, lighting equipment, and buoys of all kinds, and adapting cameras to undersea use. "We had to make the underwater cameras ourselves because there was nothing that we could use at the time," Malle recalled. "We called the cameras SM 1 (for *sousmarine*), SM 2, and SM 3 and made them from the mechanism of a hand-held Bell & Howell outfitted with wide-angle lenses." Dumas and Malle were joined by National Geographic's Luis Marden, who would be the next expedition's still photographer; Edmond Séchan, a noted cinematographer; and Pierre Goupil, jack-of-all-trades assistant to everybody. Together, they turned the *Calypso* into the best possible floating movie studio.

On March 8, 1955, they were on their way on a four-month, 22,000-kilometer voyage to the coral reefs of the Red Sea and the

Indian Ocean; the Seychelles and Aldabra islands, where the giant green sea turtles come to lay their eggs; and Assumption Island, which turned out to be a speck of white sand sitting on top of the most prodigious reef. Below this monsoon-swept dot in the immensity of the Indian Ocean, where only a handful of humans lived, the Cousteau team got to film the most dazzling underwater footage anyone had ever seen.

Simone brought Bulle, a dachshund, along. Bulle was no great diver but got himself filmed on deck when it came time to document the shipboard activities. Increasingly, Simone considered the *Calypso* her real home. The only woman on board, she was known affectionately as *"la bergère,"* the shepherdess of men and boys far from land, home and feminine company, hearing out one man's problem, giving another a well-aimed penicillin shot, getting a third out of trouble in some port. Like Dumas, Falco, Kientzy, and the growing number of permanent team members, she was beginning to hate town life and formal functions. She was happiest out of camera range, in the crow's nest, for example, scanning the sea for whales. Nothing would get by her. "She lives to spend hour after hour in the wind and the sun, watching, thinking, trying to unravel the mystery of the sea," her husband would tell inquiring journalists.

Marden was especially impressed by Dumas as a diver. Underwater, Didi lived up to his official title as the *Calypso*'s master diver with an elegance and agility that had the American dumbfounded. "Never have I seen anyone swim more gracefully or with less effort," he remembered. "Once I watched him jackknife and slip vertically downward over the edge of the reefs, with no apparent movement of his flippers. When we got on deck, I asked him how he could swim with so little movement. 'Oh,' he said, 'I don't know – I feel the water flowing along my body, sense the change of pressure and direction, and flex my body accordingly.'"

While sailing in the doldrums, the belt of calms and light baffling winds south of the equator, they came upon huge pods of sperm whales, but it was the coral jungle below Assumption Island, one day's sailing from the northern tip of Madagascar, that captivated them. Even Dumas and Falco surfaced after a preliminary glimpse of the reef to tear mouthpieces from their faces and shout, *"Extraordinaire!"*

A few arm strokes from the surface a world glowed with soft yellows, pinks, blues, and purples. The luminous transparency of the warm water teemed with life. Small green, yellow, red, blue, and black fish flashed by or hung motionless in solid grapes of schools. Bigger fish swam among the sea anemones and came to peer at the intruders' masks. A huge grouper accompanied the divers on their first survey. It was there the next day, disconcertingly appearing from behind them. At the next dive it was there again. Somebody named the 60-pound fish Jojo le Mérou, a name that echoed Marseilles underworld nicknames. Gradually, Jojo grew tamer until the divers could stroke his side and make him roll over with pleasure like a dog. Jojo became a scene stealer – and something of a pest – swimming into other creatures' close-ups.

What they had stumbled on, Cousteau realized, was a kind of Garden of Eden, a world of fish that had never seen man and therefore had almost no fear of humans. The fish stayed out of reach at first, Marden wrote in *National Geographic*. "After a few days when they saw that we did them no harm, most of the fish around our anchorage accepted us."

Cousteau forbade all spearfishing except by cook Hanen – even *he* was ordered to use very small hooks – and discouraged all hostile movements underwater. The reward was seeing fish waiting for divers to enter the water and escorting them back to the ladder at the end of a dive.

Carrying floodlights and cameras to the reef was exhilarating. Every day JYC, Malle, Séchan, Marden, and Goupil came up with footage of something neither seen nor suspected before. Malle tried to capture the extravagant hues and the mesmerizing visual poetry. Séchan went for adrenaline – shots of lurking moray eels, armor-bodied trunk-fish, poisonous lion and triggerfish, and streamlined hunters streaking in from the open ocean: sharks and jacks. Cousteau and Dumas pushed for the greatest possible depths where nearly every kind of in-vertebrate marine life of warm waters existed, from scarlet and yellow sponges and fibrillating sea fans, to plantlike pearl oysters and plumed black bushes of coral and purple coils of sea anemones. Nine men were needed to film Dumas chipping at a coral spire at 50 meters as orange- and yellow-striped fish darted in and out of the 6,000-watt floodlight.

Once, Falco, Malle, and Marden dived along the vertical reef face to 70 meters, Malle and Marden recalled with fondness their oceanic work and wanderings with Cousteau. "For somebody who wanted to become a filmmaker," the future director of *Murmur of the Heart, Lacombe, Lucien,* and *Pretty Baby* said, "it was a fantastic education. Cousteau was always a great technician, improving constantly." Marden also remembered JYC's probing mind, his way of listening to his people's discussions of how to accomplish something. "And he'd say, 'Well, why don't we do *this?*' " the American photographer recalled. "It would be 180 degrees away, but the best system. Always."

Cousteau believed the cinema was the supreme art form because movies encompassed many other art forms and because they had an almost organic duration. Painting, sculpture, and architecture, he believed, tried to defy time, to be frozen in eternity, whereas theater, ballet, music, poetry, and film used time as raw material. "I prefer to admit that we are here like a flower, to bloom and die," he said. "The supreme art has to deal with this, to cope with it and to use time as a building block in a piece of art you are making. You have to have a good script or a good text. You have to have good images, beautiful images. You have to have good music. You have to have the sense of rhythm. You have to pack all these things

164

into a neat, interesting, and beautiful piece."

Monsoon storms put an end to the Assumption Island filming. They not only endangered the *Calypso* riding on top of the razor-sharp atoll, but also roiled up the sea. Even a minor storm could cloud up the water to the point that what was filmed one day would not "match" what was shot the next day. The *Calypso* sailed north to film dolphins, porpoises, and whales near the coast of Somalia.

Mardken got to admire Cousteau's seamanship at Ras Muhammad at the tip of the Sinai Peninsula, where the Strait of Gubal leads north into the Gulf of Suez. When echo soundings indicated a shipwreck at the bottom of the strait, the captain sent out a launch equippped with a radio dish on top of its mast. The launch was told to drop anchor and, in effect, become a fixed reference point for signals bounced off its dish. Methodically, the *Calypso* began sweeping back and forth over the wreck while a crew member jotted down on graph paper the echo distances to the bottom. Little by little the outline of a ship took form on the tracing paper. Dumas and Falco donned aqualungs, went over the side, and after ten minutes came up to report that an 8,000- to

10,000-ton freighter lay tilted skyward 35 meters below.

Divers went down with cameras, soon to see the skeletal outline of the steel mast and wire stays disappearing into the blue. Further down, the elliptic shape of the freighter's stern became visible. The divers eased down past the railings festooned with aquatic growth and clouds of fish swimming in and out of portholes. On the open rear deck a 10-millimeter gun pointed to the sky. Swimming inside the hull, Dumas and Falco suddenly faced an enormous fish. It so startled them that they retreated to one of the ship's narrow passageways.

"As big as a truck," Dumas reported once they were topside. Falco believed the scales on the monster were as big as his hand. The next day, Malle also saw a "truckfish," bigger than a shark and estimated to weigh over a ton. When Marden went down and saw the enormous thing move among the mangled remains of the keel, he thought it was more than 2.4 meters long and maybe 1.5 meters high. It was covered with giant mailed scales. Big canine teeth protruded from its jaws. Falco saw an even bigger specimen, perhaps 4.5 meters long, but the truckfish remained shy. It was eventually identified as a monstrous wrasse, *Chielinus undulatus.* No record existed of this common fish growing so large, but the encounter was verified.

The ship's bell, dislodged from its foredeck standard, brought up and scraped free of oysters, revealed it to be the *Thistlegorm.* Dumas scrubbed silt and growth from the shipbuilders' nameplate, riveted to the bulkhead, and discovered the *Thistlegorm* had been built in Scotland by Joseph L. Thompson & Sons, Ltd., in 1940.

The 9,000-ton freighter became the cameramen's favorite wreck. They filmed the eerie shapes of barnacled trucks, motorcycles, locomotives, personnel carriers, shells, mines, and torpedoes loaded in her holds and stacked on her decks. From Cairo, Marden dispatched a letter to Glasgow and eventually learned from *Thistlegorm's* former third engineer that because of congestion in the Suez Canel during the waning days of the German North Africa offensive in 1941, his ship had been one of twenty vessels waiting at anchor at Ras Muhammad. On October 6 a Luftwaffe bomber operating out of Crete dropped two charges on the aft deck, setting off *Thistlegorm's* own lethal cargo. Surprisingly forty of the forty-nine men on board survived.

The *Calypso* nearly suffered the same fate

in the same waters twelve years later. She was homebound in June 1967 when war broke out between Egypt and Israel. Egyptian canal authorities allowed the *Calypso* to tie up with a number of oil tankers in the Suez roadstead. Israeli jets bombed the Suez oil refinery and shell fragments rained down around the *Calypso*. No one was inuured, but cameras and film, unloaded for air cargo shipment to France, were destroyed.

Counting the film from the Abu Dhabi and Indian Ocean trip (footage that included the shark saturnalia of the baby whale), Cousteau had 30 kilometers of film with which to fashion a full-length documentary when the *Calypso* returned to Marseilles in June 1955. While the ship spent the next four months setting up hydrographic stations throughout the Mediterranean under the direction of oceanographer Henri Lacombe, Cousteau, Malle, and a pair of film editors began winnowing the mass of film down to a passable hour and a half.

Cousteau wanted a true documentary, a film that not only overwhelmed its audience with footage of undersea wonders but also showed *how* such images were obtained, that is, showed Dumas, Falco, and everybody else

168

working. Malle wanted a movie that stretched the viewers' mind with true other-worldly poetry. The opening sequence was his, a trail of bubbles disturbs the blue stillness as aqualunged divers, in wetsuits and carrying arc torches, glide through the world of silence. The next sequence was JYC's – the magical creatures surface and scamper up to the *Calypso*'s deck, mere men in awkward costumes and breathing apparatus. The movie's concept was entirely Cousteau's, but many of the images that stay in its audience's mind had a marked affinity with the Louis Malle films that were to come.

While Yves Baudrier composed a score, Cousteau decided the credits should say: directed by Jacques-Yves Cousteau and Louis Malle. Bowled over, Malle could only express his gratitude.

Le monde du silence stunned its first audience. The world premiere was at the Cannes Film Festival, April 28, 1956 – with the *Calypso* strategically moored in the bay and the crew mingling with movie stars on the Croisette.

Films in color were the exception, not the rule, in 1956, yet here was a documentary of stunning color beauty, an adventure film with both a sense of the awesome and a feel for its own technical skill. From the introduction of divers with phosphorous torches moving through the blue-gray depths, to images of never-before-seen lifeforms on the deep magenta of coral carpets, scenes of the businesslike deck of the research vessel, of thundering along whitecaps with racing dolphins, and gazing into the purple coils of a sea anemone, the movie was one hour and twenty-seven minutes of marvels and thrills.

Here is the discovery of the *Thistlegorm*, a phantom hulk, encrusted with barnacles, being explored by a diver gliding through the quietness that is broken only by the long intakes and rippling exhalations of his breath until he chooses to add another sound by striking the wreck's bell and making it ring out with eerie clarity in the pristine blueness. Here is Jojo le Mérou in all his speckled ugliness cavorting with a diver and interfering in the movie-making. Here is the chilling frenzy of sharks feasting on the baby sperm whale, and in contrast everyday shipboard activities. The humor and intimacy with which the crew are captured result in a vivid sense of participation, of sharing not only the adventures and perils of underwater exploration but the surface work.

The film was an immediate, lasting, and worldwide success. It won the Cannes

Festival's Palme d'Or. Columbia Pictures picked up the film for international distribution, agreeing to JYC's demand that James Dugan be hired to work on the English-language narration.

More modestly, Pierre Cousteau also came out in the arts and letters in 1956. *Après le déluge* ("After the Deluge") was a collection of essays in which he exercised his mordant wit and pent-up rancor on the current political scene. "On November 23, 1946, a tall, clean-shaven gentleman in a handsome red robe trimmed with white conyskin, told me rather tartly that I was condemned to death," he began. "That was disagreeable, but it was serious. Very serious. I know of nothing more serious than conveniently aimed rifle barrels. Five months later, a small, clean-shaven gentleman – but without a robe – came to my cell to inform me that on second thought the Republic would economize twelve bullets and that my punishment was commuted to life. That was nice, but not serious. With this 'pardon,' we stumbled heavily into empty nonsense. My tormentors' talk ceased to be plausible. I could believe in the reality of the firing squad. I coulnd't believe in 'life.' "

The cold war, which saw the United States push France to approve the rearmament of

West Germany ("Young Jerries aren't just authorized to play soldiers again; they are ordered to hurry into *vertdigris* – or other more Atlantic colors – with the blessings of the true democracies"), and French acrobatics to justify keeping African colonies were grist for PAC's waggish humor. He could foresee three answers to the dilemma of what to do with the million French settlers in Algeria. There was the Muslim solution of letting the settlers stay as slaves, the biblical or Anglo-Saxon solution of exterminating them all ("the means of destruction, thank God, have progressed since Buffalo Bill"), or the Soviet solution of massive deportation ("this might be the moment to invoke our treaty alliance and ask our Russian friends to welcome in their Siberia our surplus French").

There were a satirical review of de Gaulle's *Memoirs* suggesting a Nobel Peace Prize for the general, a catechism for Communists making fun of leftist chic, excerpts of delirious hymns to Stalin, and an invitation to Saint-André-de-Cubzac ("where my forefathers tended vineyards for a depressing number of generations") to imitate Moroccan justifications for throwing off the yoke of colonial rule. There was "A letter from a Father to his Son" warning against a life as an intellectual, but no mentions of PAC's famous brother.

Jacques went to New York with *The Silent World*. While Dugan translated – Jojo le Mérou was the ohly casualty, losing his Marseillais name to become plain Ulysses – Cousteau was with Perry Miller working up an entire television series. Perry was now with CBS working on "The Adventure" and "Seven Lively Arts" series and together they came up with a concept for a running program that Jacques and Malle would do for the network. Malle came to New York and sat in on the planning sessions at Perry's Thirty-Sixth Street apartment. Nothing came of it, however. A sudden quiz scandal – President Eisenhower was shocked at the revelations that contestants had been lying about their appearances on *The $64,000 Question* – caused the networks to feel an urgent need to reassert their grip on programming. Buying documentary series from outside sources was suddenly out.

Cousteau also had to work out an arrangement to pull the short subjects Perry still had in circulation. He wanted to be able to use footage from them in future full-length films. "We worked it out because Jacques is a man of honor," she remembered. "It was understood that I would have a small interest in *The Silent World* because I had worked for years promoting him."

An ear infection forced Malle to beg off the next trip. In fact, *The Silent World* gave him a chance to make a feature film right after his return to France. "When I started making films I was very lucky because I codirected this documentary with Jacques Cousteau," he said a decade later. "He being a gentleman let me cosign with him when I was twenty-three. He didn't have to do it, and yet he did."

The idea that the ocean bottom doesn't consist of vast level plains but has mountain ranges and canyons, basins and ridges, and peaks and valleys as well defined as any on land was no longer a novelty in the mid-1950's, but the painstaking tabulation and plotting of these features were. American, British, Canadian, Russian, and Swedish survey ships were busy collecting data on ocean depths, continental shelves, sea mounts, island arcs, and ocean trenches (satellites would soon make such costly and time-consuming voyages obsolete).

Financed by the French Ministry of Education and a National Geographic grant, Cousteau and Harold Edgerton took the *Calypso* to the Romanche trench, a 7.2-

kilometer-deep gash straddling the equator in the mid-Atlantic. The summer trip yielded the first photographs of the trench bottom and, with a picture of a sea star, evidence that life existed below the surface.

The *Calypso* depth recorder found the Romanche crevasse rather easily and, with the launch used to bounce off radar signals as in locating the *Thistlegorm*, the profile of the trench was quicly determined, but how do you anchor over 4.5 miles of void? Cousteau's solution: You pay out 5 miles of nylon cord (the weight of five miles of steel cable would sink your ship) and steam slowly forward until the line is taut and exerts a diagonal drag on a special anchor. At MIT, Edgerton had built his camera housing to withstand the horrendous bottom pressure of 5.5 tons to the square inch, but on the second try saw four-millimeter-thick plate glass crack.

There were happier moments. Sixteen-year-old Philippe, all toothy grins and stepping in the way of everybody, was there for his first real expedition (Edgerton's son Bill had stayed in Massachusetts testing an experimental underwater breathing device), spearing large squids that everybody liked for dinner except his father, and in later dives off the Portuguese island of Madeira discovered *Heteroconger longissimus,* penlike eels swaying in the current like a forest of canes on their tails buried in sand and, at the slightest disturbance, retracting into the sand.

The captain and "Papa Flash" lived in a blizzard of charts and depth data as the *Calypso* cruised back and forth over the trench that, in cross section, appeared as a blunted V. André Laban and new crew member Christian Carpine purloined plaster of paris from the *Calypso* surgeon and, as fast as the data came from the depth recorder, molded a plaster model of the trench.

They were almost at the end of the work when a radio message from Boston told Edgerton that his son Bill had lost his life wearing the breathing device in an underwater tryout. Cousteau ordered the *Calypso* to Dakar, Senegal, and while the expedition continued off Cape Verde, flew with Edgerton to Boston for the funeral, rejoining the ship two weeks later.

JYC was back in the United States a month later. *The Silent World* opened to rave reviews in New York in September. In October, Cousteau was in Los Angeles to help the publicity push for an Academy Award. (In interviews, he warned overenthusiastic young Americans not to take up scuba diving without instruction.) On Oscar night, *The Silent World* won the best documentary award.

International stardom was not in the French navy tradition. Cousteau had powerful patrons in the Ministère de la Marine – Admiral Lemonnier was one – but he had even more powerful enemies, superiors who had never forgiven him for testifying in uniform on his brother's behalf in 1946.

The evidence was in Captain Cousteau's lack of promotions. Despite his Resistance medal, his command of the postwar Undersea Research Group, innovative minesweeping work, and undersea ordnance testing, he was, at forty-six, the lowest-ranked officer of the Naval Academy class of 1933. More prosaically, some of his superiors didn't know what to do with him. He had been "detached" from active duty for nearly a decade and it could be argued that his interests no longer coincided with those of the navy.

From Cousteau's perspective, the inconveniences of being a naval officer were beginning to outweigh the advantages of access to navy facilities, the powerful servicemen's network, and the modest but certain pay and perks. The navy had been his home for twenty-seven years, but his career and his ideas were turning toward a kind of oceanic frontier. He could make himself and his listeners excited when he threw out ideas about colonizing the sea, building veritable seafloor habitats, or fantasized about creating a true *Homo aquaticus,* a man living most of his life underwater with surgically modified lungs. During the first nine months of life humans grow while immersed in the fluid of the womb, he liked to say when he got worked up about his futuristic "waterman." The first crisis of human life is the moment when we pass from the liquid to the air medium at birth, he would add, saying he believed the underwater species could come by 2010 at the latest.

This was not the usual talk of tradition-bound navy clubs, of course, and as a navy officer he felt constricted in many ways. He also sensed that his growing reputation was resented. Yet for Simone's sake he hesitated to cut the umbilical cord. She was the daughter of three generations of navy men.

Simone was no typical officer's spouse, living and breathing for the code of Toulon's caste system of officers' wives. Indifferent toward protocol and celebrity, she lived out of his limelight, voluntarily, increasingly away from Sanary, from home interests and responsibilities. She was the true mistress of the *Calypso,* the only person without a title, yet the permanent and original source of the onboard sense of family, the spirit and morale of the men, or, as she called them, her "boys." To her, as one of them remarked, the *Calypso* must always sail.

To keep it all afloat, Jacques had to become impresario, business tycoon, inventor, fund-raiser, scholar, lecturer, prophet, and poet. He had to charm and bully governments, foundations, and corporate entities in a growing number of cities. Simone knew that this multiple universe away from home and ship was peopled with women who were attracted to him, women who found him the embodiment of yearnings for distant horizons and for living by one's impulses, and whose attention flattered his ego. Simone was a self-sufficient woman who made her own life important.

Jean-Michel wanted to be an architect and was about to do his two years of military service. Philippe didn't know what he wanted: one day it was engineering, the next it was cinematography, although he shared his father's youthful passion for flying and was about to receive his license as a glider pilot. Jacques and Simone knew that without the safety net the navy provided, their existence would be a perpetual highwire act. Making popular movies seemed to be the surest way to stay ahead of creditors. *The Silent World* had not only made Cousteau a household name, it had made scuba diving the new sports fad. Air Liquide couldn't turn out aqualungs fast enough. Cousteau received royalties, but running the *Calypso* proved to be frighteningly expensive, even with government contracts, foreign underwriting, industrial contracts, and the possible commercialization of new underwater gear.

Still, it had taken two years and more than a thousand dives to make *The Silent World*. A sequel would no doubt be even more costly in time and effort, as it would have to top the original in spectacular undersea images. Or it would have to be totally different. But the couple longed for the unknown beyond the prow, the hidden wonders. They were both healthy and barely hitting their stride. With the rank of *capitaine de corvette*, Cousteau resigned from the navy.

Celebrity almost immediately brought a new opportunity. There were rumors, soon confirmed, that Monaco's Prince Ranier, who had just married Grace Kelly, would not be adverse to seeing the aging director of his great-grandfather's palatial but moldy

Oceanographic Institute succeeded by a certain star explorer.

The appropriations to pay for Cousteau's expansive, high-energy directorship of Monaco's venerable Oceanographic Institute in 1957 provoked a constitutional crisis in the smallest secular but most densely inhabited state in the world.

9
THE GREAT DEPTHS

Prince Albert's cliffside Oceanographic Institute, looking high over the portside entrance to Monaco's harbor, was not the first of the great marine laboratories. Anton Dohrn, a German zoologist who studied marine life in the Strait of Messina, spent his own fortune building the Stazione Zoologica in Naples in the 1870's. To help maintain the laboratory, Dohrn set up an aquarium to attract tourists, an idea Prince Albert's great-grandson and Cousteau would elaborate on over the years.

Two widely different but propitious occurrences for the furtherance of human interest in the seas took place in 1870. The

British Parliament voted funds to send the HMS *Challenger* on a world expedition, and Jules Verne published *Twenty Thousand Leagues Under the Sea.*

At the urging of the famous naturalist Thomas Huxley and the brilliant scholar C. Wyville Thomson of the Royal Society as expedition chief, the Royal Navy agreed to send the 2,000-ton wooden vessel *Challenger* on a world tour. A century earlier, the Admiralty had sent James Cook to explore the immense reaches of the South Pacific to see if Terra Australis Incognita on Dutch mapmaker Gerhardus Mercator's chart really existed and, if so, to claim it for the Crown (a few years earlier, Vitus Bering, a Dane in the employ of Czar Peter the Great, had roamed the northernmost Pacific and established that Asia and America were not joined), but the 115,000-kilometer voyage of the *Challenger* was the first expedition concerned with what was *in* the oceans.

Crammed with laboratories, workrooms, special decks, and "all the instruments and apparatus which modern science and practice have been able to suggest and devise," the *Challenger* sailed from Portsmouth in 1872. She crossed the Atlantic several times, sailed south from Cape Town to become the first steamship to cross the Antarctic Circle, touched land in Australia, New Zealand and the Fijis, explored the China Sea from Hong Kong to Yokohama, struck across the Pacific to Honolulu, steamed south to the coast of Chile, through the Strait of Magellan, touched at Montevideo, and recrossed the Atlantic by way of Ascension Island and the Azores. The corvette returned to England in 1876 bearing notebooks filled with data, museum bottles aswim with astonishing lifeforms, and lockers full of rocks and mud dredged from the seafloor. The implication of all this so excited the Victorian scientific mind that the seas became the object of eager scrutiny. As Huxley told a dinner honoring Thomson and his crew, their expedition laid "a foundation for future thought upon the physical geography of the sea that not only had not existed, but had not even been dreamed of."

There is something atavistic about the great depths, and the publication of Verne's *Twenty Thousand Leagues Under the Sea* also spurred interest in the mysteries of the deep and its creatures. The story of the sinister Captain Nemo and his undersea voyage in the strange craft was not only a remarkable foretelling of the submarine's invention. Verne's startling imaginative powers also played on ancestral fears of sea monsters and conjured up nightmarish images of giant squids.

Cousteau carried a worn copy of the original French edition aboard the *Calypso* and saw it pass from hand to hand as crew members remembered their own first reading of the juvenile classic. In *Octopus and Squid*, Cousteau and Philippe Diolé reproduced the original Neuville engraving showing Captain Nemo and two of his men standing at the *Nautilus*'s huge observation window watching the giant cephalopod, and quoted the passage where the sub is attacked by seven giant octopuses, one of which halts the engines by grasping the propellers with its horned beak. Despite years of diving in hundreds of places, *Calypso* team members were apprehensive in 1969 when they entered the Puget Sound to film the giant octopuses of Seattle, animals as big as themselves. Seeing a giant squid in the murky water, its eyes fixed on a diver, Cousteau later said, gave the diver a mixed feeling of respect, and of primitive terror. "The myths on which we are raised die hard, even in those of us who pride ourselves most on having conquered fear through knowledge."

Knowledge, respect, and fear for the watery realm go back to the mist of time. The faint traces we possess of our most distant forebears include bone harpoons, hooks and dugouts, and since seafaring that doesn't hug a shoreline demands the recognition of patterns of currents and tides, winds, sun and stars, and the animals in the sea, contacts with the oceans are among the earliest of human records. Three thousand years ago Phoenicians in the Eastern Hemisphere and Polynesians in the vast Pacific became skilled long-distance voyagers. In 600 B.C., Phoenicians claimed to have made a trip around Africa from east to west. Later historians doubted this, especially the claim by Phoenician sailors that at one point the sun was on their right hand instead of the customary left. Of course, this is the position of the sun in the Southern Hemisphere, and instead of casting doubt on the epic voyage, the assertion strengthens its likelihood.

The systematic accumulation of knowledge of the oceans started with the wonderfully clear and agile minds of the Greeks. Their name for the Mediterranean was Thalassa, and for a while during the nineteenth century the learned name for the science of the sea was "thalassography" (Philippe Cousteau's film company was to be called Thalassa Films). Aristotle focused his remarkable intellect on the creatures of the sea and inventoried 180 kinds of marine life. Four hundred years later, Pliny the elder could account for only 176 species, but his contemporary Hippalus noted that the monsoon winds of the Indian Ocean blew first one way for half the year and then reversed their direction, a discovery that greatly reduced the length of journeys across the open sea. Medieval Arab cartographers first used the "seven seas," a phrase that reached the West through the writings of Omar Khayyám, and in 1416 Henry the Navigator of Portugal founded a school of seamanship at Sagres and launched the golden age of exploration.

A delightful cast of bandits, soldiers, adventurers, eccentric noblemen, and romantic souls occupy the center stage of the marine sciences.

In the century that followed the great discoveries of Christopher Columbus, Vasco da Gama, and Ferdinand Magellan, an Italian count became the first scientist of the sea. Luigi Ferdinando Marsiglia was twenty-one and fresh out of Padua University in 1679 when he accompanied an Italian diplomat to Istanbul. During his stay in the Turkish capital, young Marsiglia – his name is sometimes spelled Marsili – met the British ambassador, who told him he had investigated, without conclusion, the waters flowing through the Bosporus. Marsiglia questioned Turkish fishermen, who confirmed the ambassador's contention that a surface current and a reverse undertow flow through the strait. When they cast their nets near the surface, they told him, the nets were carried toward the Mediterranean, but when submerged deeper, the nets drifted toward the Black Sea. Marsiglia built a current meter with a propeller for underwater measurements and proved his hunch: Because the water of the Mediterranean was saltier, and therefore denser, it sank to form the deep current flowing into the Black Sea, and this was compensated for by the surface current of lighter water from the Black Sea.

After a military career in the Austrian army in which he saw action against the Turks, was captured and made a slave, then ransomed by the diplomat who first took him to Istanbul, only to be cashiered, Marsiglia settled in France and studied the Mediterranean. He was the first to use a dredge to raise marine animals from the deep and to establish that although surface temperatures vary, readings below 100 meters are constant. At fifty-six he published the first book on oceanography and later traveled to London, where he was made a member of the Royal Institute and was especially welcomed by Isaac Newton.

A contemporary of Marsiglia was William Dampier, a buccaneering Englishman with a similar taste for action and science. He preyed on Spanish galleons in both the Atlantic and the Pacific, visited Australia in 1686, and after his return published a picaresque account of his adventures, *A New Voyage Round the World*. The book's success encouraged him to write a sequel, *Voyages and Descriptions*, which recounted more of his privateering and also included a sober section that showed him to be a careful observer of everything affecting seafaring and of the natural history of the lands he visited. In his forties, Dampier made two more voyages as a privateer. The first was unsuccessful but the second resulted in the capture of booty worth £200,000. He died in his bed in London at the age of sixty-three.

Oceanography owes a debt to Benjamin Franklin. When Franklin served as postmaster general for the Colonies, he received complaints that mails from England were often two weeks late. The North Atlantic had been heavily traveled for three centuries, and mariners who, like Ponce de León, had gained direct experience of the great current running along the North American coast, named it the Gulf Stream, presumably because it issues from the Gulf of Mexico.

Talking to his cousin and whaling captain Timothy Folger while they were both in England, Franklin found out that American merchant captains had learned from whalemen to avoid the adverse currents on their westward trips but British packet captains had not. Even those captains who were warned about the Gulf Stream, Folger added, appeared to ignore it. At Franklin's request, Folger sketched the course of the Gulf Stream on a chart. Franklin had it printed up, along with Folger's instructions on how to avoid the stream. Copies of chart and instructions were sent to Falmouth and British packet captains eventually learned.

As for Franklin, on his next crossing to America he lowered thermometers over the side of his ship and took scores of water readings that showed the Gulf Stream to be warmer than the waters bordering it. En route to negotiate a treaty with France in 1776, he made more temperature measurements, and in Paris commissioned another Gulf Stream map, this time to help French and American captains carrying arms and supplies to the colonial rebellion. A decade later, during his return voyage to America, the seventy-nine-year-old Franklin could be seen leaning over the rail of his ship, taking the Gulf Stream's temperature again.

Johann and Georg Forster, a father-and-son team of German amateur scientists who emigrated to England in 1766, are the link between Captain Cook and the next big name in oceanography, Alexander von Humboldt. The Forsters sailed with Cook on his second voyage, and the younger Forster published an account that appeared both in London and Berlin. The German version established Forster as one of the most advanced German thinkers and accomplished stylists, and he was avidly read by Goethe and the generation of the period of enlightenment.

Fifteen years younger than Georg Forster, Humboldt was a Prussian baron with a scientific mind and an ardent admirer of the French Revolution and its republican ideals. A journey through Germany, Holland, and England with Forster wakened his romantic inclination to the tropics. In 1796, Humboldt was traveling from Paris to Cairo with the French botanist Aimé Bonpland, hoping to join Napoleon in Egypt, when, detouring via

Madrid, the unexpected patronage of the prime minister, Mariano de Urquijo, led Humboldt and Bonpland to make Spanish America the scene of their explorations.

The pair sailed for Caracas in 1800, and confirmed the existence of a link between the Orinoco and Amazon rivers deep in the jungle (the Casequiare waterway that a Cousteau team would explore 183 years later). After a long and arduous journey along the Cordilleras from Colombia to Peru, they climbed the Chimborazo to an elevation of 18,893 feet – the world record for the next thirty-six years. In Peru, Humboldt measured the currents of the coastal waters and became fascinated by the teeming life of this great cold ocean stream. Through his observations of tropical storms and his mapping of the South American volcanoes in which he showed they were set in linear patterns, presumably corresponding to vast subterranean fault lines, he laid the foundations of geophysics. After a year in Mexico and a short visit to the United States, Humboldt and Bonpland returned to Europe.

In order to secure the scientific co-operation required for publishing the results of his travels, Humboldt settled in Paris. He was courted by academies and governments, refused appointment as Prussian minister of education, discovered the decrease in intensity of the earth's magnetic force from the poles to equator, worked on his magnum opus, *Kosmos*, for twenty-one years, formed extensive theories on seismology, and died in 1859, a year after his dear friend Bonpland.

Charles Darwin was influenced by Humboldt and read his *Personal Narrative*. Although Darwin was not a marine scientist, he made a major contribution to marine biology with the theory on the formation of coral reefs that he formulated during his voyage as the unpaid naturalist aboard the *Beagle* from 1831 to 1836.

The wealth of knowledge the *Challenger* brought back resulted in an unprecedented fifty-volume dossier on the oceans. When all was compiled, it showed the ship's scientists had collected 4,417 new species, "strange and beautiful things which seemed to give us a glimpse of the edge of some unfamiliar world," Thomson noted.

The decades that followed saw explorers of many nations take up oceanography. The Russian shipo *Vitiaz* cruised around the world making pioneer observations of sea temperatures and density. Japanese scientists began studying salmon migration off the far eastern coast of Asia. Viktor Hensen led a German expedition that gave us the word "plankton," Norwegian explorer Fridtjof Nansen allowed his ship *Fram* to be frozen in the arctic ice to study the polar ice cap and C. G. J. Petersen, a Dane, developed the first theory of overfishing. Alexander Agassiz, a Swiss-American teacher at Harvard, covered 160,000 kilometers in oceanographic voyages, first in the steamer *Blake* and later in the *Albatross*, the first ship built especially for scientific exploration.

Beginning in 1885, Albert de Grimaldi, prince of Monaco, became a glamorous newcomer to oceanography. Albert was all of twenty-two when he developed a passionate interest in the fledgling science. Another wealthy young nobleman might have been satisfied to let a dilettante's enthusiasm give rise to a patron's largesse, but Prince Albert gradually emerged as a colleague of leading marine scientists and an innovator. He outfitted a series of yachts as research vessels, each better equipped and planned than the last, invented several of the techniques and instruments used for measurements and exploration, and initiated research in the Mediterranean and the Atlantic. In 1895 his *Princesse Alice* was working near the Azores when Portuguese whalers wounded a huge right whale, or cachalot. In its death throes a few meters from Albert's ship, the whale spewed parts of five colossal octopuses totally new to science. In a launch, *Princesse Alice* crew members managed to recuperate all five bodies from the sea of whale blood, and the cephalopods obtained in this unexpected manner were hauled on deck and, during the next twenty-four hours, dissected. As the prince was to write in *Remarques sur les céphalopodes,* one of his many scholarly volumes, one of the squids had lost its head, another had lost its body but its eight arms were there, each as large as a man and equipped with a hundred suckers wtih claws. "My naturalists had already explored the stomachs of these specimens and had removed, along with over two hundred pounds of debris, the remnants of several giant octopuses, fairly well preserved, which also belonged to totally unknown species," Albert wrote. "As one may suspect, the profession of these men requires a great amount of dedication: for, in their work, they are required to stir about in a purple mass, in full fermentation, littered with eyes and beaks which had resisted the actions of the gastric juices. The stench of this mass was most unpleasant. Toward the end, the naturalists' stomachs revolted in a faint echo of the event which, the day before, had given these treasures to science during the final spasm of the dying whale."

Albert was no less important as benefactor. Besides the Oceanographic Institute with its aquarium, museum, library, and separate research center in Paris, he founded the Institute for Human Paleontology, which undertook a number of major digs. The money came from the shrewd calculations of his grandmother, Princess Caroline, who in the 1860's had arrived at the conclusion that Monaco's future lay in drawing wealthy outsiders. Gambling was emerging as a favorite pastime among European aristocracy but was confined to middling towns in Belgium and Germany. Monaco had perfect climate and natural beauty; moreover, casino gambling was illegal both in France and Italy. The success of gambling was so astounding that the Casino, an immense ornate palace, soon paid all government expenses, and employed a sixth of the entire population. Albert's father, Charles III, endeared himself to his people by excusing his subjects from all taxes.

When Charles died in 1880, Albert, who once said the world needed fewer princes and more men of intelligence and learning, added the burdens of state to his learned endeavors. His aunt had married a German prince and Albert tried his hand at diplomacy by repeatedly seeking to defuse French-German rivalries.

Appalled by the barbarism of World War I, he declared Monaco neutral and spent the war years aboard his yacht in the harbor rather than at the palace because the ship afforded him more solitude. Postwar realities forced him to move closer to France – he even signed a treaty stipulating that if the House of Grimaldi failed to produce an heir, Monaco would join the French Republic. Still, his "postage stamp domain" remained very different from its embracing neighbor. There were subtle shades, characteristics, and distinctions between Monegasques living on the south side of the Boulevard de France and the French on the north side of the street. And there were hard economic differences. Tourism and gambling brought wealth to the principality. There was no military service. The leisure industries brought a steady stream of service jobs and, of course, no one had to pay taxes.

No one had to vote either, a fact increasingly resented by nativist Monegasques eager to progress from subjects to citizens. It was a dilemma Rainier ran into when he made the appointment of Jacques Cousteau as director of Albert's institute part of his realm's economic diversification.

In 1957, Monaco remained a political anachronism, a Renaissance fiefdom wiped out by the French Revolution, restored by the 1815 Congress of Vienna anxious to make republican ideals unfashionable, and living a sleeping beauty existence as a protectorate of France.

The sovereign prince of the House of Grimaldi ruled by divine right, enacting laws and collecting and spending revenues as he saw fit. Timidly, Albert had established a Council of State in 1911, only to suspend it during World War I. His son and successor, Louis II, who spent his many years as crown prince as a career officer in the French army, suspended parts of his father's laws in 1930, governed by decree for three years, and restored the Council of State, only to suspend the right of assembly at the outbreak of World War II.

Rainier, the son of Louis's daughter and an impoverished French nobleman, was no great fan of the Casino and its gaudier practices and clientele. A colonel in the French army, Resistance fighter, scuba diver, race-cart driver and playboy living in Cap

Ferrat with movie star Gisèle Pascal during the last neglectful years of his grandfather's reign, Rainier came to the throne in 1949 determined to curtail the Frankenstein monster, as he called the Casino, by finding alternative means of attracting tourists and their money.

Convinced that the long-term future lay in economic development, Rainer began by burying in a tunnel the "eyesore" Nice-Genoa railway running smack through Monaco and extending the principality into the Mediterranean with massive landfills. Digging the three-kilometer tunnel through the rock proved to be astronomically expensive. It was opposed not only by traditionalists who believed everything in Monaco should be left the way it was, but by the National Council, as the Council of State was now called. A pair of loquacious lawyers, Louis Aureglia and Jean-Charles Rey (the latter soon to be Rainier's brother-in-law), kept up a constant pressure for constitutional reform – that is, for means of tying the prince's purse strings.

Once started, however, the tunnel was a *fait accompli*. It still wasn't finished in 1956 when Rainier married Grace Kelly. A period of truce followed the Cinderella marriage, but when Rainier decided on a steep increase in the Oceanographic Institute's budget to cover Cousteau's hefty stipend and plans for modernization, Aureglia, Rey, and the National Council were ready.

Rainier, Grace, and the board of directors of the Albert Foundation considered Cousteau's appointment something of a coup for Monaco. As a diver and animal lover, Rainier had known the captain for years. Grace had not only seen *The Silent World* but also read the book during a vacation after the filming of *To Catch a Thief* for Alfred Hitchcock. The board of directors appreciated Cousteau's contacts in America, in particular with the National Geographic Society.

At a meeting with his council, Rainier argued that the institute was a vital part of Monaco "that must be sustained and built-up, whatever the cost." Once he left the meeting, however, Aureglia convinced his fellow councillors that the time had come to stand up to the prince.

Aureglia and his confreres blinked first. In a clever end run, Rainier took to the airwaves of Radio Monte Carlo and told his startled subjects he was dissolving the National Council and abrogating the right of assembly or demonstration. For precedent, he quoted Albert I and Louis II and couched his justification in terms of divine right, accusing the council of paralyzing the administration of Monaco.

Aureglia called the action a "coup d'état." Others called the prince a dictator, a reactionary, and a "destroyer of liberties." But Rainier portrayed himself as a modern man fighting for the health and wealth of Monaco against cantankerous, parochial, backward self-interests aching to despoil everybody by getting their hands into the cookie jar. Why else would the council display such indifference to the Oceanographic Institute, which had been in decline until its board of directors had convinced Cousteau to take over?

The opposition was not prepared for this public relations campaign. Aureglia's response was polite, erudite, and arcane, and the crisis petered out. Three years later Aureglia, Rey, and the rest of the opposition rallied behind their prince when Rainier got into a deadly scrap with President Charles de Gaulle over the taxing of French citizens and corporations, such as Jacques Cousteau and his diverse enterprises, claiming legal residence in Monaco. This time, Rainier and Aureglia blinked together and Monaco became a constitutional monarchy.

Cousteau's ideas for the five-story institute

were tonic. With his infectious enthusiasm, he told the board and, in private audiences, the princely household, the way to turn the institution – and, by the way, why not call it Oceanographic Institute *and* Museum? – into a self-sustaining, if not money-making, Riviera attraction, was to add new aquariums, new programs, and laboratories. First of all, why not take advantage of the *Calypso*'s far-flung voyages to collect Mediterranean and tropical species to stock a basement aquarium until it became one of Europe's finest?

On the ground floor he suggested the high-ceilinged Victorian rooms should be devoted to modern oceanography, with life-sized mockups of the new diving saucer and scale models of bathyscaphs. And how about a small movie theater showing selections of shorts? On the first floor, Albert's collection of skeletons of large marine mammals, those huge whale, narwhal, and grampus bones, should be kept, of course. Perhaps a diorama of turn-of-the-century oceanography could be built with Albert's whaleboat, the quaint instruments, and the stuffed animals like the 13-meter squid caught off Newfoundland. There could be mannequins of bewhiskered scientists in long smocks standing over a particular specimen. On the side there could

201

be exhibits of the restless oceans, animated maps of currents, explanations of why the sea is blue, why the oceans are salty, the celestial mechanics of tides, the partnership of wind and water, and so on. And why not open the windows and balconies? The view was priceless. You could see the coast from the Esterel to the Italian Riviera.

To show he meant business – and that he had no intention of adapting to the sedentary life of an administrator – he had Falco, Kientzy, and Maurice Léandri, the brother of original crew member Titi Léandri, go dolphin hunting in the *Espadon* with Captain Alinat. Falco wsasn't sure you could catch live dolphins, but JYC told him the way American marinelands did it was by lassoing the marine animals.

With the help of a pair of OFRS engineers, Falco fashioned a lasso and a kind of giant pincer. A forward platform was rigged to the *Espadon* for Falco to stand right over the prow. Nothing worked. The *Delphinus delphis*, or common dolphin, was lighter, more nervous and delicate than Florida's *Tursiops truucatus*, or bottle-nosed dolphin, seen giving performances in marinelands. On the advice of "experts," Falco tried a harpoon dipped in curare to immobilize the animal without causing it any harm.

Harpooning proved a disaster and Falco went back to an improved version of his pincers. After ranging the Mediterranean as far as Corsica for six months and discovering that schools of dolphins were just as numerous off the Nice-Monaco coast, they had perfected a technique for approaching the skittish mammals. Falco would fire the pincer, then Léandri would throw a yellow buoy as far as possible from the ship. The instant the buoy was in the water, Kientzy was supposed to dive in, and Alinat give the *Espadon* a turn to the right before cutting the engine. To avoid bruising the dolphin's delicate skin, Kientzy had inflated rubber mattresses with him in the water, and his job was to wrap the mattresses around the animal, remove the pincer, and bring the dolphin alongside *Espadon*.

On October 31 they came uppon a school of several hundred off Cap Ferrat. Falco fired his pincer at one of three stragglers and Léandri threw the buoy. Alinat veered, cut the engine, and jumped into a rubber dinghy while Kientzy splashed into the water. The dolphin had been in the pincer for three minutes by the time they reached it. It was floating on the surface, apparently exhausted by its struggles to free itself. Less than two hours later it was in a tank at the Oceanographic Institute.

Falco walked the traumatized animal around the tank. The young female was trembling and going through convulsions. As she seemed to grow weaker, they held a tank of oxygen to her blowhole. With the first few breaths, she seemed to improve. When Falco and Kientzy were about to leave for the night they saw Kiki, as they eventually named her, sink slowly to the bottom. Immediately, both men dived in and brought the unconscious mammal to the surface. With a third team member, they took turns walking her around the tank all night. Falco learned to take the animal's pulse for attending veterinarians by jumping into the water, holding the dolphin in his arms and placing his hand over the heart. Kiki seemed to thrive, cried like a child when left too long alone, and began to eat live fish. In March 1958, JYC sent Falco and crew out again to capture a companion for Kiki and commandeered the Palm Beach Hotel's swimming pool. Falco captured a male off Nice, brought him back to Kiki, but one morning found him dead at the bottom of the pool. An autopsy showed pieces of cloth and wood in his stomach. A fatally ill dolphin apparently swallows anything within reach.

The next two dolphins Falco caught, a female and a male, committed suicide by swimming at full speed into the side of the tank, smashing their skulls. Falco left on the spring *Calypso* voyage that took naturalists from Paris, Marseilles, and Monaco into the Atlantic for hydrological and biological research. Kiki thrived for a few months, then she, too, died. She had seemed to recognize and love Falco, and had he not been off on the Atlantic expedition she might have lived longer.

The Oceanographic Institute never got marineland-style dolphins. Instead, the Cousteau team learned much about the gregarious and intelligent mammals that would be valuable when it came to making TV specials a decade later.

10

THE BEGINNING OF A STRUGGLE

"You won't find the word 'pollution' in regard to the marine environment before 1960 – just as the word 'ecology' really doesn't exist before 1970," Raymond Vaissière said in the mid-1980's. "There is no literature on marine pollution before 1960. For Cousteau the pollution debate, the antipollution fight, began with the French army's decision in 1960 to try dumping nuclear waste in the Mediterranean."

Vaissière was a young Algerian-born biology graduate who, as an Oceanographic Institute new-hire, stumbled into a hornet's nest of passions over Cousteau's decision to protest the proposed disposal of radioactive material at the upcoming Barcelona meeting of the World Underwater Federation. Members of the Monaco staff were deeply divided. There were those boning up on all matters anatomical who talked about the disposal of spent plutonium-239 as the ultimate doomsday horror. And there were those – a significant majority – who believed it was suicidal for the institute's new director to take on Charles de Gaulle's Olympian *force de frappe*.

After liquidating the vestiges of colonialism and trying to wind down the divisive Algeria war that had brought de Gaulle to power, his two-year-old government was energizing itself by adding nuclear weapons to France's arsenal. To be a nuclear power – together with a strong economy, a franc as solid as gold, and regained international prestige – was the cornerstone of Gaullist statecraft, the prerequisites for challenging the increasing world hegemony of the United States and for taking bold initiatives in the new era the French president saw dawning with the end of the cold war.

The drawn-out Algerian conflict touched JYC and Simone's lives personally. As the son of full-fledged Monegasque residents, Philippe had continued his education in Monaco, but in order not to lose his French citizenship he was spending his two years as a draftee in the navy, seeing action in Algeria. At the institute, debate over the French military's proposal to dump sealed drums of spent plutonium into the Mediterranean caused strains. Those on the Cousteau side argued that such dumping would amount to the first true pollution of the sea; the half-life of plutonium was 24,300 years, meaning it would remain a danger to life for up to half a million years. And high level uranium-235 and plutonium-239 were extremely toxic. One-thousandth of a gram of plutonium, inhaled, caused fibrosis in the lungs and death within hours.

The "realists" on the staff saw the debate in immediate political terms. The principality was in the middle of its economic fight with de Gaulle. To fill the residential and office towers of Rainier's building boom, the prince had started a great offensive to attract new business to Monaco. The attraction was the absence of personal and corporate income tax, and more than American, German, and British corporate leaders, French businessmen responded – many of them "overseas" French whose repatriation after the loss of Indochina, and in 1962 of Algeria, was financed by French taxpayers. These right-wing *pieds noirs* felt de Gaulle had "abandoned" them when he finally pulled France out of North Africa. In turn, it rankled the general no end to see some of his most implacable foes escape French taxes and controls by ducking into Monaco.

To the astonishment of the realists, Rainier risked aggravating his strained relations with Paris by joining Cousteau in demanding a ten-year moratorium on dumping atomic waste in the Mediterranean. The argument was that nothing should be thrown into the sea unless the people who did the dumping knew what they were doing. "What becomes of this talk of 'limitless resources' and 'mankind's last dependence' if we are now spoiling the sea forever?' Cousteau asked. "What becomes of the hope of human occupation of the oceans? Are we letting present contingencies kill the dreams of the future?"

The World Underwater Federation grouped national diving organizations in Europe and North America. Delegates from seventeen countries met in Barcelona in March 1960 to exchange scientific data and draw up safety rules, and naturally elected Cousteau its president and presiding officer. It came as a surprise to most of the 170 delegates that Cousteau wasn't just interested in rules for dealing with sharks and the nitrogen buildup in divers' bloodstreams, but proposed to stop for a decade the disposal of nuclear wastes in the sea.

Plutonium-239 was the worse pollutant. There was also low-level radioactive waste, which included anything that had picked up induced radiation, such as uranium mining tools, gloves and uniforms of workers in fuel-enrichment plants, and cooling water from reactors. Since 1946, he told the conference, the United States had consigned a million gallons of low-level nuclear waste to the sea in steel drums. The Soviet Union was probably producing an equal amount, and the smaller nuclear powers, Britain and France, proportionately fewer quantities. And there was the disposal of obsolete weapons, including nerve gas. More than 30,000 bombs and cannisters containing poison gases, along with mostly German munitions that had been dumped in 90 meters of water between Sweden and the Danish island of Bornholm after World War II, were beginning to show up in Baltic fishermen's nets. And the U.S. Department of Defense was disposing of outdated war matériel by loading it aboard obsolete Liberty ships, towing the vessels to designated offshore sites and sinking them.

Vaissière would remember the astonished and sometimes pained looks greeting Cousteau's speeches and lobbying in Barcelona. "The oceans were primordial, untamed, and all motion in 1960," he recalled. "No one was sensitive to pollution problems. The sea was rich and splendid and savagely eternal, and here comes the pioneer and foremost promoter of exploring the deep to say man was perhaps mismanaging the oceans. The real astonishment is that the French army actually agreed to reconsider its plans for dumping nuclear wastes in the Mediterranean."

Shortly before the World Underwater Federation was formed in Monaco in 1959, Cousteau had been called to his brother's deathbed in Paris. With his nephew, JYC had spent a last few hours with Pierre Antoine before his brother slipped into a coma. Jean-Pierre had turned twenty three days earlier and saw his father entrust him to his uncle as the two brothers make their peace. Three days later the fifty-two-year-old Pierre Antoine died.

Librairie française, a small Left Bank press, published two of PAC's books in 1959. *Les Lois de l'hospitalité* ("The Laws of Hospitality") is the tragicomical story of the wrong way ("we should have sought refuge in Spain") flight of five Parisian collaborators, three wives, and a ten-year-old orphaned boy through the collapsing Third Reich and, in mid-winter 1944-45, across the German, Italian, and Austrian Alps toward a hoped-for detention in a U.S. prison camp. *En ce temps-là* ("In Those Days") is a quick sketch of PAC's youth ("my father was deplorably liberal"), and career in political journalism that skips the war years and becomes a diary of his long wait for trial, his sentence, time on death row, and eleventh hour reprieve. The author never finds himself guilty of anything more serious than gullibility and a risible sense of honor. His children are barely mentioned, his famous brother only as JY or Jacques-Yves, and only twenty-four hours before his scheduled execution does the prison journal reveal inner turmoil, with an entry about his mother praying for him. Two months after the sentence was reduced, a letter from JY provokes despair and entries that made sense only to the diarist, but hinted that in 1946 Jacques interceded with the judiciary and had something to do with commuting his brother's death sentence. Without quoting from the letter, Pierre writes that it opened once more a deep wound in him, a hurt that was stupid and unacceptable, yet wouldn't go away because his future looked so bleak. "Perhaps Jacques-Yves now understands he should have let me face the firing squad, that that would have been more human."

PAC's widow kept the never-published

manuscript of the Marcel Proust book. Françoise married Nicholas Poliakoff, a Russian Jew, over his mother's objections. The Poliakoffs had three sons, divorced, and in her mature years, Françoise again used her maiden name. Jean-Pierre attended medical school and became a renowned Parisian cardiologist.

Captain Cousteau spent the summer of 1959 sailing to the New World and measuring his growing authority and popularity. Hooting tugboats, sirens from ships and docks, and the waterworks from a city fireboat gave the *Calypso* the traditional New York harbor salute on August 29 as she sailed past a fog-bound Statue of Liberty to take part in the first World Oceanographic Congress. Thousands of scientists, journalists, city officials, and navy representatives visited the former minesweeper while her master addressed the convention. From New York, the *Calypso* sailed up the New England coast to the Woods Hole Oceanographic Institution, then south and up the Potomac river to be feted by the National Geographic Society.

It was a heady trip. The world was discovering skin diving and, as *Time* magazine reported in a cover story on JYC, the sport that now had one million dedicated

U.S. skin divers was "almost the single-handed creation of a lean (6 ft, 154 lbs), visionary Frenchman named Jacques-Yves Cousteau." Celebrities from Lord Louis Mountbatten and rocketeer Wernher von Braun, to Clare Boothe Luce and Gary Cooper were strapping air tanks to their backs, frog fins to their feet, and with rubber mouthpiece between their teeth, discovering a "fascinating new playground, alive with beauty and tinged with danger."

Wherever he went Cousteau found himself surrounded by avid fans who plied him with questions (Sample: "Can you compress air into tanks lots smaller than the ones we have now?" Answer: "Yes, but it is too expensive – the demand will have to be greater"). He called manta rays and barracudas overrated killers, admitted sharks were a more puzzling matter, but that the last thing a diver should do was to flee. "The good diver stays and faces the shark." With rigorous training, diving was safer than motorcycling, he said, calling the best divers people who weren't especially powerful but reflective, methodical individuals who calmly did all the right things.

The trip was also the occasion for shakedown trials of the diving saucer. A ballasted model without crew aboard was lost in March 1958 when a sudden lurch by the *Calypso* caused the cable lifting the saucer out of the water to snap. The craft was found the next day a kilometer beneath the surface, too great a depth to attempt salvage operation. Now the DS-2 (for diving saucer # 2) was being tested in the clear blue waters of the Caribbean.

Albert ("Bébert") Falco was not only good at catching Mediterranean dolphins, he was also becoming the expert pilot of the saucer. Cousteau had to marvel at – and admit to being envious of – Falco's mastery of the new undersea craft. With Bébert at the nozzle controls, a ride along the Leeward Islands of Guadeloupe was a trip through an enchanted dimension. The saucer moved like an airplane. Falco could make it hopscotch over reefs, glide on its nose, play dead on the bottom to observe never before seen animal forms, veer, tilt and cruise up, down, forward, and backward.

On the return across the Atlantic, Cousteau and Edgerton tried a new method of photographing the deepest point, the 8,600-meter Puerto Rico trench. They used "kytoons," helium-filled balloons bearing an aluminum foil radar target, to provide stationary reference points for mapping the seafloor and, once the trench was located,

40,000 feet of cable of progressively greater strength. Edgerton's six-hundred photos revealed traces of life even at this great depth.

Papa Flash got to ride the diving saucer with Falco off West Africa, but trouble with state-of-the-art cadmium power cells nearly caused a disaster. At 120 meters the saucer hit the bottom and stayed there. The instruments went dead and in the silence they heard bubbles, like boiling water in a kettle. Only the jettisoning of emergency weights allowed Falco and Edgerton to rise to the surface. The bubbles they had heard were discovered to be gas developing inside the cadmium cells that had caused the battery cases to explode. Cousteau ordered conventional batteries installed after the *Calypso* returned to Toulon on Christmas Day, 1959.

The new decade saw the Cousteau organization work on both sides of the future ecology fault line. The *Calypso* spent part of 1960 studying both radioactivity and the laying of a natural gas pipeline in the western Mediterranean.

The summer brought heightened international tension. The shooting down over Russia of an American U-2 spy plane culminated in the sudden cancellation of a planned summit conference in Geneva between President Dwight Eisenhower and Soviet leader Nikita Khrushchev. The United States, Britain, and the Soviet Union had laboriously negotiated a ban on nuclear tests in the atmosphere and underwater when France exploded its first bomb in the Sahara – China was rumored to be the next member of the nuclear club – and the two super-powers threatened to resume atmospheric tests.

Oceanographers saw the dusting of world's seas with radioactive fallout from a new round of atmospheric tests as potentially catastrophic, but before John F. Kennedy had been in office one hundred days, the superpower rivalry was vaulted to a different frontier. On April 12, 1961, Major Yuri Gagarin became the first human to orbit the earth in a space vehicle. No wonder the young President's mind and words were on new dimensions a week later when he presented the National Geographic Society's gold medal to Cousteau.

"He is one of the great explorers of an entirely new dimension and I can imagine his satisfaction in having opened up the ocean floor to man and to science," Kennedy told the Rose Garden gathering that included Simone, the National Geographic's Melville Grosvenor, and part of the Washington diplomatic corps. "I can think of no more a felicitous award than this to the captain, your wife, the representatives of France, Mr. Ambassador, and the Geographic." The medal inscription eloquently paid tribute to Cousteau. "To earthbound man he gave the key to the silent world." In response, JYC called it much more than a personal award and paid tribute to the team effort of his crew and his friends at the National Geographic, the Woods Hole Oceanographic Institution, and MIT.

Cousteau held unorthodox views on the subject of industrializing the ocean depths. He disagreed sharply with proponents of the fashionable view that the sea contains endless riches. The oceans were no bargain basement for humanity, he said. The supply of food and minerals to be hauled from the oceans was finite, a fact that demanded a rational approach. Fishing was an example of irrational, stone-age harvesting. "Ages ago man selected the most productive wild animals to domesticate – the horse for power, the goat and cow for milk, the chicken for eggs, and all of them – plus the pig – for edible flesh," he stated. "Stock farming is the logical next step in the sea, that is 'farming' seafood instead of pursuing wild creatures." As for mining the sea bottom, he was cautious. He had heard of a pair of South Africans mining diamonds with a suction pipe similar to the vacuum cleaner he had used at Grand Congloué, but mining for raw materials would be difficult and very expensive. "The sea isn't going to give us anything without a hard struggle and vast capital outlays," he continued. "However, the day may be coming when we shall need whatever minerals can be taken below."

At the same time, contradictions were beginning to gnaw at him. He had successfully lobbied against proposed French nuclear waste dumping (and spoke out against the actual dumping in Pacific waters by the U.S. Navy), yet the *Calypso* was France's official oceanographic vessel, and as such brought him essential funds. At what cost? After an ill-starred biologists' voyage to Brazil – a 26,000-kilometer round-trip beset with costly mechanical mishaps – to dredge, trawl, and dive for flora and fauna between Recife and the Uruguayan coast, the *Calypso*'s 1962 program included seismic refraction work between Nice and Corsica. Seismic refraction was a polite way of saying undersea bombings. By setting off massive explosives, geologists created sonic shocks that allowed them to draw the profile of the sea bottom and to determine the composition of the subfloor strata.

The exercise transformed the *Calypso* into a floating powder keg, with enough TNT to sink herself and two accompanying work vessels. When Cousteau saw the marine holocaust that seismic refraction left behind, he was so appalled that he started a crusade to have TNT banned from undersea geophysics.

Yet at the same time he was deeply committed to man's presence in the sea. He was convinced that in a few short decades humans would not only work underwater but would spend part of their lives there, performing vital tasks. He could imagine communities, vast industrial complexes, and even new nations arising under the sea. Our species had gone through an aquatic stage before. Maybe it was time to complete the cycle by returning to the sea.

11
HOMO AQUATICUS

Cousteau's *Homo aquaticus* was born of frustrations, as were the aqualung, the diving saucer, and the lengthening list of special equipment conjured up, prototyped, tested, and if possible, put into commerical production by his successive corporate entities. The aqualung came about because Cousteau wanted to stay underwater longer and be able to dive deeper. The diving saucer was the result of the *Calypso* skipper's impatience with having to rely on Harold Edgerton's deep-sea camera contraptions instead of being able to see with his own eyes. "From 280 meters down," Cousteau noted in the saucer logbook during one of the first descents in 1959, "everything is to be discovered."

Space was the new frontier, quickening the pulse of science and firing both public imagination and American-Soviet rivalries. Yet no one besides the Piccards and a handful of others had ever peered into the briny depths of the oceans. The U.S. Navy was set to acquire the Piccards' newest bathyscaph, the *Trieste*, to try a manned sinking into the Mariana trench in the Pacific, but even if successful such a descent would be no more than a six-hour excursion. What Cousteau wanted to know was whether humans could *live* on the ocean floor.

The answer was obviously affirmative. John Scott Haldane and the British Admiralty had established in 1907 that man

221

can live in twice the density of the atmosphere for a long period and be decompressed rapidly without danger. But what Cousteau wanted was human occupation of the seafloor, true "aquanauts" or "oceanauts." The wealth and creativity humanity is seeking was not to be found in orbital projectories, he said a few months after Yuri Gagarin, sitting hunched in a tiny capsule, became the first man to orbit the earth in 1961. "In ten years there will be permanent homes and workshops at the bottom of the sea where men can stay for three months at a time, mining, drilling for oil, coal, tin, other minerals, and farming seafood and raising sea cattle." What he could foresee beyond 1971, he said, were hundreds of thousands of aquanauts, a new breed of humans living and working half their lives under the sea. "More important than the huge space and wealth, they will draw new thoughts and creativity from a whole new world. And hopefully we may enter an era that deserves the title, civilization."

The yellow cylinder in which Albert ("Bébert") and twenty-eight-year-old newcomer Claude Wesly lived 12 meters below the Mediterranean in September 1962, was a bit roomier than the capsule John Glenn had used six months earlier to become the first American to orbit the earth. The barrel, named Diogenes after the Greek philosopher who lived in a tub, was the size of storage tanks buried under gas stations. The *Calypso* towed the cylinder to a bay at Frioul Island off Marseilles and lowered it to a preselected site. With reporters and photographers watching on closed-circuit television, Falco and Wesly swam down to their new home.

Every day the two oceanauts left their seabed station for several hours to work at deeper levels. To relieve possible boredom, they had radio and TV hookups to the surface and received daily visits from Cousteau and scuba-diving doctors and journalists. The experiment was called Conshelf, short for Continental Shelf Station.

When Bébert and Claude were brought to the surface one week later with all the time-consuming precautions, it was evening. Cousteau was there at the top of the ladder, scrutinizing the two men's faces for signs of metaphysical change. After all, they were the first humans to have experienced seven days of weightlessness since vertebrates emerged from the sea nearly 500 million years ago. The service boat sped toward the lights of Marseilles. On shore, JYC took Bébert's arm and walked him on busy streets to see him reestablish contact with life on land. JYC couldn't wait any longer and asked his friend what was his impression of living underwater. Groping for words, Falco answered, "Oh, Captain. Everything is ... everything is moral down there." Nearly a quarter century later when Cousteau was addressing the first planetary conference of space explorers from thirteen countries, he would mention Falco's response that evening and say astronauts and divers not only shared strong reactions to weightlessness, but had also passed through a "kind of moral gateway that made them see national and tribal disputes as ridiculous, as something mankind must learn to leave behind."

A month after the Conshelf experiment, Cousteau was in London taking the World Congress on Underwater Activities by storm. A new kind of man was evolving, *Homo aquaticus,* who would dwell among his own kind in submerged towns and swim about on his daily labors. "Diving has gone beyond sport; it is now a worldwide movement," he told the gathering of several hundred marine experts. "The imperative need now is to place swimmers underwater for very long periods, to really learn about the sea. I think there will be a conscious evolution of *Homo*

224

aquaticus, spurred by human intelligence rather than the slow blind natural adaptation of species. We are now moving toward an alteration of human anatomy to give man almost unlimited freedom underwater."

The new species would come shortly after the year 2000, he prophesied. Water people would be born at the bottom of the sea, possess lungs filled with an incompressible liquid, and breathe by means of a blood-regenerating technique. They would be able to swim to a depth of about a mile. To go beyond that would not be feasible since the presssure of 170 atmospheres would compress and literally wreck the body, but it was the stretch above the one-mile depth that humans would be interested in. "Virtually all the food and raw materials we could exploit on the ocean floor exist in this zone of the continental shelf and the continental slope."

Was he going off the deep end? To one conference delegate who dismissed *Homo aquaticus* as "science fiction," Cousteau revealed that the National Aeronautics and Space Administration, which the Kennedy administration had just established, was thinking along similar lines and developing an "artificial gill" to allow spacemen to function in hostile environments without breathing. The NASA gill, he explained, was a capsule of chemicals, to be worn under an astronaut's armpit, which would take over the lungs' job of filtering carbon dioxide out of the blood and replacing it with oxygen. Future "menfish" would inhale water instead of air. To overcome the collapse of lungs underwater, there would be some sort of mechanical assistance to extract oxygen from the sea.

A few months later when his old friend Jim Dugan asked him about the science fiction reference, Cousteau in turn asked what was wrong with science fiction as a presentiment of reality. "Ever since Jules Verne, and lots of people before him, the informed human imagination has projected what is to come. Actually, I was trying to be conservative in talking about the underwater future in London. Why, there were people there who wanted to talk about milking whales in regular underwater dairies! At the underwater congress a man asked me what *Homo aquaticus* could expect to find under the sea that we have not discovered already. The question was fairly breathtaking. We know practically nothing about the depths of the ocean!"

In June 1963, Conshelf II thrust Cousteau oceanauts deeper into the sea and for a longer period of time. This time five men lived on a coral ledge in a star-shaped home 12 meters below the Red Sea northeast of Port Sudan.

This ambitious demonstration project of an underwater village and seabed work station, far from a home base, swelled the crew to forty-five men, plus Simone. The trade organization of the French oil industry, increasingly focusing on offshore drilling, was a major underwriter of the $1.2 million (1963 dollars) project. Again, however, the only way Cousteau was able to make budgetary ends meet was with a movie contract. The result would have to be a full-length documentary.

The Starfish House was a five-room bungalow on telescopic legs anchored to the bottom of the Shab Rumi lagoon. It was pressurised to equal the surrounding water pressure, which meant the entrance was a liquid, always-open bottom "door." The leader of the oceanauts, Raymond Vaissière, would establish a marine biologist's dream, a complete undersea research station, complete with fish pens he could flipper out to. The four others were chief diver Claude Wesly of Conshelf I experience; André Folco, a handsome industrial designer; and Pierre Vannoni, a former customs agent – both chosen for their calm, compatible personalities – and, for contrast, Pierre Guilbert, a bearded cook and paterfamilias rustling pots, pans, and flippant one-liners.

Besides Starfish House, so named because workshops and living quarters branched off from a central main chamber, and a garage for DS-2, the project featured a two-story, rocket-shaped Deep Cabin anchored to the sloping reef 30 meters below the surface. Here, Kientzy, now a ten-year veteran of Cousteau expeditions, and André Portelatine, the voluble director of Nice's famous scuba-diving school, were to spend one week under 3.5 atmospheres of pressure, breathing a mixture of air and helium and making daily dives to depths of 100 meters. The point of the Kientzy-Portelatine exercise was to test the theory that a helium booster station could take divers to much deeper encampments without too great risks of nitrogen narcosis. Would they have clear brains at these depths or be overcome by rapture of the deep? Since the seven oceanauts could not be brought up in a hurry in case of an accident – to do so would result in their deaths from the effects of decompression embolism – they were color-coded. They wore silver wetsuits; everybody else suited up in black.

Conshelf II was a hellish experience for

everybody except the quintet in Starfish House. Only they had air conditioning. The support crew on board the *Rosaldo*, the utility ship anchored above with its noisy array of ever-running generators and compressors, and aboard the *Calypso*, worked around the clock in blistering heat that reached 120°F. They were dazed with fatigue, constantly losing weight, and occasionally fainting on the job.

Pierre Goupil, who had been Louis Malle's assistant on *The Silent World*, was head of the film crew. Philippe, who had just obtained his *baccalauréat* from the Lycée de Monaco and planned to study engineering, was part of the camera team, which literally got to fight off sharks and, a novelty, isopods, or sea mosquitoes, an agile planktonic crustacean with a bite as fearsome as that of piranhas.

During the installation of the Deep Cabin, also pressurized to equal 3.5 atmospheres and with an open "liquid door," Raymond Coll was making repairs to outside power, telephone, TV, and instrument cables, and Pierre Servelo, an electrician who was on only the second dive os his life, was doing work inside when the structure began to slip, snapping the wires to the surface and thudding on down the reef slope. The Deep

Cabin fell off for nearly half a kilometer, until it struck a ledge 42 meters down and came to a stop, leaning against the reef. Coll's backpack tanks and one of his flippers were pinned between the steel cabin and reef while inside in the darkness Servelo realized water was rising in the lower chamber toward him. He heard banging and scuffling outside and thought divers were coming to his rescue. It was Coll cutting himself free from his backpack and pulling his foot out of the trapped flipper.

Rescue was on the way. Jean Alinat and Albert Falco suited up and came stroking down when they saw Coll, without aqualung and only one flipper, slowly rising with distended cheeks. He was gradually lowering the pressure in his lungs. To have retained more of his last inhalation before letting go of his aqualung mouthpiece would have fatally ruptured his lungs. Alinat and Falco reached the cabin and brought young Servelo to safety.

For Kientzy and Portelatine the worst proved to be the humidity. Conshelf II had been planned for March when the Red Sea waters are at their coldest. It was mid-July instead and the Deep Cabin was a sauna. They slept little. To cool off Kientzy donned his aqualung and went swimming among the sharks. JYC promised to send down blocks of ice.

Nearly everybody was on night shift. Tropical waters come alive with the most extraordinary animals at night and the camera team was after exciting footage. They had improved lighting equipment, including a stiletto light developed by the OFRS. This narrow intense beam has the power of mesmerizing fish in midwater, allowing divers to gather unharmed specimens with their bare hands.

Coll and Christian Bonnici, an intense, driving worker, mechanic, and self-reliant diver who was to spend a decade with Cousteau, were holding floodlamps at a depth of 33 meters one night as Goupil and his assistant, Gilbert Duhalde, prepared to film marauding sharks. The pack began circling the men, moving in and growing in numbers until there were some seventy sharks.

The antishark cage held only three people. Goupil rang the alarm to have it hauled up. Next, he shoved Duhalde, the least experienced diver, inside and, with Coll and Bonnici, got on top. As the cage slowly rose, the three men sat back to face the narrowing circle. Suddenly the sharks attacked. The men struck back with cameras, lights, and shark billies. The cage broke water with the frustrated sharks thrashing on the surface in a frenzy. No one was hurt.

The filmmakers concentrated on the silver-suited oceanauts gliding through translucent waters into caverns, on brilliant shots of fantastic fish – huge parrotfish in bright, flashing blue-green and orange colors, triggerfish – and compositions of plantlike animals such as Gorgon's heads, a member of the starfish family, shaped like a small bush with thousands of slimy branches, that can walk away, and, if caught in floodlight, contract and vanish into a coral crevice, or startling huge urchins with radarlike scanners on top. Goupil and his team also filmed the diving saucer, headlights beaming, gliding toward the camera and, from inside DS-2, its deep probes, the Deep Cabin coming into view and then slaloming over 300 meter-deep plateaus and mesmerizing prehistoric-looking berycids in stiletto light, larval jellyfish, swimming worms, and many-faceted hatchetfish. Goupil also had a diver sweep a fine silk net through a fog of plankton, transfer the living organisms to a clear container, and then with special lights, filmed the gossamer movement of a million microscopic lifeforms.

The captain himself was the tireless

232

overseer of everything. He lived practically without sleep and during the four weeks lost 10 kilos. For rare moments of relaxation, he went riding the diving saucer with Falco. The onion-shaped garage allowed the DS-2 to be serviced and used totally underwater. Based in the submerged dome, the saucer was never immobilized by bad weather. During one deep plunge in the DS-2, JYC and Falco came upon a tangled and struggling bed of living crabs at the base of the reef. They skimmed over what seemed to be hundreds of millions of crabs, each the size of a man's fist, and thought it ironic that hundreds of millions of half-starving people lived in the lands bordering the nearby Indian Ocean.

In free-diving, Kientzy and Portelatine reached almost the depths of Cousteau and Falco in the saucer. Despite a constant ear pain, Portelatine was determined to dive with Kientzy to the depth they had planned, 110 meters. Here, in the lambent stillness of crystalline water, they were breathing eleven times the volume of air they would on the surface. This meant they emptied their double set of tanks at a rapid rate. Before shooting back up to their cabin, Kientzy made a push to 119 meters – the height of a standard thirty-story building. He didn't enter this record in their log and only confessed to it when it was all over. Such dives would be too hazardous from the surface, but since Kientzy and Portelatine reached these depths without experiencing nitrogen narcosis, they had vindicated the undersea work station concept.

JYC swam down to the Starfish House four or five times a day, spent four entire days there, while Simone and a doctor scuba-dived down twice a day. Visitors included Philippe, oil experts, French and U.S. navy planners and biologists. Vaissière and his crew laid on a champagne dinner on July 12 for the Cousteaus' twenty-sixth wedding anniversary, an occasion JYC would remember for the flat champagne as double atmospheric pressure kept the bubbles imprisoned in the wine.

The 3.5 pressure in the Deep Cabin played a puzzling trick. By the middle of their week, Kientzy and Portelatine noticed the water rising in their lower sleeping deck. A telephone check with the topside showed this could not be, since the pumped-down oxygen and helium was constant, and equal to the water pressure. Kientzy wrestled a bottle of helium off the outside rack and released the gas in the cabin, pushing the water back down with the added pressure.

The water rose again, however, and threatened to flood them in their sleep. Sevelo calculated the answer. Helium, the next-to-lightest gas in the atomic table, was seeping into the television cable and escaping to the surface.

The oceanauts came up July 14, Bastille Day, to exhausted cheers from the support crew. The Starfish House and Deep Cabin were refloated and dismantled, but the DS-2 garage was left for possible reuse. After a ten-day rest, the Conshelf group and visitors left. Cousteau was happy to have pioneered a submerged colony, Vassière was convinced that marine biologists around the world would soon demand ocean-bottom laboratories, the oil industry representatives believed underwater stations might be cheaper and safer than offshore drilling platforms, and the navy experts thought of future antisubmarine warning stations and undersea coastal defenses.

World Without Sun was the cinematic record of Conshelf II, a ravishing ninety-three-minute excursion to an otherworldly realm that lived up to the encore moviegoers had come to expect from the director of *The Silent World* and had more than one reviewer reach for Jules Verne metaphors. The sights of the diving saucer, slipping from its underwater garage and dropping step by step down the stairway of the continental shelf to observe wonders never seen before, provided some of the most breathtaking sequences. Yet the film's intent was to show that humans can live in the sea and that the sunken continental shelf, which projects from the shores of all the continents, represents, in its innumerable resources, a wealth that humanity cannot afford to ignore.

Columbia Pictures again became the international distributor. At a news conference in New York for the December 1964 American premiere, Cousteau told reporters he had an intense dislike for the word "documentary," and that neither *The Silent World* nor *World Without Sun* taught facts. "If you notice, there are hardly any 'facts' in them at all," he said. "In *World Without Sun* we never even identify the locale as the Red Sea. As soon as you are specific, the poetry disappears." In fact, his two films had been consciously designed to make humans look awkward so that audiences would see the beauty and diversity of nature.

World Without Sun won the 1964 Oscar for best documentary. It also ran into something that would periodically dog

PHOTO: DR. J.P. COUSTEAU ARCHIVES

Daniel's 85th birthday and Calypso *cake.*

In the Galleries of the Oceanographic Museum in Monaco, director Jacques Cousteau joins Prince Rainier, Prince Albert and Princess Grace of Monaco at the Museum's fiftieth anniversary in 1960.

PHOTO: BETTMANN NEWSPHOTOS

The 102nd Charter Anniversary ceremonies at the University of California in 1970 are disrupted when a youth casually requests an autograph of Jacques Cousteau.

The funeral of Philippe. Jacques and Simone are on the right.

The Captain gives the signal for release of the mooring rope from the research ship Calypso *on August 27, 1986, as the ship left Miami for a five-year "Rediscovery of the Earth" mission.*

JYC on the Rediscovery expedition, 1986.

Father and sons. Jacques, Daddy, and PAC at St-Andre de Cubzac during the early days of the war.

...nary, 1946. Cousteau (in car) and l. to r. Simone, Philippe, ...an-Pierre, Jean-Michael, and background, right, Francois and ...izabeth.

Daddy, at 72, at Torquay.

*Simone and Yuki
aboard the* Calypso.

Cousteau 2; Monaco 1. Soccer match between Cousteau and Oceanographic Museum teams. Below JYC and Simone, l. to r.: Ruth Dugan, Andree Bertino, the wife of the late Cousteau collaborator Serge Bertino, and James Dugan.

cques and Simone in llywood in 1956.

This twenty-three foot high structure houses two men underwater for about ten days. Carried on board the Calypso, *it was placed at a depth of one hundred feet.*

Cousteau as a maker of nonfiction entertainment for big screen and television – accusations of staged reality, synthetic confrontations and less than honest "creative" editing. In 1956, *New York Times* veteran film critic Bosley Crowther had gone out of his way to place *The Silent World* above various Walt Disney nature films, citing such "hokey sequences" in Disney's *Living Desert* as a mating dance of scorpions and, in *Water Birds,* a rhapsodic ballet of grebes as examples of "putting music to cleverly cut assemblages of real-life shots to achieve a theatrical sensation."

The closing scene of *World Without Sun,* however, offended Crowther to the point where he consulted oceanographers on its veracity. His credulity was challenged, he wrote in his December 23, 1964 review, by this climactic scene which showed the saucer, at a depth of 1,000 feet, move through a tunnel into a wholly enclosed underground lake, where it surfaced and Falco opened the hatch. Wondering whether Cousteau wasn't perpetrating a hoax here, he wrote that oceanographers doubted such a deep-sea cavern could exist, and, if it did, whether the atmosphere in its air "bubble" wouldn't be noxious methane gas rather than air. He went to some length describing the scene, saying that since the shot was made from the exterior, a camera was presumably set up in advance, and he wondered whether some of these scenes hadn't been filmed in a studio aquarium or tank. Another scene that bothered him was one that showed the camera move from the interior of Starfish House through a window and away in the night. "It is too bad that this obvious faking should finally excite one's doubt and mar one's compolete enjoyment of this otherwise plausible film."

Two weeks later the *Times* ran a three-column letter from a deeply offended Cousteau. If Crowther had paid attention, JYC wrote from Paris, he would have seen that the sequence beginning inside the undersea house and continuing outside was in reality two matched-up shots. In fact, the tracking shot away from the house porthole was so difficult that Goupil tried four times and Cousteau four times, with his son Philippe towing him away from the window with a string around the ankle. As for the enclosed underground lake, the film never said it was at a depth of 1,000 feet. Quoting "We're going up" in the dialogue between Falco and himself, Cousteau maintained common sense, plus visual and verbal descriptions of the upward voyage, would tell any viewer that tunnel and underground cavern were higher up (how much higher up the letter didn't say). In his rebuttal, Crowther said he had gone back to see *World Without Sun* a second time and that he had managed to get Cousteau on a transatlantic telephone. A second viewing convinced him that ninety-nine out of a hundred people would get the distinct impression tunnel and cavern were at a great depth, "and I suspect that is precisely the impression Mr. Cousteau wants them to get." On the phone, however, Cousteau had acknowledged that the tunnel entrance was only "a few fathoms beneath the sea" and that the cavern was not an airtight pocket. "So my original objection to the staging of this incident is not altered," Crowther concluded. "It still tends to deceive, and provoked some gnawing skepticism as to the validity of the rest of the film. This is too bad, because *World Without Sun* is so exciting it doesn't need a tricky 'kicker' at the end."

Cousteau would not forget the incident. In his 1970 book *Shark,* coauthored with Philippe, he spent three pages describing how they had filmed the receding window and habitat back in 1962.

In 1965 there was a Conshelf III, a globular structure seven meters in diameter capable of accommodating six men. It was sunk 108 meters – nine times the depth of Conshelf II three years earlier – below the Mediterranean off Villefrance-sur-Mer and Cap Ferrat. With André Laban acting as *chef de mission*, Philippe as cameraman, and Oceanographic Institute physicist Jacques Rollet compiling medical and physical data on everybody, they and Coll, Bonnici, and new team member Yves Omer spent twenty-eight days at the base making daily dives to 130 meters, simulating oil swellhead repairs that oilmen considered impossible under-water. They breathed a mixture of helium and oxygen, or "helox," that prevented rapture of the deep, but brought new complications. Breathing part helium at these depths meant losing heat conductivity and body heat seventy-seven times faster than in a normal atmosphere. New vests made of incompressible foam rubber helped maintain body heat, but extra heaters had to be brought down.

Ten thousand kilometers away, off La Jolla, California, the U.S. Navy was conducting its parallel experiment, Sealab II. For publicity purposes, the two undersea habitats were hooked up by telephone so

Laban and Philippe could talk to astronaut Scott Carpenter 67 meters under the Pacific. To help rid Laban and Cousteau Jr. of the characteristic Donald Duck squeak caused by breathing part helium, they were given neon and oxygen, "neox." A storm caused a real emergency by threatening to gnaw away at the lifeline cables running over the Cap Ferrat cliffs out to the stable A-frame and into the ocean. In case the cables broke, Laban was to seek to resurface the sphere by breaking out a two-week supply of atmosphere-regenerating chemicals and jettisoning ballast. Once free from the bottom, the oceanauts were to bed down in sleeping bags and cover themselves with blankets and clothes. Without the electric heaters they might freeze to death in a few hours in helium. At the height of the storm, which innundated the Riviera with torrential rains and provoked rockslides along the coastal corniches, Falco and Kientzy climbed out on the A-frame and strung new stays up to save the cables.

Conshelf III cost $700,000, involved 150 technicians and a dozen vessels. It sent Cousteau heavily into debt. *Expérience Précontinent III,* as the resulting feature documentary was called, was not given a theatrical release and instead became a television special. The English-language version was written by Jim Dugan and Irwin Rosen, and it brought Cousteau in contact with David L. Wolper, the Hollywood television producer National Geographic's Melvin Payne felt comfortable working with on the specials the society sponsored. Called *The World of Jacques Cousteau* and narrated by Orson Welles, the Conshelf III television program ran on CBS in May 1966 as a National Geographic-Wolper Productions special.

Cousteau called Conshelf III "one of the first steps in man's economic occupation of the ocean floor." Conshelf IV would have five men stay two weeks at essentially the same depth but dive to 175 meters – the height of a forty-story building – and be less dependent on surface support systems. Conshelf V, announced for August 1966, would be established at the drop-off line of the continental shelf at 193 meters. From here, five men would attempt dives to 295 meters (the height of a seventy-story building). Future oceanauts, Cousteau believed, could live in underwater habitats at 215 meters and make dives to 426 meters (the height of the Empire State Building). Eventually, the ties to the world above could be entirely eliminated, giving oceanauts "the true freedom of the deep."

Conshelf IV and V never happened, but in October 1968, Cousteau signed a development contract with the de Gaulle government to build a surface-independent and mobile undersea settlement called the Argyronète.

In Greek mythology, Argyra is a sister nymph to *Calypso,* a naiad who deserted the shepherd Selemnos and left him so heartbroken that Aphrodite took pity on him and transformed him into a river, granting him the power to cure the sickness of the heart. Whoever bathed in Selemnos River found oblivion from the sorrows of the heart. To Cousteau, the Argyronète was a $1.5 million contract with the Ministry of Industrial and Scientific Development and part of his grandest plans to have undersea settlers engage in undersea farming, mining, oil drilling, geological and biological research, and, perhaps, a deep-sea Disneyland.

To build the 300-ton, ten-man sub that would become the home for four oceanauts diving and working extensively at depths to 700 meters, or half a mile, JYC reorganized the OFRS and renamed it Centre d'Etudes Maritimes Avancées (CEMA). Facilities were built in Marseilles to carry tank dives to a theoretical 1.650 meter "saturation" and to test instrumentation for very deep seafloor stations.

The Argyronète (Greek for "silver spinner" and the name of an aquatic spider) was never built. In the late 1960's, Cousteau found new challenges and opportunities that made him change course. He turned from doing scientific research to popularizing it. Fifteen years later he would utterly condemn the idea of colonizing the sea, claiming the undersea environment is not hostile to man, "but it is not ours."

12
SHOWBIZ

There is a curious mixture of irritation and contempt among scientists for scientists who become popular stars, the late Jacob Bronowski being an exception. Jacques Cousteau and Carl Sagan have suffered peer scorn and studied ostracism because they made television series about the oceans and the universe. The Scripps Institution of Oceanography in La Jolla, California, won't let Cousteau near its labs and classrooms lest he corrupt young scholars with showbiz dross. Despite diligent service on seven of the National Academy of Sciences panels and committees, Sagan has never been invited to join because colleagues dismiss him as a mere popularizer. This is curious because popular enthusiasm for science is exactly what science needs.

In Monaco, in January 1966, JYC and Simone entertained a lanky television executive from Hollywood and his wife, a former opera singer. Bud Rifkin, the vice-president of David Wolper Productions, had already made his first fortune selling off his and his partners' syndication company to United Artists and would soon make a second in the budding cable TV. Simone, who had little regard for women in general, took a liking to Teddy Rifkin and they went shopping and out to lunch together while the men talked business.

Rifkin's proposition sent Cousteau's imagination spinning. David Wolper Productions produced all the National Geographic television specials. Wolper was a thirty-seven-year-old transplanted New Yorker who had been on the fringes of big-time Hollywood for a decade, while moving toward the center stage of television as treasurer, vice-president, and president of a number of ephemeral production companies. He loved nonfiction television and made his first impact with *The Making of the President* documentary in 1960. A perfectionist and friend of documentary filmmakers, he talked nuts and bolts with cameramen after office hours and lost money backing a number of them. Wolper had weathered his first battles with the networks. After he had completed a film titled *The Race for Space* in 1960 and secured a sponsor, Shulton, for CBS airing, ABC, CBS, and NBC announced that, as a matter of policy, they would henceforth only broadcast documentaries produced by their own news divisions. Independent producers were stunned, but Wolper managed to convince Shulton to buy time for *The Race for Space* station by station around the country.

Rifkin was something of a scuba diver himself, and as the new vice-president of Wolper Productions he had screened the Conshelf special and told his boss there was a TV series in this Jacques Cousteau. Before taking off for Europe with Teddy, Rifkin had called Melvin Payne at National Geographic and gotten the lowdown on the French explorer. Payne had been quite frank: The only problem Wolper Productions would have was controlling Cousteau's cost. "He always spends infinitely more money than he's allocated and we have a hard time keeping tab," Payne explained.

Rifkin repeated none of this to his gallant host. What he did tell Cousteau was that he was quite sure he and Wolper could sell one of the networks on a Cousteau series. What kind of money are we talking about? JYC inquired casually. With Payne's warning clearly in the back of his mind, Rifkin said the way to proceed was for Cousteau to come up with about twelve or fourteen projects, like the shark, the coral reef, and that they could then share the world. Wolper Productions would take the English-speaking world, plus Latin America, and Cousteau could have the rest. Rifkin was not going to get into any French bookkeeping, but for *his* share of the world he'd imagine he was talking about maybe $300,000 per espisode. Twelve episodes at $300,000 each came to $3.6 million ($10.8 million in 1987 dollars).

The Rifkins stayed in Monaco a week. They were barely back in Los Angeles before a package arrived with typed-up outlines for twenty-five projects. Wolper and Rifkin were soon in New York trying to sell one of the networks on the idea, and to sign a contract with JYC's energetic attorney, Lee Steiner.

"I got an offer from all three networks,"

247

Rifkin recalled, "except that CBS only wanted to do one hour at the time. NBC wanted to give me an order for one year and I kept saying there's no other way to do this, because once the expedition starts, you can't start and stop it. Someone has to make a commitment for twelve episodes spread out over three years and just let it run."

Cousteau and Philippe came to New York to be in on the negotiations with their lawyer. Rifkin liked the younger Cousteau, feeling that his devil-may-care attitude was just right in a twenty-six-year-old. Philippe wasn't exactly in on the negotiations, but he was there talking with his father far into the night about the things they could do if Rifkin could pull it off.

Philippe also met Perry Miller, who after several years with CBS had joined WNET, the New York public television station, and was about to make her own debut as a producer-director. Talking about children had never been part of Perry and Jacques's conversations, but she knew how he felt about his sons. She liked what she saw. "Philippe was very much like him, always very sort of teasing and ironic about his father," she remembered. "He was not going to be part of the hero worship."

ABC-TV's Tom Moore was the only network president who, in Rifkin's words, "sparked" to the project. Moore, a drawling Mississippian, was the broadcast industry's hero of the day for saying that by preempting network schedules with presidential news conferences all the time "Lyndon Johnson is just stealin' money right out of our pockets." In the case of the Cousteau project, Moore's eyes seemed distracted from the bottom line because he was ready to discuss Rifkin's terms. The negotiations went into high gear. JYC was unyielding. He had to have twelve hours so he could do the *Calypso* the way he wanted it, in order to get the equipment he needed, and as Rifkin said, once the *Calypso* was sailing they couldn't stop and go. Moore and his executives and lawyers met with Cousteau, Rifkin, and Steiner in conferences that dragged into the night, and were followed by all-night discussions in the Cousteaus' hotel room.

To complicate matters, in the middle of the negotiations, Philippe fell in love with a tawny-haired fashion model. Janice O. Sullivan was a green-eyed Californian living in a world of fashion shows and Upper East Side parties while quietly wondering whether she would find a man of substance in New York. At an after-theater party a friend whispered to her, "There's the greatest guy here. Go follow him around." That was easy enough, she remembered. Philippe towered over most people at the party and his outdoor glow set him apart from the winter-pale New Yorkers. He told her he was from a family of underwater explorers, but that meant nothing to her.

Philippe and Jan began having dinner together every night. JYC often tagged along to discuss contract details. On such occasions, father and son soon spoke staccato French, each turning to Jan from time to time to apologize for boring her. She found the captain charming but the hours of jabbering in French gave her headaches. Somehow, Jan and Philippe managed to discover each other. In May he left for Paris and two months later she joined him for an idyllic summer.

The $4.2 million contract Cousteau and David Wolper Productions signed with ABC for twelve hour-long television films changed everything. The deal made possible the most ambitious multiyear expedition to all the world's oceans. The TV episodes would not be documentaries but adventures. Scientists lived adventures that were sometimes thrilling and even dangerous, but the "how to" aspects of scientific explorations were tedious and boring. *The Undersea World of Jacques Cousteau,* the overall program title, would be made up of individual sixty-minute true stories – not as lessons or documentaries, but as nature adventures. Each segment would relate to an oceanographic problem, or challenge, and the story line would tell how the issue was solved.

The contract provided that Les Requins Associés (Sharks Associated), JYC's corporate filmmaking entity, was responsible for shooting the material and that all editing and postproduction finishes would be done in Los Angeles by Wolper Productions, with Philippe Cousteau acting as liaison and onshore adviser to the succession of overseers Wolper assigned to the series – Alan Landsburg, Jack Kaufman, Warren Bush, and Marshall Flaum. There were options for additional episodes beyond the four-a-year run of the three-year contract through 1970. Les Requins Associés had 100 percent control of the Europe-Asia-Africa markets and could sell the series in these markets for whatever the traffic would bear.

First Cousteau delicately negotiated the release of his ship from her various duties with the French government, including seismic refraction work and the supervision

251

of the laying of a controversial pipeline carrying red mud from a Marseilles aluminum factory to a deep-water dumping site. Next, he ordered the *Calypso* to undergo major refitting and remodeling. Each of the two 2,500 horsepower engines were reconditioned, the davits were removed and reconstructed to support heavier loads, a modern electrical system was installed, and the crew's quarters were rebuilt into separate cabins accommodating two persons each. Winches and scoops made for scientific research were replaced by storage space for two new P-500 minisubs. Called "sea fleas," these one-man units were built by OFRS so they could latch on to one another for enough power to tow a debilitated diving saucer in an emergency. On the upper deck, a new stateroom was added for JYC and Simone. A television room was outfitted, and new radar, larger windows, and closed-circuit TV were installed. While in the United States, Philippe added ballooning to his aeronautical skills and a hot air balloon was ordered for aerial filming. In October, Albert Falco took the various new pieces of equipment on a three-month shakedown trip to the Red Sea aboard the *Espadon*.

When the summer was over for Jan and Philippe, she flew back to New York determined to put him out of her mind. Gone for months at a time and wedded to his growing role in the expanding Cousteau universe, he had no permanent place in his life for her or any other woman. Not that he was easy to forget. He was his own man, someone who didn't want to exist on the fringes of his father's reputation, someone with his own verve and magnetism, his own mind and ideals.

As an only child of a Los Angeles family, Jan had grown up depending emotionally on friends rather than family, and the clannishness of the Cousteaus was new to her. Here were father, mother, and two sons dedicated to action and accomplishments. Three weeks after Jan and Philippe had said goodbye at Orly airport, he phoned from Monaco and asked her to marry him. "I said yes before he could change his mind," she recalled.

JYC and Simone were furious. This fashion model wasn't good enough for their Philippe. There were scenes between mother and son, between father and son, but in January 1967 in a filial revolt that stunned everybody, Philippe married Jan in Paris. His parents didn't come to the wedding and JYC's somewhat pointed wedding gift to his American daughter-in-law was a crash

253

course in French, ten hours a day of private lessons for six weeks. Jean-Michel was already married, but Anne-Marie was at least French. They had met while Jean-Michel was studying architecture and since his graduation he had no part in the film operation. His father, however, tried to draw him into his orbit and suggested the freshman architect skip the traditional years in a large architectural firm and concentrate instead on marine design, on futuristic adaptations of Conshelf habitats, condominiums built out under the sea. Anne-Marie, a native of Rodez, in central France, was to become a photographer.

Before the newlyweds had spent a fortnight together, Philippe was off to begin filming the first installment of the new TV series. Instead of feeling sorry for herself, Jan moved deeper into her husband's world. Uninvited and unpaid, she showed up at the Avenue Wagram Cousteau office, answered phones, typed, and in general tried to make herself part of the project. Jean-Michel and Anne-Marie arrived from Madagascar, where he had organized visas, supplies, and a land base for the upcoming Indian Ocean filming. Anne-Marie spoke no English, but Jan spent a lot of time with her sister-in-law, learning the quirks of the Cousteaus distended family life, and the ways of Parisian driving, housekeeping, and shopping. "Actually, I was lucky," Jan said in retrospect. "Because Philippe was away, I couldn't depend on him to be my interpreter. So, knowing I had to do it myself, I was doubly motivated to learn the language and adapt to a new environment. We develop new muscles and new strength as a result of independence." Her only mortification was that she never got her sea legs. She tried every known remedy against seasickness, but none worked.

The TV series threw JYC and Philippe together in Los Angeles several times and bystanders like Rifkin were appalled by the drawn daggers between father and son. More than ever Philippe sought to be his own man. He still resented his parents' hostility toward the woman of his choice and bristled at peace overtures.

To get a head start on whale filming – and to put a soothing distance between himself and his wife and his parents – Philippe took Jan to San Diego and established a location base there. He rented a Cessna aircraft and with Jan and a pair of gray whale experts, Wally Green and Ted Walker, flew down the west coast of Mexico. It was too late in the migratory season to get anything on film, but they decided which of the Baja California lagoons were the most promising for filming the gray whales' love nests and nurseries.

In Monaco, meanwhile, the February 17, 1967, sendoff of the refurbished *Calypso*, her master and crew of twenty-seven was a carefully scheduled media event. It almost didn't take place as JYC suffered two fractured vertebrae in an auto accident. Everybody insisted the departure be delayed or that Captain Roger Maritano, who had been interim skipper since 1960, slip the *Calypso* off quietly. But as in 1936, Cousteau refused to listen to doctors or anybody. He told Simone that what he and his spinal column really needed were the strokes of silky tropical waters.

Too much was at stake, and on February 18 everything went according to plans. After a news conference and a farewell reception, Prince Rainier and Princess Grace, among others, came on board a *Calypso* crammed with crates of new gear. The photo opportunity had the Rainiers give Simone a farewell present, a St. Hubert hunting dog named Zoom. JYC spoke of the upcoming voyage. Earlier expeditions had been for specific purposes. This time the *Calypso* would be gone for years on an errand that, like the sea itself, was boundless, unending. This was a kind of permanent mission to explore and to tell. He said television was the best means ever offered someone like him who found that part of the joy of making discoveries was to be able to tell about them. "I would love to convey to the public as much of my love for the sea as I can, and to help others to realize the sea is not only a great resource but a source of inspiration."

After the guests had left and balloons were released, the *Calypso* cast off. Maritano was at the helm and JYC in his cabin flat out on his back. Zoom proved to be of such exuberant energy that Cousteau found him too big and frisky for the cramped ship. The dog eventually became everyone's pet, even of a pair of sea lions caught off South Africa, of which Zoom was initially insanely jealous.

There was a new sense of excitement on board and, JYC felt, a new order of magnitude. The oceans were so vast, and there was so much to learn. This was his dream come true.

The *Calypso* slipped through the Suez Canal and joined *Espadon* in the familiar waters of the Red Sea. Cousteau was eager to test the new equipment and his sore back. Just past Shadwan Island he cast anchor one morning and ordered crew and equipment overboard for a tryout.

With the exception of the diving saucer, everything was new. The aqualungs had been redesigned to become elegant hydrodynamic diving suits, glistening black with yellow striping down arms and body and with a headpiece with built-in light and radio telephone. To propel themselves, divers had electric scooters, sometimes with lights and cameras mounted in the nose. And there was the Galeazzi tower, a submersible decompression chamber of Italian design. Swung over the side and lowered to the divers' work area, the Galeazzi tower allowed them to remain at the pressure of the work area while they were being hauled up and to stay inside the chamber while they gradually decompressed.

For surface scouting, the first prototypes of small inflatable runabouts of skiffs, soon baptized Zodiacs, were propelled by powerful outboard engines. Besides closed-circuit television for both surface and under-water monitoring, there were color-coded backpack tanks with various helox mixtures for deep dives. Despite the pains of his slowly healing back that sometimes made moving pure agony, even in the balmy Red Sea waters, JYC dived with the rest of them.

For the serious filmmaking they had in mind, they carried thirteen underwater cameras, six commercial dry-land cameras, and a variety of special automatic cameras for deep filming, plus untold amounts of waterproof lighting and miles of cables. In personnel, it translated to five cameramen and their assistants, all divers.

Two Cousteau inventions proved to be a bust. To find heads and tails in the kilometers of film being shot, JYC had the idea of having a diver describe what he saw and filmed via telephone to a tape recorder on board ship. It didn't work because the density of the air a diver must breathe at 33 meters or more deforms the human voice and turns the descriptive commentaries into Donald Duck squeaks. Also slightly ahead of its time was his computer, an electronic device attached to a typewriter keyboard that would code film sequences according to subject. Thus, if the editor needed a wrasse swimming left to right, all he'd have to do was to punch up the right negative edge number. All very good, except that they never got the programming right.

In Djibouti, they picked up Ludwig Sillner, a stocky German amateur diver and photographer who was a ballpoint pen representataive in Arab countries. JYC had

259

first met Sillner in Port Sudan in 1963 and had been impressed not only by Sillner's skills as a photographer but by his command of Arabic in its various Yemenite, Saudi, and Omani dialects. Sillner hated the crowded crew's quarters and rigged himself a tent on the spar deck out of green tarpaulin. When it rained at night, he was drenched, but he said better alone and wet than in a crowd and dry.

In Massawa, Ethiopia, at the end of August, they picked up Philippe and his hot air balloon, shipped from Sioux Falls, South Dakota. The balloon proved useful in scouting passages for the *Calypso* through reefs and atolls, for filming turtles on the islands between Madagascar and the coast of Mozambique, the subject of the third episode. It was 120°F in the shade when they reached Massawa. The deck planking was so hot and Zoom's whimpers so pitiful that his two-legged friends took to carrying him around in their arms.

The ABC contract didn't quite cover the expenses of all this, plus the rotation of crews that French maritime law mandated for ships not making yearly calls to their home ports. But Les Requins Associés had quickly sold the series in the major European markets.

It was *L'Odyssée sousmarine de l'Equipe Cousteau* in France and *Geheimnisse des Meeres* in Germany. One dive could, of course, yield footage for more than one episode – sharks and coral reefs came together in the Red Sea and were indeed the subjects of the first two segments – but the ratio of dives to usable film averaged an appalling ten to one.

Time and again, the *Calypso* would come across phenomena worthy of being investigated only to have them disappear before film crews could get into the water, despite the fact that everybody was trained to have equipment ready. JYC adapted quickly to television, to what David Wolper's L.A. office said it needed. "He understood and changed his own technique," Wolper remembered, and by the early 1970's the Cousteau team was such a top-notch filmmaking machine that a five-month trip to the Antarctica resulted in four one-hour television films and a full-length feature. Visiting journalists liked to talk about the easy camaraderie surrounding Cousteau. In reality, it was a grueling grind that resembled army boot camp.

Some subjects defied even military discipline. It seemed nonsensical to even guess where whales – the subject of the fourth

261

telefilm – would resurface once they had been spotted. Still, at the first yell of "Thar she blows," suited-up divers jumped into Zodiacs, gunned the outboards to get ahead of where they guessed the whales would be, jumped into the water, and aimed cameras on oncoming shadows. From the shipboard, all they could get on film were glistening backs.

By trial and error, a technique involving the use of two zodiacs slowly evolved that first television summer on the Indian Ocean. The only way to get any footage of whales was to get ahead of them and perhaps slow them down. While one Zodiac tried to get ahead, the other rubber boat put cameramen in the water in front of the whale as it swam around, above or under the men. Nothing altered the whale's progress: The divers could climb on its back and grab hold of a fin, but the leviathan continued to move forward. The Zodiacs backed up to pick up the divers and begin the game again. "We chased a whale, we jumped into the water, waited a second or two for our masks to clear, and began shooting," André Laban recalled, "and when we ran the developed film, all we'd see would be a whale's tail – and that only if we were lucky."

A further complication was that humans

have never been able to interpret a whale's movement, reaction, flick of a fin or tail, so that divers had no idea at any given moment whether the animal was merely bothered by the whining outboards or seething with anger. "When a dog snarls or a lion roars or a rattlesnake rattles, you know what to expect," JYC said. "But a whale? A sperm could be in a frenzy of rage for an hour before he decides to put an end to us with a flick of that incredible tail, and we would have no way of knowing it." Philippe felt humpback whales somehow tolerated the human presence underwater because they took extraordinary care to avoid hitting divers. The size of a whale in the water made a diver's mind rebel, JYC thought. "There is no experience on dry land that can compare with it."

There were accidents. Yves Omer suffered a dislocated knee and Bernard Delemotte, a bearded blond diver who had just joined, nearly drowned when a gray whale in the Pacific charged their Zodiac. Delemotte once tried to lasso a baby whale and managed the stunt of riding a whale like a horse until he was thrown into the water.

Cousteau almost gave up on fishing sperm whales, but recording any moving creature was never easy. Michel Deloire, a chief cameraman through the 1970's, and Albert Falco filmed octopuses in 1972, but they could seldom film the same species on different dives. Getting frontal views of dolphins swimming alongside the *Calypso*'s prow was impossible until a specially constructed arm holding a remote-controlled camera aimed backwards at the prow was rigged up. A 1971 attempt at attaching a camera with a harness to captured dolphins and setting them free to join their schools was a flop. The dolphins couldn't reach cruising speed. Also, film taken from the released dolphin's back proved totally void of interest. Footage of mother and calf sperm whales swimming alongside the *Calypso* in the Indian Ocean in 1967 proved, upon developing, to be of poor quality.

Pressure to get enough footage for four hours of finished film a year resulted in successive fracturing of crews. Philippe's enthusiasm for the Pacific gray whales persuaded JYC to let his son split off in 1968, lease his own ship, and produce the Pacific whale segment on his own. Philippe's chief cameraman was Jacques Renoir, the great-grandson of the impressionist painter, who proved to be the most talented of a long line of Cousteau cinematographers, to whom

JYC would turn an entire project in 1970. Philippe's Pacific team subdivided in turn, with one crew spending three months on barren Guadalupe Island, 250 kilometers from the west coast of Mexico, shooting elephant seals while Philippe and his team concentrated on the whales in Baja California's Matancitas and Scammon bays. The latter proved a nearly impossible assignment. To get close enough to film whales mating or giving birth was impossible, and shooting from a rented Cessna was no good either as the plane's engines frightened the grays. An attempt at hanging a cameraman below the plane in a vertical parachute almost ended in tragedy when the traction cable broke and its buckle struck Philippe in the face with such force he had to be fished out of the water unconscious.

Budget breakdowns were hard to make. By 1972, however, Les Requins Associés accountants estimated that maintaining two film crews at different locations cost just under $2,000 a day.

A day's – or especially in tropical waters, a night's – shoot started with a general huddle. Everybody kicked in ideas of what shots had to be made to complement what was filmed the day before or, with new sequences, who would try what. Captain

Cousteau offered up a preliminary plan for general criticism. Deloire, Renoir, Dumas, Falco, Kientzy, and others commented on the chances of achieving the objective. Dumas was especially good at coming up with scenes showing what an animal could do. His most tantalizing work was with octopuses. He tested their reaction to a mirror placed in front of them (one octopus extended an arm and tried to wipe out the image of itself like a windshield wiper, and when it didn't work returned distressed to its hole) and their ingenuity in getting their favorite food, a live lobster, out of a glass jar (after turning red in anger and puzzlement at sensing the glass wall between itself and its prey, another octopus eventually removed the lid with its arms).

Events often telescoped parts of different telefilms into each other. The captain and crew were shooting the highlight of a sunken treasure hour in the Caribbean in 1968 when one of two half-tamed sea lions starring in another segment swam away. The disappearance led to a whole new twist. News reports from Puerto Rico told of a fisherman who had captured an unusually friendly but starving sea lion. The seal had promptly eaten half the man's catch and, to recuperate his loss, he had sold the seal as a pet to a

266

family whose young son had recently lost his dog. A crew member was dispatched to Puerto Rico and the event led to a sequence featuring Cousteau giving the sea lion its first car ride as he bought it back from the family and returned it to the *Calypso*.

Buying expert advice, whether it meant flying in eminent zoologists or hiring local fishermen, became standard practice. Eugenie Clark of a Florida whale institute was in the Indian Ocean for the sperm whale shoot, and Walker joined Philippe for the entire gray whales expedition. Cambridge University's Anna Bidder, an expert on the nautilus, a fossil of the octopus family found only in the waters off Fiji, New Caledonia, the Philippines, and parts of Indonesia, joined the *Calypso* for a voyage in 1971. A year earlier, Albin Dziedzic, a research engineer in acoustics, and phonetics expert Bernard Gautheron contributed to the dolphin filming. But it was members of the Imragen tribe, a nomad people of the desolate coast of Mauritania, that provided the most photogenic collaborators. Renoir got to shoot a living illustration of man's age-old affinity for dolphins – unforgettable images of these African fishermen, wearing only loincloths, and the glistening dolphins hunting mullets together in the sunbaked surf.

When both JYC and Philippe were together on a sequence, the older Cousteau gave the general orders of the day and Philippe translated these into specifics for Renoir, Deloire, and René Barsky, a diver-cameraman who, with Deloire, filmed the whale shark, the world's largest fish off Mombasa, Kenya, and, with Falco and Bonnici, chased a species of small dolphins known to be almost unapproachable in a zodiac without ever catching up with them. Once Philippe, Deloire, Renoir, Barsky, and their assistants and, in the case of night- or deep-diving, their gaffers, were in the water, JYC directed from topside via closed-circuit TV and radiophones in the men's helmets. Conversation was limited most of the time to one-way orders from above as the sound of air bubbles and the increased density of the air made the divers' speech difficult to understand. Watching on the monitors, Cousteau jotted down specifics and a very first draft of a descriptive narration. After a dive, which usually lasted forty-five minutes, he would use his notes to interview the divers, thereby adding to the narrative while everybody's impressions were fresh, and suggest new scenes. During the filming of risky shark sequences, the cook, doctor, mechanics, and other topside crew members invaded the TV room and hovered behind the captain, staring at the two screens, he once said, "like bullring aficionados at the moment of truth."

Shooting the stuff was the most thrilling part, according to Cousteau, because it was an emotional roller coaster of despair and hope. "We can spend three months waiting on *Calypso,* unable to do any work, and then suddenly the weather turns perfect, the animals are there and the film can be picked up in twenty-four hours," he told *The New York Times* in 1972. Jan remembered his uncanny ability to arrive for his close-ups at Philippe's locations as the weather changed. "He always brings good weather. It may have stormed for days, the boys are playing bridge, Monopoly, Scrabble, getting restless. Then the captain comes and the sun shines. When he leaves, the bad weather often returns."

To journalists, JYC affected a studied indifference to land-locked postproduction problems of editing the kilometers of film into exciting television fare (the ratio here was often seventy-to-one of exposed negative to final cut). In reality, he was very protective of his image, and very aware of David Wolper Productions' ability to improve audience understanding, and to shape a progression out of diffuse footage. John Soh was the editor and once he had assembled a rough cut of one or two episodes, JYC would come to Los Angeles, sit through screenings, and make comments before the final narration was written and Soh would finish the telefilms.

There were quick changes at the corporate level during the first year. Wolper left the company to pursue big-screen production; Rifkin became president and the firm was renamed Metromedia Producers Corporation (MPC).

Disneyizing; the anthropomorphism of animals by giving them human forms and attributes, is a constant peril in nature films and a delicate subject in the Cousteau series. While Cousteau himself would bristle at the mere suggestion of staged entertainment and claim his true asset to be his credibility as an explorer, his films of undersea life are not only anthropological but philosophical – that is, screenfare that arranges exotic images in such a way as to make a point. He believed our age-old Disneyizing of nature, our urge to describe species as good and bad, is at once a human greatness and a terrible weakness. To see lions as noble creatures is itself ennobling, but to take an octopus from its element and reduce it to a gelatinous mass by throwing it in the sand and then judging it to be devoid of beauty and intelligence is criminally stupid. His moral point was that for most of human existence we have barely known anything about the creatures of the sea, that we have approached them only with hooks, nets, spears, and harpoons.

In *The Undersea World of Jacques Cousteau* he marveled at the sensory system of such animals as sharks and took pains to show that creatures like manatees can be cultivated to trust humans. Sharks see no better than man in the water at night, but they have sense organs we lack. They can sense vibrations in the water's hydrostatic pressure, "taste" chemicals, and are far better than we are in perceiving minute changes in the environment and in distinguishing degrees of sensations. He wished to cross the chasm that separates humanity from animality, and described how he has sat in the *Calypso*'s nose observation chamber and seen dolphins swimming alongside press eyes against the glass. He has wondered about the spark in those eyes – "the keen look, both melancholy and mischievous and so different from the icy fixity of a shark's stare" – as well as about their curiosity about us. Could dolphins, he has asked, be the ones with whom we finally

271

bridge the gap and restore to life its primordial unity?

He has been awed by the *change* in our perception of whales – from seeing them as monsters to seeing them as gentle giants – and said man will honor himself in being able to feel respect for the largest creature on earth, in being able to touch and perhaps understand it.

Whether fiction or documentary, prime-time television thrives on subjects that can be shaped into morality plays. Ideas become dynamic when they are turned into emotions – confrontations, affection. A Cousteau TV hour is a slice of aquatic life with the dull bits cut out, factual observations structured into information that will astonish, amuse, and possibly influence. It is therefore not surprising that former collaborators will cite chapter and verse of coaxed animals and fabricated events. To make fish perform – that is, have them swim toward or away from a camera – they must be lured with food. Sharks are enticed into camera range with bloodied morsels, manatees with water weeds, dolphins with live fish. According to Delemotte, so much of the 1973 *Hippo, hippo* footage was so tame that in order to get a troupe of Zambian hippopotamuses to look anything like a ferocious herd, he and

Yves Omer had to poke and push them into Philippe's camera range. Crocodiles would move and look menacing only when Delemotte and Omer threw fire sticks at them. The touching story of an orphaned baby whale in the 1979 telefilm in the St. Lawrence River was a total fabrication, according to Canadian cameraman Jacques Leduc, who shot part of the footage.

War destroyed some of the earliest *Undersea World of Jacques Cousteau* film. After sailing the Indian Ocean from the Maldives to the Seychelles and circumventing Madagascar shooting sperm whales, sharks, and coral reefs during the spring of 1967, the *Calypso* put in at Mombasa for a drive shaft repair and continued north into the Red Sea for a visit to the Conshelf II site – the undersea garage was still there, with coral growing on the roof – and an unexpected return to France for a July 1 crew change. Radio reports crackled with news bulletins of rapidly deteriorating relations between Egypt and Israel. Cousteau decided to fly ahead and got on a plane out of Cairo on the first day of the Seven-Day War.

With the *Espadon* and scores of other ships, the *Calypso* was anchored in the south-end lineup waiting for transit when vessels

273

already in the Suez Canal were bombed and sunk, closing it for what proved to be seven years. Egyptian authorities agreed to allow some of the *Calypso*'s precious cargo – film, cameras, and electric scooters – to be unloaded for forwarding by air. The crates were barely on the dock, however, before strafing by Israeli war planes hit them and destroyed their contents. Two weeks after the war officially ended, the *Calypso* was again a sitting duck in the middle of aerial hostilities. Shell fragments fell all around her and Zoom went into hiding below deck for hours.

After crews were exchanged by air – Alain Bougaran replaced Maritano as captain, Raymond Kientzy took over from Falco as chief diver – it was back to the Red Sea and the Indian Ocean to try to pick up replacement footage. Philippe and Serge Foulon, a younger diver who would ride an orca, or killer whale, off Vancouver Island in 1972, improvised a program and, in a first departure from the *Calypso*, an investigation of an inland lake. A team helicoptered over barren stretches of Djibouti and Ethiopia to Lake Assal, a body of water so salty that Philippe and Foulon could only get under its surface when weighed down with 30 kilos of lead each. The lake bottom proved to be covered with beautiful gypsum crystals and to contain a school of coral fish living in inland waters. The salinity burned the two divers' faces and hands to the point where they had to be hosed down between dives to relieve severe skin rashes.

In December, while they tested new sea fleas and the *Espadon* was repatriated around the Good Hope (on the deck of a German freighter), JYC was in New York to promote the upcoming debut of *the Undersea World of Jacques Cousteau.* The goals were manifold, he explained. His expeditions sought to expand knowledge that would help threatened species. He looked for unusual animals thriving on the sea, and traced the evolution of the oceans in fossil rocks dating back millions of years. "From cages made from Plexiglas we will film life that is serene, savage or beautiful," he said in the pretitle introduction to *Sharks,* the first installment of the series. "We will explore the graveyards of the sea for whatever treasures are hidden, knowledge or gold. Each time we dive, each time we enter the sea, we learn something new. It is the promise that lures us, and we have never been better equipped to see, to learn, to record. This voyage is the culmination of my life's work, to explore and unravel the mysteries of the sea."

Philippe and Jan watched the premiere in San Diego, a week before they, Renoir, and Ted Walker set out on the leased *Polaris III* to film the migrating gray whales of the Pacific.

Jan had no official position and in the beginning just watched from the Baja California land base. She learned to handle a camera, tried out an aqualung, and ended up carrying film and laundry back to Los Angeles by plane.

Meanwhile, the *Calypso* reached Europa, a coral island between Madagascar and Mozambique, in whose underwater caves the coelacanth is supposed to live, and on whose beaches sea turtles mate and lay their eggs. The coelacanths were believed to have been extinct for 70 million years until a living specimen was caught near Madagascar in 1938. No "fossil fish" were found, but the ponderous lovemaking of the giant turtles was filmed.

A pair of fast-moving killer typhoons forced the *Calypso* to leave anchor from above the razor-sharp reefs, stranding a camera team on the beach. A radio message from the *Calypso* told the stranded men to abandon their camp and bury themselves in the sand. Winds and rains hitting 140 miles an hour destroyed their camp.

The *Calypso* sailed 100 kilometers east to seek shelter at Tuléar, on the Madagascar coast, when her starboard propeller shaft broke. To get moving again, Bonnici, Coll, and Bernard Chauvelin suited up and jumped into three-meter waves to work one hour on screw and shaft. More repairs were necessary in Tuléar. The Robinson Crusoe castaways were picked up eventually.

After a call at Port Elizabeth, South Africa, to pick up JYC, the *Calypso* spent February 1968 exploring small offshore islands overrun by penguins and gannets, and in Walker Bay, sea lions. Because of their formidable teeth, divers first went down in shark cages. The seals proved to be cautious but curious animals in their own element, weary of fish handouts. With a lot of splashing, slipping, and laughing the crew managed to capture with nets two young male sea lions on Sea Island near Cape Town. Called Pepito and Cristobal, the pair traveled to America on the *Calypso*'s deck.

It was the *Calypso*'s fifth Atlantic crossing. During the voyage radio messages told captain and crew that Daniel Cousteau had died. Françoise and Jean-Pierre, Jacques's niece and nephew had tended their grandfather during the last months of his life. He had died at home on Avenue de la Motte-Picquet a few months short of his ninety-fourth birthday.

Approaching Ascension Island, midway between Africa and Brazil, the team witnessed rehearsals for the Apollo space shots, daily rocket launchings from the island's U.S Air Force base, and caught fish for Pepito and Cristobal. Each seal required 10 kilos of fresh fish every day. After making landfall in Natal, Brazil, the *Calypso* continued north to the Caribbean, where Falco and Coll built pens for Pepito and Cristobal. The sea lions became more friends than prisoners, and swam first with harnesses and eventually freely with the divers. After seven months of communal living – and Cristobal's escapade to Puerto Rico – they were set free and their story became the fifth Undersea World installment. As Cousteau said at the end of the show, Pepito and Cristobal's adventure proved that man and seal could live in harmony if man so chose.

Sunken Treasure, a mad hunt for $50 million still on the bottom of the Spanish Main, became opus 6. A wily Frenchman sold JYC, Dumas, and crew on spending time looking for the *Nuestra Señora de la Concepción,* which went down in 1641 while sailing through the treacherous reefs of the Silver Bank between the Turks and Caicos Islands and the Dominican Republic.

The idea sent spasms of gold fever through the crew. A vote held in the mess was unanimous in favor of the treasure hunt, but JYC agreed only on condition that the search would end after one week.

A lot was known about *Nuestra Señora de la Concepción* because an eighteenth-century American privateer named William Phips had located and lifted $1 million worth of gold from the wreck. As in the Grand Congloué operation sixteen years earlier, a compressor was loaded on to a small barge, and a vacuum cleaner so powerful it could suck blood out of a man's arm was used at the wreck site. Divers, who called the suction airline "the monster," worked twelve hours a day in relay teams, each staying down one and a half hours vacuuming. After two weeks, the wreck was still not identified. After eighteen days, 300 tons of sand had been sifted. Crews agreed to go on short rations and to avoid taking showers in order to stay. They pooh-poohed a threatened storm and rode it out on the site. A cannon was found, goblets, plates, and finally a weight of a kind used to measure and double-check the cargo of galleons. Brought up and polished it had the year 1756 stenciled on it. The wreck they had toiled over was over a hundred years newer than the ill-fated *Nuestra Señora*.

JYC could afford to be philosophical since, either way, he had a film. *Sunken Treasure* ended with him making a solitary dive while in the voice-over narrative he says success and failure are so much alike that whether treasure hunters find their treasure or not, they usually find out something about themselves.

13
CONSCIOUSNESS

The remaining telefilms were made in the Americas. Philippe's gray whales and the elephant seals of Guadalupe Islands contributed an hour each. There was a segment on Lake Titicaca, the world's highest lake, which took the *Calypso* through the Panama Canal and down the Pacific coast of South America, and programs on octopuses, on the speed and diving ability of dolphins, groupers, and orcas, plus a wrap-up hour called *the Living Sea*. Both the captain and
280

Philippe knew how to be lyrical and thrilling in their reports on windswept horizons and the mysteries of the deep, and both looked terrific on screen.

Turning sixty, Cousteau was ever more craggy and wispy-haired, but the sweep of the Gascon nose and the jut of the jaw were there with the projection of intellectual strength. At thirty, Philippe was an arresting physical presence with his blue eyes set deep in a perfectly sculptured face, full beard and mane of brown hair flecked with gold. To say they complemented each other was the cliché most journalists and visitors repeated. In reality, the relationship was emotional and highly charged, with JYC holding back his son and Philippe rearing up and trying to get even. Alternately, Jacques threw cold water on his son's ambitions, telling him he wasn't ready for more responsibilities, and egged him on, encouraging him to find his own way. In 1969, Philippe broke away and set up his own film company in Los Angeles.

And there was Jean-Michel, less sure of himself, hovering in the background, organizing the difficult expedition to Lake Titicaca, and carrying out the thankless jobs of finding and contracting for supplies, smoothing out relations with often touchy governments – suspicious Peruvian navy personnel accompanied the special train bringing diving saucer and sea fleas to Lake Titicaca – arranging mail and communications, and at rotation time, shepherding homeward-bound crews from wharves to airports and picking up the incoming replacements.

Jean-Michel emphasized his architectural talent. He designed *la balue,* a 3-by-4-meter Plexiglas cage for filming sharks, named after Jean Cardinal Balue, the fifteenth century secretary of state to Louis XI, whom the king threw into an iron bird cage for treason. Jacques told Jean-Michel to concentrate on marine technology and found him a job designing a marine museum aboard the laid-up tourist attraction *Queen Mary* in Long Beach, California.

Jean-Michel and Anne-Marie lived in a big rented house in Los Angeles. Anne-Marie didn't like L.A. and missed her family in France. They often didn't have money for the bare necessities. There were odd jobs for Jean-Michel, including involvement in a program to teach blind youths to scubadive and to test their advantage in murky and dark waters over sighted divers, who often lose their bearings and panic. Most of the time, however, he was not needed by the Cousteau organization. Like Philippe, Jean-Michel was torn between a desire to cut free and to win his father's approval, hating to exist on the fringe of his father's reputation yet unable to strike out totally on his own.

And Jan kept the two brothers apart. Jealous of Philippe's position in the Cousteau orbiat, Philippe the physical person, Philippe the diver, the filmmaker and obvious heir apparent, she felt only her husband had earned his rank as crown prince. Who was jealous of whom? Philippe bristled at being thought of as the *fils à papa*, the derogatory French term that implies the son of an influential father is usually a wimp if not an incompetent. Jean-Michel, on the other hand, sensed that the American psyche attached little condescension or mistrust to someone because he or she happened to be the offspring of a celebrity. Americans loved fame, even by refraction. You couldn't lecture in France because you happened to be the son of a famous explorer. In America, Jean-Michel realized, you probably could.

Jan had grown up under the influence of an ambitious, loving mother who had married too young and had taught her daughter to be aggressive and self-motivated. Jan could only accept the second-in-command position for her husband. Adapting to the Cousteaus' bohemian ways, the constant movement, the uncertainty about future contracts had been difficult for her. As a model, she had known her bookings months in advance; now she had to adapt to what she called "this on-your-toes life." She felt she had earned her place in her husband's world and now found it exciting and stimulating.

Philippe found out the hard way how difficult it was to make a splash of his own. Bud Rifkin had warned him: Jacques Cousteau is the star, not you. Philippe and Jan moved from their first rented apartment in West Hollywood to L.A.'s swank new Marina del Rey seaside community. Philippe was determined to make his Thalassa Films a success, but everything he tried became a bargain basement reflection of his father. Whenever he called network programmers or independent producers to pitch a project, people expected him to do low-budget underwater movies.

For a time he wondered whether he shouldn't leave filmmaking altogether and upgrade his various pilot's licenses to perhaps become a commuter airline pilot. What essentially rankled Philippe was his father's unwillingness to give him more responsibility. When they talked about it, JYC urged Philippe to find his own way. The advice might have carried more conviction, Philippe thought, if JYC wasn't counting on him quite as much to make *The Undersea World* a success.

Among the French colony's professionals Philippe thought of going into business with were André Rosselder, the boss of the Air Liquide subsidiary U.S. Divers, in suburban Anaheim; Robert Bardey, the stringer for French television and sometime importer of Zodiacs; and realtor Isabelle Rodoganachi. With these and other friends, Philippe and Jan discussed projects on weekends aboard the boat Philippe bought, while Rifkin and Metromedia producers served as weekday sounding boards.

Philipe's return to the paternal fold was neither humiliating nor total. Father and son got together again because the captain needed Philippe and because Philippe realized these were wonderfully productive years for his father, a time for him to perhaps begin summing himself up, to reflect and to write. JYC had felt Philippe's absence as a cruel loss, not on the operational level where Jean-Michel functioned, but as idea man and inspired filmmaker half his own age. The captain was not ready for the elder statesman's role. Although Philippe was soon to be vice-president of the Cousteau Society that became the umbrella organization for the far-flung empire, be continued to reside in California and, until 1974, kept Thalassa Films active. What would finally reconcile the two, or make JYC and Simone accept Philippe's marriage, was the birth of Alexandra, Philippe and Jan's daughter, in 1976.

Something profound was stirring with the new decade. The industrial world moved toward the final turn of the century with its first serious reservations about industrialism itself. Air pollution and the environment provided a way of talking about specific fears, but the uncertainty was deeper. People began thinking differently about themselves in relation to the world around them, and in a few short years environmental concerns would prove to be an agent of broad change in many countries' economic, social, and physical fabric. The Cousteaus gravitated naturally toward the environmental movement, but did so from different angles and at different speeds, the captain from seeing garbage floating in the Atlantic literally a thousand miles from any land, Philippe from a love of wildlife.

Philippe got there first. California with its youth cult and affluent idealism had nurtured David Brower and his Sierra Club, which had kept dams out of the Grand Canyon and played a major role in promoting the 1964 Wilderness Act and the Endangered Species Act that President Nixon had just signed, but Philippe's empathy and deep commitment to whales was intensely personal. The most thrilling moments in his life had been in the water with whales, once watching a stream of modulated bubbles rise from a humpback's blowhole (this meant the whale was talking, possibly talking to *him*). Another time a mother humpback swimming straight at him with her baby pulled back her fin so as not to hit him. The leviathan could have killed him many times over and the gesture, he felt, was extraordinary.

An earlier moment of insight had come when he and a crew stayed on a tiny uninhabited reef in the Red Sea and discovered voracious crabs hauling away swallows' chicks from their nests in the sand. The vanity of human attempts to favor one lifeform over another, and of dividing animals into good and bad species, appeared to him in all its absurdity then and there, as did the cataclysm of his and his comrades' arrival in this microcosm of a world. The need to let things be dawned on him when he saw a storm reduce the population of an entire island to nothing, sweeping all life away in a few hours.

The landing of Americans on the moon in July 1969 crystallized Jacques Cousteau's thoughts on ecology. The confirmation that the moon is a sterile satellite, devoid of air and water and therefore utterly unable to support life, brought home to him the need to preserve the soil, water, air, and plant and animal life on this planet to prevent their deterioration to a lunar state of lifelessness. JYC was not the only one to realize that images of earth in all its fragile blue oneness would perhaps help man leave behind his tribal childhood and, if not lead to global brotherhood, at least point out the absurdities of nationalism. His focus was the seas, the cradle of all life, and when seen from space the oceans were so obviously fluid, elusive, and interconnected. "We can see for ourselves that the earth is a water planet. There is a limited amount of water on our globe – no more, relatively speaking, than a single droplet of water on an egg – but nonetheless the earth is the only known planet to be washed with this vital liquid, so necessary for life. The earth photograph can drive a second lesson home to us; it can finally make us recognize that the inhabitants of the earth must depend upon and support

288

each other. The dust of distant planets has been baked and doused with chemicals in the desperate quest to discover life, but we have discovered only that we are alone in the solar system, and perhaps in the universe."

Raymond Vaissière, who since Conshelf II had become director of biology at Monaco's Oceanographic Museum and a teacher of marine ecology at Nice University, remembered how forcefully Cousteau made his point that once we have seen earth from space we must conceive it as a whole, and the obvious corollary, the oceans' delicate balance. Cousteau's authority was unique. He had covered 150,000 miles of sea, he told a U.S. congressional hearing, and he was appalled by the pollution the *Calypso* had encountered, not just oil spills in coastal waters but trash floating in the mid-Atlantic. "People do not realize that all pollution ends up in the sea. The earth is less polluted. It is washed by the rain which carries everything into the oceans, where life has diminished by 40 percent in twenty years. Fish disappear. Flora too."

He decried the ecological effects of brutal modern fishing techniques. "The ocean floors are being scraped. Eggs and larvae are disappearing. In the past, the sea renewed itself. It was a continuous cycle. But this cycle is being upset. Shrimps are being chased from their holes into nets by electric shocks. Lobsters are being sought in places where they formerly found shelter. Even coral is disappearing."

What sent chills down the spine of Vaissière, and such other participants brainstorming in Monaco as Britain's Barbara Ward, was Cousteau's argument that ideas spread so slowly that people were causing pollution faster than they could become aware of it, and that people tended to think their need to exist and to multiply was sufficient reason and justification for anything they did. From her perspective as an economist, Ward had come to practically the same conclusion. Economic development and conservation were interrelated, and the balances of the environment were so delicate that human actions and interactions could have potentially catastrophic and even irreversible effects.

Cousteau was no harbinger of clocks ticking toward a Last Judgment. Damage to marine life *could* be stopped. In Monaco in 1970, he said the United States and the Soviet Union were making considerable efforts, that European countries were starting to act. "Some scientists are sure it is too late," he said. "I don't think so." He resented the notion of survival, of people looking to the oceans as a kind of parachute of last resource. The point was not survival in some twilight nightmare but utilization of the dynamics of science, the paradoxes even of the modern world, to save it.

He would never join the wilder shores of environmental activism that thrived on doomsday chic and hated to admit *anything* could go right. Fearing no doubt that the larger public would not take their crying wolf seriously, committed ecologists were opposed to recovered animals being taken off endangered species lists or international conferences of scientists admitting a couple of decades of sewage treatment construction had actually resulted in cleaner rivers and, in parts of the Mediterranean, a healthier sea. Cousteau was a rationalist, a believer in intelligence. "Today, in the fury of misguided progress, destruction has become exponential, hysterical, catastrophic," he would say in 1976. "But, paradoxically, the same science and technology used for reckless pilfering of resources have also developed all the means, all the solutions, to reverse the trend. Although the situation at the dawn of the industrial age, more than two hundred years ago, was far less serious than it is today, it was hopeless because there was no technology available to reverse the trend."

He alternatively ridiculed governments and appealed to their better judgment. He talked about the jealous insecurities of new Third World nations and "the exacerbated pretensions of national sovereignties" when it came to the planet's oceans. That the care and management of ocean space and resources had a strong international component went without saying since waves and currents move, fish migrate, and even geophysical elements displace themselves on the ocean floor. The oceans, he kept repeating, are one ecological whole, and their problems must be solved with a view to the whole or they cannot be solved at all. With the transformation of traditional uses and the introduction of so many new uses of the oceans, the traditional law of the sea, based on the freedom of the high seas and national sovereignty of narrow strips of coastlines, had been rendered totally obsolete. Yet without a world agreement on a certain number of basic rules, he wasn't optimistic.

In 1971 he met Georges Pompidou and tried to persuade the new French president to support a Pan-European solution to pollution. The meeting taught him a lesson. "Cousteau, never forget that a President can do nothing," Pompidou told him. "It's the lobbies, the technocrats who make policy." JYC took the advice to heart. Politicians, he realized, act only *after* a disaster.

In Geneva, he testified with his old friend Jacques Piccard before a United Nations environment conference and in Washington pushed for making the new "Sky Lab" a monitor of ocean polution. He called upon the fourteen industrialized nations that he estimated were responsible for 80 percent of the oceans' degradation to join forces and act quickly. A year later, he had an agreement with the Goddard Space Center in Maryland and Texas A&M University for the *Calypso* to study oceanic pollution, and with NASA for satellite mapping of the shallow, mostly coastal, waters of the oceans where most ships, including the new huge supertankers, travel most of the time. He advocated a global remote sensing system using satellites and permanently assigned aircraft to monitor the seas. The satellites would collect data from thousands of instrument buoys, drifting or anchored. By 1973, he had inflatable, parachutable buoys anchored off Monaco and others ready for deployment off Spain's Atlantic coast.

His attitudes toward his own country became aloof in the early 1970's in response to shifting opportunities, and as a result of a contract cancellation he resented as a personal affront. The French government's cancellation of the Argyronète program in 1971 came like a thunderclap from a blue sky. On September 9, François Ortoli, the minister of Industrial and Scientific Development, without explanation, ordered a halt to public funding of the mobile seafloor station. Indeed, the same day Premier Jacques Chaban-Delmas told a TV audience that in the face of President Nixon's devaluation of the dollar two weeks earlier, the aim of domestic policy was to protect production and employment. Cousteau eventually sued for 9 million francs ($1.6 million) in indemnities and a symbolic franc for damages to his reputation.

He was in many ways outgrowing his Frenchness. Although he could delight an audience on a jetliner cabin with the charm, sparkle, and sense of maverick idealism and risk that somehow add up to tony Gallicism – and shrink into superior anonymity if the plane was full of fellow French – this was not a quirky display of calculated reverse snobbism. He increasingly enjoyed the respect and recognition that proverbially belong to prophets when not among their own kind. He had structured the Cousteau group to give him special freedom. Increasingly, he lived in perpetual motion, one day giving a speech in one city, racing to a business meeting on another continent, and finishing the week aboard the *Calypso* at sea. He functioned well in a free-floating cosmopolitanism and loved to fly off on an impulse and without warning.

If he had a headquarters it was his office at the Oceanographic Museum. Prince Rainier's building boom and opened-arms investment policies, which was giving the the Larvotto skyline the appearance of Miami Beach, coincided with worldwide inflation to remake the face of Monegasque tourism. Without losing the international glitter set, the principality attracted the less well-to-do but expanding middle classes. Day tourism rose 200 percent in the 1970's and the Oceanographic Museum drew over 300,000 visitors a year, paying not only the cost of innovations but the director's salary that the councillors had found so outrageous in 1958.

Cousteau's office was a bare room with a few photographs of ships on the wall. His desk was a plain board supported by two trestles. Appointments were difficult since time and place didn't mean much to him, although underlings maintained he always did what he was supposed to do, but that in the midst of doing it something interesting might waylay him.

A fifty-year-old murder mystery made him detour to a God-forsaken island in the Pacific and resulted in perhaps the oddest *Undersea World of Jacques Cousteau* episode. A Frenchman in San Diego told him about the lighthouse keeper on Clipperton Island, a speck in the Pacific no more than five kilometers across and lying 1,100 kilometers southeast of Acapulco. Nobody had wanted Clipperton. Not the Spanish navigators who discovered it; not the Englishman, John Clipperton, for whom it was named; not the French government, which put forth a claim but was sorry it did after two expeditions could find no way to navigate a ship into its lagoon; not the United States, which claimed it and then pretended it hadn't; and not even the Mexican government to whom it defaulted. The story of the Mexican lighthouse keeper was so gory JYC had the *Calypso* head for Clipperton in 1970 to film its enormous sharks and, if possible, put together a whodunit. In 1910, Mexicans had occupied Clipperton with about a dozen soldiers. They built a lighthouse, installed a lighthouse keeper, and left the mini-army with their wives and children to protect the Mexican claim. The First World War and the Mexican Revolution put an end to supply ships. The Clippertonians fell ill with scurvy and starvation. The three strongest men set out in a boat, hoping to make it to Mexico, only to capsize and become food for the sharks. The lighthouse keeper stealthily rounded up all the firearms and disposed of the sick weak men so that he could have all the new widows to himself. Tradition branded him a sadistic maniac who kept the women and children paralyzed with fear, promising that if a ship ever appeared on the horizon he would kill his harem and throw them to the sharks so they couldn't expose his savagery. One night, however, one of the women crept up with a pickax and murdered the lighthouse keeper in his sleep. The very next day an American ship showed up and rescued the survivors.

The Cousteau crew not only filmed what they believed was the pickax but took it back for forensic analysis. They found an aging Mexican who had been one of the children, flew him out to Clipperton, and filmed him retelling his childhood nightmare.

Cousteau spent more and more time in the United States and, aboard his beloved ship, off its coasts. The *Calypso* had reached San Diego in February 1969 and spent the next year and a half making telefilms from California to Alaska, the Pacific off Mexico, and after the Clipperton episode, a trip to the Galápagos Islands. The voyage along the west coast of North America brought the *Calypso* to her birthplace, Seattle – duly celebrated by the local media – and her master and crew under the spell of a blue-eyed mermaid named Joanne Duffy.

The search for opportunities to film the Puget Sound's giant octopuses led to the local diving club and to Duffy, a twenty-one-year-old diver and marine biologist who, as JYC noted, not only looked striking in a bathing suit but handled eight-armed "monsters" as big as herself as if they were trained dogs in a circus. She guided the crew on a tour of underwater bays and inlets around Tacoma, coached giant cephalopods from their crevice homes among the algae and anemones, and for the Cousteau cameras, played with them, made them her friends, and showed how gently they should be petted. "It has to be done very gently," she explained. "It is hard to keep in mind that octopuses of the size and weight of these are really fragile animals, highly developed and with a sensitive nervous system. They seem to succumb easily to nervous disorders. If a diver is too rough with an octopus, even

298

without actually hurting it physically, it happens that the animal goes into a state of emotional shock and sometimnes dies." Cousteau had to ask if she had ever been repulsed. "No, never," she answered. "I don't know why. The only thing I can say is that, as far as I am concerned, the octopus is the most beautiful creature in the sea. Even when it is not moving, it is something marvelous to look at." Joanne Duffy would take up an entire chapter in *Pieuvres, la fin d'un malentendu* (translated as *Octopus and Squid: The Soft Intelligence*), the third book Cousteau wrote with Philippe Diolé, a stocky diver, archeologist, and author of numerous volumes on marine explorations.

On the Galápagos Islands, which since Darwin has fascinated naturalists, they concentrated on an animal that most people would find less than cuddly, the marine iguana. What intrigued JYC was that to find food these fossil reptilians had returned to the sea some 100 million years ago and learned to dive. It was all the more remarkable because the Galápagos climate is characterized by the tropical anomaly of being surrounded by low ocean temperatures caused by the chilling Humboldt Current.

Still interested in the idea of altering human physiology to create if not a true

Homo aquaticus then at leastg a better diver, Cousteau went to work with the gentle "dragons." Together with UCLA specialist George Bartholomew, JYC wired a male iguana to an oscilloscope and took it for a dive. They discovered that during a dive a marine iguana can slow its heart from fifty to four heartbeats a minute and even stop its heart altogether for three minutes. The penalty after such a dive is that the animal must lie for hours on sunbaked rocks to reoxygenate its blood. With human divers carrying depth meters and filming the plunging animals, the team also established that marine iguanas can dive to an amazing 28 meters, the height of a six-story building.

After the Galápagos, the *Calypso* sailed through the Panama Canal to New Orleans and the Gulf Coast. Les Requins Associés and Metromedia had to keep the shows coming and, after three months' shooting in the Caribbean, the *Calypso* headed back to Marseilles in September 1970. The open-ended expedition had lasted almost four years and covered over half a million miles.

Almost immediately, ship and crew made a pipeline survey for Italian and Tunisian natural gas interests, and resumed dolphin filming in the Mediterranean. A year of dry-dock overhaul and substantial alterations to accommodate a helicopter allowed Jacques and Simone to spend their thirty-fourth anniversary with old friends in Juan-les-Pins and to promise they would be back the next year for their anniversary.

On July 12, 1972, however, they were off to Antarctica, an arduous voyage through wind-force storms, pristine icy beauty, and life teeming at the edge of death. Everything was water – water solid, water liquid, water vapor in fog and cloud, but also humble, fragile water. Jacques was shocked to find various nations' scientific stations surrounded by heaps of litter and to hear the hypocrisy of geophysicists claiming their offshore drilling in this last virgin continent was for scientific purposes when their own sailors and drillers admitted they were looking for oil.

Cousteau would call the dives he made under the Antarctic Circle the most exciting of his life. The Antarctica trip produced four television hours and a full-length documentary, caused the accidental death of Michel Laval (Cousteau ordered the *Calypso* to Ushuaia, Argentina, so he could accompany the body back to Paris by plane), damaged the much rebuilt but now thirty-year-old *Calypso*, and ended in 1973 with another year's dry-dock overhaul in the Todd Naval Shipyard in Galveston, Texas.

It was in the United States that Cousteau began a new venture that made him say his life was taking a new turn. The America of counterculture effervescence, Vietnam War protests, and massive legislative efforts to address the "motherhood" issues of the environment, from coastal zone management to clean air, was the America of grassroots pragmatism, advocacy groups, and benign tax laws for nonprofit organizations of popular enthusiasm. America had powerful environmental groups that knew how to influence and be part of the political mainstream, groups like the National Wildlife Federation and the Sierra Club, the Union of Concerned Scientists and the venerable Audubon Society, plus chapters of Friends of the Earth, the British-born movement that existed in twenty-four countries.

The American way was very much in the Cousteau grain. He understood that the ammunition of "issues" politics was information – detailed, accurate, and plentiful – to discredit an opponent and to satisfy the mass media. The claims and campaigns of those who first drew attention to conservation problems had a way of being either modified or reinforced by studies and deliberations of scientists that led to legislative, regulatory, and judicial results. What had impressed him more than Earth Day, April 22, 1970, when, with the support of President Richard Nixon, demonstrations had been held throughout the country to remind people of polluted air, water and land, was the swift passage of the Clean Air Act, the creation of the Environmental Protection Agency (EPA), and the rest of the fabric that gave the movement real players and structure.

What was so different from European ways of influencing policies was the American emphasis on building legal constraints on industrial, economic, and energy behavior, on imposing "social responsibility" and accountability on large institutions. Hundreds of followers of Ralph Nader – mostly college students and recent graduates – poked into the affairs of business and government and produced books on subjects ranging from antitrust violations to water pollution. Whereas European environmentalists pointed to changes in government spending, resolutions at party conferences, white papers, and other indications of shifts in public policy, American reformers understood the only way was to develop a body of environmental law.

What Cousteau had in mind was an organization to fight for the preservation of the planet, a three-pronged instrument for taking on politicians and world leaders, for supporting the research that made the difference, and in the vernacular of the time, for raising the consciousness of people through the media, books and education programs. The oceans were sick through overall mismanagement, but ignorance was the first cause. Education, therefore, was the solution. He saw television as the main artery to popular conscence – with *The Undersea World of Jacques Cousteau* he could reach 40 million people in one night – but television was a largely passive means of persuasion. What the times so obviously cried out for was persuasive activism.

JYC was convinced that world leaders were systematically lying about the environment and energy matters. The thing was to catch them at it. If some government agency somewhere said an experiment was not harmless when in fact it was, the organization he had in mind would come out and say so, through the media and grassroots efforts. It could not be he alone saying so. His organization would have artists and writers, as well as qualified scientists – "all the people who contribute to the progress of the human mind," as he liked to say.

The oil crisis that followed the Arab-Israeli war late in 1973 took the wind out of the environmentalist sails. As the shortage of oil became a major problem in many parts of the world and growing fuel shortages gripped Western Europe, Japan, and North America, environmentalism and newly enacted anti-pollution regulations suddenly looked out of place. There was still widespread support for cleaning up the environment, but that support was facing severe strains. The catalytic converter that made cars run cleaner also made them consume more gasoline.

Typically, Cousteau refused to wring his hands. He deftly jumped not so much to the other side as ahead of the issue. The oceans, he said, could solve the crisis.

The force of the tidal and temperature changes in the sea could be harnessed. Metal ores and raw materials of every kind in virtually inexhaustible quantities could be mined at the ocean bottom and farmers in diving gear could provide mankind's food from plantations below the surface. The possibility of getting methane – a major ingredient in natural gas – from fast-growing kelp intrigued him particularly. Seaweed grew at the fantastic rate of nearly one meter a day and 94 percent of the energy it stored could be converted to methane.

In 1974 the Cousteau Society was founded in Bridgeport, Connecticut, as a nonprofit organization dedicated "to the protection and improvement of life." Within a year, it boasted 120,000 members and was in the middle of the Ford administration's energy battle. The $6-billion energy research budget approved by a U.S. House-Senate conference committee was a "declaration of war with the Cousteau Society," its founder declared. "We will support off-shore oil development only if enough money goes into solar-energy research, but in this bill there is only peanuts." The society polled 72,000 members on energy. Over 32,000 replied. Of these, 26,000 felt solar energy should be heavily funded, while only 3,700 thought nuclear energy should be encouraged. Jacques Cousteau was the society's president; Philippe, who had in mind to publish a yearly inventory of life on this planet, was vice-president.

"I am entering a new phase in my life," JYC told the *Christian Science Monitor* a few days later. "I have been a fighter against the elements. Now I am a fighter against the system when it is wrong."

306

14
DEFEATS

Cousteau's fighting spirit was unflagging and the newest endeavor, so very much fashioned in his mold, yet another success. Yet the mid-1970's were a time of activities hanging fire, of growing pessimism and of defeats. There were "no go" projects, notably a North Pole expedition, and there were smart bouncebacks, and a politicization of his ecology involvement that culminated in his almost running for election in France as a "green." His and Philippe's search for a place where they could illustrate the consequences of a people catastrophically ruining the environment led them to Easter Island and a forty-first TV hour of brooding despair.

The big shocker was ABC's cancellation of *The Undersea World of Jacques Cousteau* in 1976. The reason had nothing to do with Cousteau, but, perversely, with the network's sudden success. Since the beginning of television, ABC founder and chairman Leonard Goldenson would do practically anything to get the network out of perennial third place. Doing practically anything meant taking more chances than front-running CBS and middling NBC, and taking chances attracted gifted, gregarious, and persuasive new people. ABC was the place to be in the 1970's and the alumni of its golden era were to be among the most successful movers and shakers in the U.S. entertainment industry a decade later. Innovation led to success, especially with formula teenage shows. It was therefore next to impossible for the network's programmers to preempt the regular weeknight lineup of *Starsky and Hutch, Happy Days,* and *Laverne and Shirley,* ABC's top-rated shows, in order to broadcast another Cousteau episode.

And the hustle, the allure and excitement of fast-track careers that saw talented people hopscotch from networks to production to programming and, in many cases, back again, constantly lost Cousteau his best Hollywood talent. With his miniseries *Roots,* David Wolper was back in television, but as head of a production company that employed 125 people. A heart attack in 1978 would make him scale back to an operation with a staff of two. Bud Rifkin had left Metromedia to start a cable company that he and his partners would sell off to Time Inc. to become the rudiments of Home Box Office (HBO) cable television. Alan Landsburg was on his way to becoming an independent producer with winning prime-time shows, and Warren Bush retired in Florida. Marshall Flaum, a gifted writer-director-producer who had freelanced for Wolper and Rifkin, was Cousteau's co-executive producer and it was to him at Metromedia that Les Requins Associés delivered all film for editing, scoring, and narration.

The ABC derailment came just as the Cousteaus had acquired a seaplane. To increase their mobility and range, they had bought a World War II PBY Catalina marine reconnaissance flying boat that Philippe piloted. They had spent most of 1975 roaming the Caribbean, from the Yucatán peninsula and the coast of Belize to Jamaica and, after a return to Monaco, had started filming underwater archeology around Greece.

But American audiences were beginning to find *The Undersea World* offerings uneven. As much as the four Antarctica segments attracted top ratings, other installments had viewers tune out. Reviewers were no help. They talked about scripts getting a bit purple, of music too often turning momentous, leaving the visual content to carry the episodes. The eighth season had started with *Life at the End of the World,* a look at the remaining twenty-seven Quwashqar Indians of one of the Tierra del Fuego inlets who in 1850 had numbered 4,000. *New York Times* television critic John O'Connor said the protection and encouragement offered by JYC and crew to the threatened last five families didn't appear to go any farther than an eagerness to get the material recorded "Leaving the good ship *Calypso,* with its extraordinary paraphernalia, including a helicopter, Mr. Cousteau has expensive recording equipment dragged into rundown huts to ask a slew of Anthropology I questions," O'Connor wrote in 1974. "Later, the poor Indians were seen trying to sell souvenirs to British sailors. The narrator intoned: 'Rosa had labored long stitching her bark canoe. Nobody will buy her boat. Her picture is taken.' The implication was that the sailor taking the picture could have been a bit more sensitive. But what of the Cousteau crew that was taking a far more elaborate picture of the situation? Their sensitivity amounted to little more than sympathetic clucking. After getting all those nice shots of sad faces, the luxurious *Calypso* sailed off into the sunset."

If commercial television in the United

States was unforgiving, the selling of *The Undersea World of Jacques Cousteau* in other countries was both easier and more disappointing. The series was firstrate television and it starred a true media personality. Camera-work and editing faultlessly captured far-flung drama and wonder. Movie directors often thought there was more to learn in a Cousteau special than in ten big-screen films. "He's a greater filmmaker perhaps than ecologist," Canada's Jean-Pierre Lefèbvre said after eighteen years of Cousteau watching. From the Soviet Union to Japan, *The Undersea World* was a TV staple. In Germany, *Geheimnisse des Meeres* was invariably an 8 P.M. offering; in France *L'Odyssée sousmarine de l'Equipe Cousteau* came on at 9:30. There were exceptions. The series ran in Scandinavia, but Cousteau was French and, in television terms, France was remote. South Africa TV bought only a selection; in the Philippines there were reruns of reruns. Developing countries paid only a pittance and Les Requins Associés ended up giving away the rights to several territories.

In the United States, Cousteau switched to public television. Taking his cue from the French series' name, the program was retitled *Cousteau Odyssey* – abroad there were no seams in the long-term continuation – but the magic seemed to have gone and American critics roundly panned the first installments. They were hardly any kinder to *Oasis in Space*, a Public Broadcasting Service (PBS) miniseries coproduced by the Cousteau Society.

JYC's new associate was Andrew Solt, a British-born former journalist and David Wolper apprentice who had made his mark as producer-director of a number of ABC adventure documentaries. *Oasis in Space* was a pained comedown from major network exposure. The Cousteau Society sought corporate sponsorship for the six-hour miniseries, but when major corporations found out what the PBS broadcast was really about, they all pulled back. "No one industry wanted any part of indicting another," Philippe said. PBS could come up with only $126,000 for the six half-hour programs and the Cousteau Society had to dip into its own coffers to make up the rest of the $420,000 budget.

Examining such threatening global catastrophes as chemical waste poisoning, the pollution of the oceans, the population explosion, and mass starvation, *Oasis in Space* was a radical departure. Gone were South Sea sunsets and balletic underwater scenes. *What Price Progress?*, the opening program, showed a Canadian pulp mill spewing mercury-laden wastes into a stream used by local Indians and illustrated the consequences of such industrial pollution with pictures of twisted and deformed victims of mercury poisoning in Minamata, Japan. Written by Solt and introduced by Philippe, the series mixed documentary footage with round-table discussions with such pundits as Barry Commoner, Robert Heilbroner, Margaret Mead, and "futurologist" Herman Kahn. In announcing the series in February 1977, *The New York Times* wondered whether the magic of the Cousteau name would be enough to attract a sizable audience for this sort of exposé while at the same time wishing Americans would heed the grim message of *Oasis in Space*.

At international conferences and public demonstrations, in speeches and interviews, the Cousteaus repeated the message. The captain shocked a 1976 Barcelona gathering of Mediterranean nations by saying their sea was in its death throes, and was shocked in turn by the speed with which twelve of the sixteen attending countries signed a convention and protocols to prevent, abate, and control pollution in the Mediterranean. A year later, he persuaded the International

313

Committee for the Scientific Exploration of the Mediterranean to have the *Calypso* undertake an unprecedented survey of the Mediterranean and Black seas to try to come up with an answer to just one big question: How could such a large body of water change so dramatically, becoming so contaminated in forty years? Philippe told *Le Point* one explanation might be that from the Ural rivers emptying into the Black Sea to Lake Victoria emptying into the Nile, more than 600 million people flushed their garbage into the Mediterranean. "You may object there's nothing new in that," he told the newsmagazine. "For one, there were fewer people in the past, and, more important, there were fewer toxic products. And all that in an ocean that doesn't regenerate. So, the Mediterranean will be the first to die and become a warning to the world." In Los Angeles, JYC said the three most important problems were overpopulation, food, and energy "and how we figure out to share these things." In New York, he marched with Margaret Mead in a Sierra Club-sponsored World Environment Day and, at the United Nations, joined British naturalist Peter Scott in denouncing nuclear power. On his own he denounced the movie megahit *Jaws*, calling the scare movie an insult to sharks.

New York City afforded the pleasure of sometimes seeing Perry Miller – now Perry Miller Adato – and to joke about the competition she was giving him on PBS. Married to Neil Adato, a Westport, Connecticut builder, Perry was the producer-director of some of public television's most noted films on artists, writers, filmmaking, architects, and painters. She was finishing *Georgia O'Keeffe*, a one-hour film that would be premiered on the expressive abstract painter's ninetieth birthday at the National Gallery in Washington. Her next project was a series on women in art.

The Cousteau films resulting from the year-long Aegean voyage were more traditional than *Oasis in Space*, but their message was another environmental warning. If he went to the waters surrounding Greece, with financial help from the Greek government, he said, it was because he wanted to dive into the past, to touch with his own hands and see with his own eyes the evidence of man's age-old insensitivity to his environment. "The island of Día off Crete's northern coast is nothing but a bare rock today," he told an Athenian news conference. "Nobody lives there. Nobody could. Yet Homer tells us it was once a thriving cultural center. Theseus,

315

after slaying the Minotaur, took Ariadne to Día on their honeymoon. A volcanic cataclysm finished off the island, but even before that the timber and soil had been exhausted and the population had deserted the place. They could do that then."

He was persuaded that the last 15,000 years of human history had been one long drawn-out disaster. The record of Neolithic and historical man, as engraved in fossil records, in deep-sea cores, and in buried and submerged clues discovered by archeologists, was one long-running lament of irreversible destruction. The idyllic Greek islands were stripped of their forests in order to build ships. Europe's wolves, bears, and woods were laid waste. Another great forest, the Sahara, was turned into desert by nomads and shepherds eight thousand years ago. Countless animals were eliminated by Asians invading the Americas across the Bering Strait. Less than five hundred years ago, Bartholomeu Dias described the Cape Verde Islands as a paradise; today they are bare.

The Cousteau Odyssey was a three-way coproduction of KCET, the Los Angeles public broadcast station, TV-1 in Paris, and Bavaria Atelier in Munich. The corporate sponsor for the American broadcast, as KCET's Phillis Geller noted with some irony, was an oil giant, Atlantic Richfield. John Soh was still the editor, although he shared credits on some segments with Henri Colpi, a New Wave director turned editor.

The *Calypso*'s first charting of the sea bottom off the southern tip of the Attica peninsula yielded a twentieth-century find that Cousteau quickly realized would make for a nice whodunit opener for the new program. Near Kea Island, his soundings, scans, and plottings revealed a large sunken vessel that was quickly identified as the *Britannic*, a sister ship of the *Titanic*, that sank in November 1916 following a mysterious explosion deep in her bowels. The British claimed she was a hospital ship; the Germans stated that the huge ocean liner, camouflaged as a medical vessel, was nothing more than a munitions carrier.

The *Britannic* had still been on the ways in a Belfast shipyard in 1912 when on her maiden voyage the *Titanic* had struck an iceberg, and sank near the Grand Banks of Newfoundland with a loss of 1,513 lives. Work had been suspended on the sister ship, design changes were made, and a special inner hull was constructed that, her builders maintained, made her unsinkable. When the explosion occurred, the *Britannic*, painted white with a green stripe and giant red

317

crosses on her sides, had been outward bound from Italy to pick up the wounded from the Allies' disastrous Dardanelles campaign. Only twenty-one of the 1,061 doctors, nurses, and crew on board perished, but for an "unsinkable" ship three football fields long to go to the bottom in less than an hour there might be something to the Germans' claim that she was secretly carrying munitions. No single piece of enemy ordnance alone could possibly have done the job.

The *Britannic* was lying nearly 125 meters below the surface, too deep for anything but elaborate helox dives, and the location was simply marked off on the *Calypso*'s maps while JYC flew to London to raise more money and perhaps find survivors of the 1916 sinking. In the meantime, the *Calypso* sailed to Día, where Albert Falco, going down in the saucer, found a submerged harbor. Here, too, special equipment would be needed, and it was not until the spring of 1976 that the *Calypso* was back with a new vacuum cleaner for the Día excavation and with the Galeazzi tower, oversized tanks for breathing mixtures of helium, nitrogen, and oxygen for the *Britannic* filming.

In the meantime, there was the enigma of the Atlantis, the mythic island or continent supposed to have once existed in the Western Sea. It is mentioned by Plato, and Solon was told about it by an Egyptian priest, who said it had been overwhelmed by an earthquake and sunk beneath the sea nine thousand years before his time. After making an agreement with the Greek National Tourist Organization and archeological authorities, JYC announced he would shoot two films on his quest for Atlantis. According to the late Spyridon Marinatos, the former general inspector of the Greek Antiquities Department, Atlantis wasn't some mythical island in the Atlantic Ocean, but most likely was an island civilization destroyed by a volcanic upheaval in the Aegean close to Thera Island in about 1500 B.C., when the Minoan civilization on Crete was almost at its peak. In 1970, Marinatos had discovered well-preserved frescoes on walls of unearthed two-story buildings on Thera that led him to speculate that an eruption had destroyed the greater part of the island and might have killed 30,000 of its inhabitants.

The only survivor of the *Britannic* sinking to answer Cousteau's Britain-wide newspaper appeal was Sheila MacBeth Mitchell, an eighty-six-year-old great-grandmother from Edinburgh who had been a volunteer nurse aboard the ocean liner-turned-hospital ship in 1916. She proved to be game enough to come to Greece with JYC and to try to go down in the saucer with Falco. Despite valiant efforts, Falco never managed to take her deeper than the halfway mark because of problems with breathing and seasickness. She nevertheless asked the *Calypso* divers to retrieve her sixty-year-old alarm clock from cabin 15. Cousteau made three helox dives to the wreck himself and from his and other divers' evidence tried to solve the mystery. His hypothesis – and that of the resulting *Cousteau Odyssey* premier show – was that the *Britannic* had indeed been a hospital ship when she was struck by a mine laid by a German submarine a few weeks earlier. The explosion had hit the liner's coal bunker, setting off a second explosion in the coal dust.

Vacuum cleaning in Día's Bay of St. George yielded hundreds of amphoras, pottery, copper and silver plates, marbles and woods from four wrecks for the National Archeological Museum in Athens and the location of a sunken Minoan jetty, indicating the harbor had been in use before 2000 B.C. Together with footage from around Thera, it also yielded two hours of television that critics found unsatisfactory and full of calculated titillation. *Calypso's Search for*

Atlantis found that volcanic eruption offered the most plausible theory for an earthquake – tidal wave combination burial of Atlantis, but failed to solve the puzzle. "Mr. Cousteau's purpose in all this is clear," *New York Times* critic John O'Connor wrote. "The dedicated environmentalist is using ancient civilizations as a warning to today's wasteful world to watch out or we, too, may go down the cataclysmic drain. But, just as clearly, he did not gather enough solid material to justify hour-long productions. And, considering that these fulfill his programming contract for the current season, the obvious padding becomes all the more questionable for public television."

Easter Island, the forsaken rock with its mysterious stone figures, lost in the vast expanse of the eastern Pacific, has fascinated successive explorers and haunted the imagination of historians, dreamers, science fiction writers, and parapsychologists. Who were the original people who had either sailed 3,700 kilometers out from the coast of Chile, or 1,700 kilometers east from Pitcairn, the nearest inhabited island, and brought with them yams, bananas, sugarcane, coconuts, sandalwood seedlings, and poultry and, over the centuries, grown to become a population of 20,000 with a written hieroglyphic script and elaborate social and religious structures? Why had they carved and hauled ever bigger images in stone up hillsides and sat them into position so they always turned their backs to the sea? Why was the quarry at the northeastern end of the 14-by-20-kilometer island abandoned with large numbers of statues in all stages of completion. In the enigma of Easter Island Cousteau found the darkest parable of *Homo sapiens* crazily destroying the environment that gave him life.

When Dutch admiral Jacob Roggeveen discovered the island on Easter Sunday in 1722, he found a people in the middle of a civil war, an exhausted population estimated at less than four thousand. Fifty years later, Captain Cook arrived to find a straggling group of six hundred poverty-stricken people only thirty of whom were women. Death from introduced diseases, capture by slave traders, internecine warfare, and voluntary emigration reduced the population to 175 in 1872. Chile annexed the island in 1888, and the remaining native islanders were confined to one village and 5,000 acres for subsistence living. The island's remaining 30,000 acres were leased to the Compañia Exploradora de la Isla de Pascua and devoted to the grazing of sheep and cattle.

Since the *Calypso* was busy in the Mediterranean with the "scale model" survey of the oceans' health, the Cousteaus' Easter Island expedition was airborne. Philippe, Jan, and an advance research team put together the Easter Island story. For an estimated five hundred years, the Polynesians had lived an idyllic life, multiplying, farming the fertile island, and carving their stylized effigies, apparently ancestors they worshipped. As they cultivated the island they cut the trees. The leveling of the forest, however, caused erosion of the land. Many tried to emigrate but since they had destroyed the forests they had no wood to build boats. The 1955-56 Thor Heyerdahl expedition had carbon-dated a legendary war between "the short-and the long-ears" – probably original settlers and newcomers stratified into upper and slaving classes – as having taken place less than a century before the arrival of Europeans.

Philippe, who brought Jan and four-month-old Alexandra along, interviewed William Mulloy, an American anthropologist on the island. Mulloy believed that as overpopulation and land erosion brought harder times, the social order had become rigid. The priests had become the rulers and imposed their obsession with statue-carving on the people. Carvers became another privileged class and the statues grew from 50 tons to an awesome 400 tons. The last trees were felled to make sleds, and hibiscus vines were cut to make hemp so a mass of peasants could drag the giant stone effigies into a ring around the island, always looking inward.

One day the slaving masses revolted. In the Rano Raraku quarry, tools and unfinished statues lie as though the work had been suddenly interrupted and never finished. The long-ears and the sculptors sought refuge behind a long wood-filled ditch they set on fire in the eastern part of the island. But the furious mob soon crossed the ditch and murdered priests and carvers. During the years of chaos that followed, the standing statues were toppled; the only images that remained upright were the unfinished ones in the quarry, which, having not yet been given eyes, had no taboo power. Chilean museum officials also believed the statues, previously thought to have been carved without eyes, indeed had inlaid eyes of red volcanic rock and white coral that were knocked out during a revolt against the cult that built them.

A feudal society rose out of the revolutionary ashes. Clashing families occupied the remaining plots of land and the last productive fishing grounds. Intruders were killed and eaten. Those who survived the cannibalism escaped to the sea cliffs where they lived in caves. They forgot how to read and used the old hieroglyph tablets for firewood. It was these straggling survivors that Roggeveen stumbled upon upon in 1722.

Philippe and his research team discovered many of these caves, littered with human bones. He also talked to the few natives still on the island. They knew nothing of their forebears. Heyerdahl had established that the earth-oven in which the long-ears were said to have perished was actually the defense ditch containing ashes. Philippe and crew filmed everything, telling themselves they had the beginnings of a very dramatic documentary.

Philippe brought a new flying machine to Easter Island, a gyrocopter that looked something like a toy helicopter. While in the air with it, the engine overheated and he crashed, smashing a kneecap. He was flown to Los Angeles for surgery and lengthy convalescence. "With that injury, we both came face to face with mortality," Jan remembered. "Before, we had thought we were golden children. Afterward, Philippe was in pain twenty-four hours a day. It changed him a great deal. There was a quietness then, a turning inward." Still, he promised to go back.

Blind Prophets of Easter Island, as the TV hour was portentously called, exerted a strange power of fascination with its moody shots of the statues with their upturned faces and long ears. But out of his element, Cousteau was reduced to playing another tourist, asking questions of Mulloy and other experts. His summary of the lesson of Easter Island, however, was among his most stirring pronouncements. "The consequences of ignorance, like the consequences of irresponsibility, are fatal," he said. "We must learn from the melancholy parable of Easter Island. We must recognize that the resources of our island earth are equally finite, and that humanity's unparalleled creative gift seems fatally linked to its own self-destruct mechanism. Here, in the endlesss sea, a vagrant cell of human life anchored itself – with all the vital connections it needed to link it to the rest of the earth – created a civilization, then vanished, leaving a handful of survivors with no conscious recollection that it had ever existed. Shall this happen again, on the larger island earth? Shall our nuclear power plants melt down, or our toxic wastes infect the waters, or our stockpiles of missiles be triggered, to leave our cathedrals and homes and workplaces empty of life, like the quarry at Rano Raraku? Or shall we pass on the riches of human invention and wisdom to living inheritors? Perhaps the islanders were right – we are not the victims of a god of evil; we are victims of the evil we bring upon ourselves."

15
BLUE PLANET

The Easter Islanders' tale may be one hack in humanity's 15,000-year sawing at the branch it is sitting on, but Jacques Cousteau was too inventive, too nimble of mind and too big of a media star to flounder in utter hopelessness. He had too much going for him, including a large audience. At times he wasn't at all sure life is heading in any discernible direction. He was a somewhat baffled agnostic – agnostic in the dictionary sense of believing metaphysical knowledge is beyond our grasp. When he looked under a microscope he could be overwhelmed by the beauty, perfection, and complexity of life. The biological diversity, the earth's trillion lifeforms, each solving the riddles of survival in a prodigal way, left him both humbled and awed.

He couldn't share Christians' belief that man is created in God's image and is a chosen species. We may have bigger brains than other species (although we haven't necessarily heard the last word on cetaceans' brainpower), but our future seems at times to beckon with shimmering promises. Increasingly, he quoted Pierre Teilhard de Chardin, the Jesuit thinker of his father's generation who made the Vatican uneasy because of his faith in science and evolution. Teilhard believed there are three infinities – the infinitely small, the infinitely large, and the infinitely complex. We have complexity going for us, Cousteau said. Although he didn't believe there was no discernible sense in anything, he shared astrophysicists' conviction that since the Big Bang the direction of the universe is toward the ever more complex.

A lot of things were going his way and he was full of daring propositions. One was to launch a new discipline – ecotech. Even if ecology and economics appeared as absolute enemies, reconciling the two was not only logical, it was a necessity if life was to continue. "Both sciences have the same duty: the art of harmoniously managing our household, the water planet earth. Both can do little without the help of technology and technology goes wild with economic and ecological controls." Ecotech meant jumping ahead and finding ways of bringing together such competing and apparently antagonistic interests as the oil industry and wildlife groups, a nation's merchant marine and its labor unions. Ecotech meant finding antidotes to most of the problems inherent in development and progress.

If "ecotech" wasn't quite a buzz word, "ecopolitics" was. The environmental movement was growing more overtly political in many countries in the late 1970's. The French municipal elections in March 1977 saw environmental candidates emerge as a serious political force, polling 12 percent in the first round of balloting. This was insufficient to take them into the runoffs, but it impressed the established parties.

It surprised Cousteau. "I don't believe in political parties, but on the other hand, you can't ignore possible popular groundswells," he told the Monaco correspondent of the Riviera's big daily newspaper, *Nice-Matin*.

"My politics is people's happiness, nothing else, which is why I need the broadest base possible. Inevitably, the defense of life passes through the loops of political solutions." A month later, he was invited to address the Massachusetts legislature and told a Boston news conference politicians were increasingly receptive to ecological ideas. He was gratified by President Jimmy Carter's decision to postpone the use of plutonium-fueled nuclear reactors, by the Environmental Protection Agency's water-quality projects, by antinuclear drives in Europe, and by the eighteen-nation Barcelona conference on ways to stop marine pollution.

Thinking ecotech, he said the free enterprise system could survive only if its abuses were eliminated. "Business people and corporations are very well organized," he said. "They have their Harvard Business Schools which teach elaborate methods and all the tricks to take advantage of the economy. It is when the balance between people and industries is not achieved that the destruction of the environment occurs." Harvard didn't resent his digs at its business school. In June 1979 he shared the university's commencement honors with West German Chancellor Helmut Schmidt, astrophysicist Subrahmanyan Chandrasekhar, and South Africa's Bishop Desmond Tutu.

The entrance of Europe's "greens" into the electoral fray was a new strategy (the fledgling West German Greens were ready to contest elections in Baden-Württemberg; the Ecology part of Britain lost its first contest and made an alliance with trade unions). The strategy was passionately debated, with moderates saying environmentalists had to get inside the power structure, and radicals objecting that the electoral approach corrupted and sapped the movement of its grassroots strength. Cousteau was uncharacteristically ambivalent. He campaigned for France's ecology candidates in the 1978 parliamentary elections, but after much soul-searching refused to become a Green candidate three years later.

The Cousteau Society was one way of being influential without being political. Its purpose was to save the earth and humanity from itself, not an easy thing. Global in its concerns and outreach, its weapons were information and persuasion. Its cutting edge was "ecopolitics." The society has an office at Avenue Wagram in Paris, but in its thrust and effectiveness, its structure, methods and organization, the society is American. Cousteau was aware of this and, when in

France, said Europe would be for later. Besides, Europe had foundations similar to his, ones that he supported and watched with interest. He was not always clear on just how the Cousteau Society would achieve specific goals, but he was a spirited chairman. "We are fighting not for survival but for quality of life, for happiness," he said. "People can only be happy if they marvel at nature, if they marvel at creation, if they marvel at what surrounds them. If they love creation, if they protect it, if they extend their minds to other people's jobs and to animals' lives and to other planets. An extension of mind is an extension of everything." He had a way of infusing ideas with enthusiasm, of connecting seemingly unconnected facts, of overwhelming by drawing the big picture. He loved to see the offices on New York's Third Avenue and L.A.'s Beverly Boulevard, busy places bedecked with photographic murals of the oceans and of the *Calypso* crew in action, bubble with activity.

Being a nonprofit organization meant being on perpetual fund-raising drives. The soliciting, the worldwide mailings for support and donations overlapped with accounting, subscription, and production activities for a bewildering output of the *Calypso Log*, *Calypso Dispatch*, and the children's *Dolphin Log* magazines, calendars, posters, records, and tote bags – crew jackets, T-shirts, *Calypso* pins, decals, and model kits were to come later. Cousteau and Alexis Sivirine published a coffee table book on the *Calypso*, complete with cutaway drawings, pull-out blueprints, and hundreds of color photos.

JYC folded most of his activities into the society, including the funding for the missions and the operation of the *Calypso*, CEMA, the television production, and the responsibility for acquiring new equipment. He also folded his multiple incomes, publishing and TV royalties, oceanography, marine engineering, and percentages of profits from Air Liquide for the manufacture of aqualungs and gases into the organization in return for an open expense account.

In 1978, Norfolk, Virginia, and two Florida seaports, Miami and St. Petersburg, vied for the honor of becoming the Cousteau headquarters and, more prosaically, for the tourist dollars a planned Cousteau Society Research and Educational Center would bring. JYC, Philippe, and the society's advisory committee played it cool, saying there was no need to relocate, but if they could find a community that offered the now 160,000-member society the facilities that would make it more efficient, they would move the membership headquarters from New York. Norfolk, the world's largest naval base and less than two hours' drive from Washington, was most enthusiastic, and its business and civic leaders agreed to finance a feasibility study on the Cousteau Center which, Mayor Vincent Thomas said, would "complement everything else that has been done downtown in the past ten years" and help bring tourists to the largely undeveloped waterfront. Miami, which was planning a major complex and would have a science and marine center, asked Cousteau to situate his facility there. St. Petersburg, where the *Calypso* had spent four months in 1975, was the first to drop out of the competition when local interests were unable to raise money for a feasibility study and the Cousteau Society proved unwilling to help finance it.

Unlike such activist groups as Greenpeace, the Cousteau Society shunned "ecoterror." Thoroughly pacifist in outlook, it felt its highest mission was to educate the world's decision makers about the ecological consequences of their action or inaction. It believed, with its president, in the pyramid of life, as it called a fused humanity. "However fragmented the world, however intense the national rivalries," JYC said, "it is an inexorable fact that we become more interdependent every day. Now as never before, the old phrase has a literal meaning: We are all in the same boat."

The society had far-flung fans and *was* a voice in the halls of power. When Roman Polansky won a libel suit in a London court in 1976 against *The News of the World* after the newspaper had said his late wife, Sharon Tate, the actress slain by the Charles Manson "family" in Los Angeles, had practiced witchcraft, the film director ordered the token $165 judgment paid to the Cousteau Society. Celso Oliveira, the governor of the Brazilian state of Paraná, said he had learned from the society that the ammunition in "issue politics" was indeed information, and that his own barrage of detailed, accurate, and massive info had led to a modest cleanup of Cubatão, one of Latin America's largest petrochemical centers and one of the most polluted communities in the world. In the United States, Senator Lowell Weicker, a Republican from Connecticut, believed the society had brought a change of perception in the Washington leadership.

The committee JYC had envisioned that contributed to the progress of the human mind had been formed by 1978, an almanac on prudent resources management was in the works, and a Bill of Rights for Future Generations was being drafted for submission to the U.N. General Assembly. Harold Edgerton led the scientists' majority on the committee. The others were Henry Kendall, another MIT scientist; H. Stanley Thayer, a New York University philosophy teacher; and from the West Coast, Edward Wenk, the director of the program for social management of technology at the University of Washington, Seattle, and the Scripps Institution of Oceanography's Andrew Benson. The arts and letters were represented by composer-singer John Denver, author-entertainer Dick Gregory, and the most famous of them all worldwide, science-fiction writer Ray Bradbury.

Mose Richards, who would coauthor several illustrated books with JYC in the 1980's, was the editor of *The Cousteau Almanac*. This was an ambitious inventory and guide to global resources, with contributions from nearly a hundred individuals on topics ranging from energy, population, and wildlife to coming ecotech attractions, and containing "wave-making" suggestions for grassroots groups interested in specifics. People from such diverse quarters as the Worldwatch Institute, the Quebec Fisheries and Marine Service, Survival International, a political analyst firm, Arthur D. Little Inc., Italian government agencies, the Fermi National Laboratories, and the Interfaith Center on Corporate Responsibility contributed, together with individuals like Isaac Asimov and Saul Stienberg. The Cousteau Society and Doubleday published the 838-page *Almanac* in 1980.

The Bill of Rights of Future Generations contained in the *Almanac* was largely the work of Thayer and two other New York university teachers, Gabriel Nahas and E. Allen Farnsworth. It proclaimed:

1. Future generations have a right to an uncontaminated and undamaged earth and to its enjoyment as the ground of human history, of culture, and of the social bonds that make each generation and individual a member of one human family.

2. Each generation, sharing the estate and heritage of the earth, has a duty as trustee for future generations to prevent irreversible and irreparable harm to life on earth and to human freedom and dignity.

3. It is, therefore, the paramount responsibility of each generation to maintain a constant vigilant and prudential assessment of technological disturbances and modifications adversely affecting life on earth, the balance of nature, and the evolution of humanity in order to protect the rights of future generations.

4. All appropriate measures, including education, research, and legislation, shall be taken to guarantee these rights and to ensure that they not be sacrificed for present expediences and conveniences.

5. Governments, nongovernmental organizations, and individuals are urged, therefore, imaginatively to implement these principles, as if in the very presence of those future generations whose rights we seek to establish and to perpetuate.

Cousteau tried to persuade President François Mitterand to make the declaration a part of the French Constitution six years later and for 1987 hoped to line up two countries to submit it to the U.N. General Assembly.

As a clearinghouse for trends and perspectives, the Cousteau Society helped cross-fertilize ecotech ideas. Bringing biotechnology to the sea, for example, promised a rich harvest of food stuffs, pharmaceuticals, bulk and fine chemicals, materials, and fuel. High-tech work with controlled mass culture of marine seaweeds, microalgae, and bacteria would produce specialty chemicals, drugs, and agrochemicals, but what excited JYC was such low-tech biomass projects as growing spirulina in recycled village wastes. Sold in health-food stores in North America, Japan, and Europe, this blue-green microalga is a natural concentrated food, the richest-known source of vitamin B_{12}. When dried it contains about 65 percent high-quality assimilable protein and compares favorably with egg protein. Spirulina is the most easily produced of all microalgae and has been eaten by humans in Africa and Central America for thousands of years. What was interesting and worthy of a pilot project was that villagers could grow spirulina in units so small they could benefit the villagers only and not become another monoculture to be monopolized by outsiders. Other algae, JYC discovered, could be used to produce methane gas or as food for goats and sheep. "The end product of agriculture," he grinned when talking to inquiring journalists, "may be sheep."

If humanity were to have a tomorrow, globalism and futurism were two sides of the same desirable coin. JYC believed passionately in the rights of future generations. He was convinced there was not going to be a sudden and total collapse of the environment because humans had a way of correcting their mistakes, if sometimes at the last moment only, but what saddened him was the certainty that we would leave a poorer world to our children. With Lester Brown, the president of the Worldwatch Institute, he agreed we were borrowing from the future more and more, economically and ecologically, and that the big question was really whether we had the appropriate institutions to even create a desirable future.

We would just stay even, it seemed, even if we took bold and imaginative steps to improve social and economic conditions, to reduce fertility, and to find wiser ways of managing the globe's resources. But if we merely continued current policies, we were falling behind because actions postponed meant foreclosed options. The opportunity to stabilize the world's population below 10 billion by 2050 was already slipping by, and similar chances were being lost in agriculture where the carrying capacity of land was shrinking in Third World countries.

Cousteau sensed future economic classes might not be divided into haves and have-nots but into "knows" and "know-nots" and that information was a revolution. "Few of us may be blessed with genius, but all of us are blessed with common sense," he wrote in the introduction to the *Almanac*. "The ability to reason is equitably distributed among housewives, farmers, accountants and students, as well as among the Platos and Einsteins in our midst. Facing today's environmental emergencies, the people of the world must use this common sense and arm themselves with better information than ever."

The Cousteau Society was dedicated to understanding problems and to finding commonsense and ingenious solutions. JYC favored such technical progress as tele-conferencing and video telephones because they might reduce air travel, and the creation of a global information utility operating via satellite on a subscriber basis and flexible enough to operate within different types of political regimes.

Miniaturization, indeed anything that promised more with less, was an obvious technological blessing. Finding opportunities in apparent calamity was another. If the increased burning of fossil fuel created a "greenhouse effect," then use the greenhouse. Plant gardens on rooftops, develop desirable vines to climb over houses during the summer to function as natural air conditioners, develop a sod capable of withstanding parking loads and replace asphalt parking lots with it. Raising the temperature of the earth a degree or two will also increase the rate of photosynthesis in all but the hottest deserts. It will make for longer growing seasons in temperate latitudes, reforest mountainsides farther toward the poles, and increase photosynthesis even more, thereby tying up more carbon dioxide and finally stopping or reversing the greenhouse effect.

The interconnectedness of the seas led to concerns for the world's great rivers and their modern discontent. These freshwater arteries of the land were playing a crucial role in the health of the oceans, fertilizing the sea with salts and nutrients, but also carrying human and industrial pollutants into the deep water. As Philippe had told astonished editors of *Le Point,* the shallow, nearly enclosed Mediterranean received the wastes from 600 million people from as far away as the Ural and Rwanda.

The *Calypso*'s year-long study of the water conditions of the Mediterranean led to a ten-month airborne investigation of the Nile in 1978. Philippe was in charge of a fifteen-man team that left the *Calypso* docked in Monaco but took along four-wheel-drive vehicles. Zodiacs, scientific instruments for sampling water pollution at tributaries, outlets of the main stream, and spots above and below every important commercial center, plus film equipment for a two-hour *Cousteau Odyssey* special.

Christened the *Flying Calypso* and first introduced to Cousteau TV spectators in *The Sleeping Sharks of Yucatán*, the PBY was the ideal base of operations for an expedition that would cover the entire 6,700 kilometers from the headwaters of the Kagera River above Lake Victoria to the Nile delta. Built in greater numbers than any flying boat of World War II, the Consolidated PBY Catalina had been used by a dozen Allied countries as reconnaissance, bomber, anti-submarine, transport, and navy rescue. Nearly 3,300 PBY's were built in the United States and Canada and several hundred more under license in the Soviet Uniuon; the British, Australian, and free Dutch Indonesia forces also used them.

Powered by a pair of 1,200-horsepower Pratt & Whitney engines for takeoff, the plane had a 3,500 kilometer range and, fully fueled, still carried a crew of seven and 1,000 kilos of freight. Pilot and copilot were in a cockpit below and just ahead of the wings and the pair of thundering engines. Behind the cockpit was a compartment for the navigator and radio operator while a flight engineer was stationed in the superstructure below the wing. Side by side waist gunners' pits, covered with sliding panels, the Cousteau crew had long since discovered, were ideal for film. At low altitudes the cameraman could stick half his body outside and film straight below.

Colin Mounier, who had been part of the Antarctica expedition, headed the cameramen, newcomers Christian Boe and Henri Alliet. The sound engineer was Yves Zlotnicka, a balding Parisian who liked to lie awake nights at camps to record a library of bizarre jungle noises. Their photography was breathtaking – shots of jungle life, the wildlife of the Sudanese savannah, swarms of lake flies rising in a massive swaying colonnade into a hurricane higher in the air than the white PBY was flying, human civilization along the banks of the Nile, unchanged since biblical times, Khartoum and its mosques, the Aswan Dam, the Temple of Ramses II, and the newly controlled flow of the river toward its mouth.

The findings were not encouraging. The good news was that the Aswan Dam had transformed a million hectares of desert to cropland, improved navigation below the dam, and might lead to the development of rich fishery from Lake Nasser, the 5,000 square kilometer backup lake created by the dam. The bad news was that the silt held back in Lake Nasser impoverished the downstream soil. Lacking silt the river flowed faster, causing greater erosion of its bed. The controlled flow weakened the Nile's impact at the delta; the Mediterranean was beginning to back up into the river and destroy the fertility of the delta. High-quality land on the coast was being lost as fast as marginal land in the desert was being gained.

While Philippe logged air miles over the Sudan, Cousteau Sr., Falco, and a seaborne crew were engaged in the danger and romance of undersea fortune hunting. The object of their treasure hunt was the S.S. *Natal*, a French oceanliner that, after a collision with a freighter off Marseilles, sank on the night of August 30, 1917, with a loss of more than a hundred lives. A lot of facts were known about the *Natal*, but the rumors, which Falco had first heard from fishermen as a boy, were more intriguing. On her fateful last voyage, the then thirty-six-year-old steamship was supposed to have carried fifty-five cases of gold ingots, a treasure that Jacques calculated would be worth $15 million in 1978 dollars.

The bottom of the ocean approaches to Marseilles was littered with wrecks and it was only after Alexis Sivirine located the *Natal*'s blueprints and turn-of-the-century photographs in maritime archives that they had any idea what profile to look for with *Calypso*'s side-scan sonar and Harold Edgerton's newest invention; an EEG scanner capable of sending up pictures of the sea bottom 100 meters down. They spent all of July x-raying all kinds of wrecks, including one they dubbed the *False Natal*, and were about to give up when, on August 2, the sonar picked up what looked like the object of their covetousness. JYC and Falco went down in the diving saucer. It was indeed the *Natal*, but the wreck was lying on a sandbar below the reach of scuba divers. They circled the wreck. On subsequent dives Falco glimpsed suitcases through a gaping hole in the first-class cabins. There was no sign of gold ingots, or of any other objects of value.*

* After a sixteen-year search for *Nuestra Señora de Atocha*, a Spanish galleon that sailed from Havana in 1622, foundered in a hurricane, and sank off Florida, treasure hunter Mel Fisher

Efforts to bring the rule of law to the sea engaged Jacques Cousteau personally for a quarter century. On this issue he sought out such world leaders as Valéry Giscard d'Estaing, Helmut Schmidt, Jimmy Carter, and Leonid Brezhnev to try to persuade them to be a little less like the Easter Island figures, mute and frozen in history, each perhaps aware that nation-state pyramids are obsolete but unable to imagine a different world.

It was an issue he ultimately fudged.

Since the first United Nations conference on the Law of the Sea in 1958, Cousteau had been an outspoken advocate of the notion that everybody not only had to cooperate to nurture the life-giving oceans but that everybody *shared* them. The living, moving sea, he said in 1981, should not inherit the failed vision that history records of endless possessive boundary disputes among nations but should offer the possibility of an open and dynamic interrelationship among men.

Both the first and the 1960 follow-up Law of the Sea conference failed to resolve two key issues – the seaward limit of a nation's

and his son, Kane, in 1985 found the ship and its cargo of gold bullion and silver estimated to be worth $400 million, the biggest modern day sunken treasure booty.

territorial waters and the right of coastal countries to fisheries beyond their territorial sea. The failure of a third U.N. conference in 1974 to agree to anything other than to continue meeting, combined with the energy crisis and the search for new resources, aggrandized national claims. Countries proceeded on their own with offshore developments and invented exclusive economic zones (EEZ's) extending two hundred miles from their shores. Ships and aircraft were allowed passage through and above such EEZ's, but the seabed resources, notably minerals, were declared the property of coastal states.

The issue split nations in new ways. Many coastal states in Africa pressed for 200-mile EEZ's and offered landlocked African countries access to the sea and its living resources, but they were less magnanimous with the seabed mineral resourcess of the continental shelf. Living resources pose particularly difficult problems in international law. The general mobility of fish, sea mammals, and birds along coasts or between coastal and oceanic waters called for a flexibility that contrasted with the "fixed" assets of marine minerals.

What really divided developing and developed nations was what Cousteau wanted most – an international ocean authority and a legal regime for the seabed. Three basic questions were involved – the area to be governed; the legal nature of the regime and its relationship with coastal states; and, finally, the nature, structure, and function of the authority. Poor countries wanted a strong international authority and industrialized countries, especially the United States, pressed for a much weaker authority that would simply grant licenses to individuals or corporations permitting them to mine the seabed. Some mineral-exporting Third World nations feared that deep-sea nodules mined for copper and cobalt would reduce their own revenues. The poor countries, now a majority in the United Nations, wanted to be able to control an authority that could enrich or, in the case of some mineral-exporting countries, impoverish them. Rich nations, on the other hand, dismissed the prospect of investing heavily in deep-sea technology for the benefit of others.

The failure of the Caracas U.N. conference on the Law of the Sea angered Cousteau to the point where he accused "incompetent diplomats and delegates" of representing the world's land-masses and not the world's seas. "At the Law of the Sea conference, there was a lot of law but very little sea," he told a Cousteau Society Involvement Day gathering of 3,000 in Anaheim, California, in May 1976. "International by essence, the sea is about to be sacrificed by a treaty that will surrender enormous areas for the good or bad will of each country, and that will not regulate deep-sea resources, and that will only soothe the conscience of delegates with its parody of environmental recommendations."

Delegates to the Conference on the Law of the Sea – UNCLOS in U.N. Newspeak – doodled at their two annual meetings until 1981, when the United States and West Germany enacted legislation that would regulate and therefore encourage commercial activities on the ocean floor. When the ratification of a Law of the Sea treaty seemed a distinct possibility, Cousteau called for a delay so the concept of EEZ's could be modified and the idea of an ocean authority be given one more chance. His proposal tried for Solomonian justice: there would be an international ocean authority issuing rules but coastal nations would be responsible for implementing the rules in their economic zones. "That's the dream that we're trying," he said.

Before anything could be debated, however, the Reagan administration effectively withdrew U.S. participation in the UNCLOS talks in order to reassess the issues and the American negotiating position. The changed American attitude was related to deep-sea mining, and France and Britain in turn joined the U.S. and West Germany in enacting interim legislation.

Regulation of the coastal zones, Cousteau said in defending the ocean authority idea, was much more critical to the health of the seas than the concern for ocean-floor problems. The Cousteau Society came up with a Global Ocean Policy paper that proposed a modification of industrial fishing and demanded that large swaths of the planet's coastlines be kept free from development. Knowing the world's poor countries were suspicious of any initiative coming from developed countries. Cousteau talked to Mexico's president, José López Portillo, about a Mexican leadership role in setting up the UNCLOS international ocean authority. He also talked with President Ronald Reagan and President François Mitterand, and touched upon the subject with Chancellor Helmut Schmidt. "At the moment the only difficulty is a false difficulty," JYC told the *Christian Science Monitor* in 1981. "The difficulties arise when the nations talk about the exploitation of minerals in the deep ocean, which means outside of the economic zones. I see nothing wrong about dredging nodules from the bottom of the ocean. But it is not economical at the moment. It is only justified for strategic reasons in the United States and in France and Japan – three countries that have already invested a lot in this field – because they understand that some of the minerals are in short supply."

A government is the ultimate incarnation of power. Whether monolithic or pluralistic, it recognizes no law superior to the one it chooses to write. In the early 1980's there was pressure on international law in the United States as right-wing sentiments openly began to question the validity of legal rules in international conduct, and U.S. Ambassador to the United Nations Jeane J. Kirkpatrick, in distinguishing between "forces used to conquer and victimize and forces used to liberate," came close to reviving the doctrine of the "just war." The need for American EEZ's was cloaked in strategic justifications and hints of future "resources war" necessities. There was little Cousteau could tell Reagan that would persuade the President to yield to an international authority the right to decide

352

whether an American company could exploit the continental shelf or the midocean ridges.

In the short term, seabed mining was a development whose time had both come and gone, but it might come again in the next century. Third World nations favoring the proposed treaty's notion of the seabed as "a common heritage of mankind" liked to mask the crude fact that they didn't have the technology to exploit the seafloor. Nor, for that matter, did the industrialized world.

The commercial exploration of the ocean floor belonged to heady 1960's visions. Cousteau's Conshelf programs had provoked a surge of interest in the private sector. Westinghouse and General Electric had built several deep-diving submersibles but quietly dropped the subject when the commercial viability didn't prove feasible in any time frame that the corporate world could live with. Mining companies couldn't see exploration work getting anywhere without taxpayers' money. T. S. Ary, president of the Mineral Exploratory Division of Kerr-McGee Corporation, bluntly told the Reagan administration, "The fair market value of a dream is zero." The 1979 discovery by a team of French, American, and Mexican scientists descending in the French submersible *Cyana* of extinct hydrothermal vents surrounded by mountains of metal sulfides off Baja California remained just that – a scientific discovery giving geologists new insights into the way continents are being formed and destroyed but devoid of any foreseeable cost-effective commercial spin-off.

Although the German firm Preussag, on a work contract for Saudi Arabia and Sudan, brought up 15,000 cubic meters of Red Sea sediment from hydrothermal vents for possible shipboard refining of its metal granules, ocean resources remained a subject of scientific journals and Pentagon war games scenarios only. The scale and suddenness of the mid-1980's fall of oil prices would turn Big Oil manic depressive. Kerr-McGee, which would see its credit ratings lowered because of its particular vulnerability to collapsing oil prices, joined the most financially robust giants in chopping capital expenditures by half. Seabed mining would become a receding dream.

The U.N. Convention on the Law of the Sea was promulgated in April 1982 and quickly signed by 117 nations but not the United States and some twenty others, chiefly industrial states. It created an International Seabed Authority whose policies were to be set by an assembly of all signatory states and an executive council of thirty-six states, half chosen on the basis of geography and half on the basis of interest. The authority would contract with states or firms wishing to explore the seabed, but it would also conduct its own operations through an agency called the Enterprise, which would have the right to acquire the technology of any other contractor on commercial terms. Eleven months later, President Reagan issued a proclamation establishing the American EEZ. The decision was couched in cold war rhetoric. The Soviet Union had reached self-sufficiency in supplies of most strategic materials and had secured sources for the remaining few, whereas the United States had to import manganese, a fundamental metal in all steel and most cast irons; cobalt for high heat and wear resistance to jet-engine superalloys; and nickel for its widespread use in aircraft and shipbuilding. With a stroke of a pen, Reagan quadrupled the ocean area over which the United States exercised jurisdiction – making it the largest such area under any nation's control.

By 1984, 138 countries and twenty-one international organizations had signed the UNCLOS, but the rejection by the United States, Britain, and West Germany cast doubt on whether there would be enough money for the treaty's enforcement. To Cousteau it was another opportunity missed. Yet when he was invited to the White House in 1985, he said nothing to President Reagan about his ardent wishes for one ocean belonging to all humanity. He lauded the President instead for the environmental laws that had come into effect during Reagan's term as governor of California. The compliment was returned. "Captain Cousteau perhaps has done more than any other individual to reveal the mysteries of the oceans that cover more than two-thirds of the surface of our planet," said Reagan. "It is therefore likely that he will be remembered not only as a pioneer in his time but as a dominant figure in world history."

Did Cousteau believe himself above the fray?

When Brice Lalonde, the leading ecology figure in French politics, asked him to run as the Greens' leading candidate in the 1981 presidential elections, the possible Cousteau candidacy caused a stir of excitement. JYC asked friends and family for advice – his nephew Jean-Pierre, who had a good grip on French politics, was against the idea – and locked himself in his Paris apartment with a copy of Plutarch's *Lives* and 80,000 letters from supporters before convincing himself he would be more effective outside the political system. French ecologists viewed him with a mixture of awe and suspicion, admitting he was an ace at structure, organization, and fund-raising while finding him terribly cautious and suspicious. "Our lack of organization disappointed him," Lalonde recalled. "He had wanted more empirical structures, something less ideological."

In the 1970's Cousteau grew more reserved, more philosophical. He was not like the stone, gathering moss and leaving behind an estate and a moment, he liked to say. Nor was he like the rose, trying to make each instant beautiful and fruitful, to ornament himself, to produce. More and more, he was like the wind, organized nothingness. He believed the more disinterested he was, the more sensitive he could be to life.

What added to the aloofness, his inner-directness, was the bitterest loss he ever suffered, the loss of Philippe.

16
FATE

Philippe was bringing the *Flying Calypso*
down for a landing on the Tagus River.
Lisbon and the estuary shimmered in the late
afternoon sun as he throttled back and swung
south to look for a stretch of straight river.
They were 18 kilometers upriver, near the
suburb of Alberca, and at the end of a short
test flight over the Tagus, the second longest
river of the Iberian peninsula (the Ebro is the
longest). John Soh was still cutting the Nile
film but JYC was negotiating with Canada's
National Film Board and doing the St.
Lawrence River; in L.A., KCET was looking
for financing for a Mississippi special. Rivers
were a promising subject, although the
Flying Calypso's next mission was strategic
support for Albert Falco and a series of
diving saucer experiments.

It was Thursday, June 28, 1979, and
Philippe was just back in Europe from
Norfolk. Sixteen months of ardent wooing
by officials of the Virginia port had paid off,
and on June 2 the *Calypso* had been given a

tumultuous welcome, complete with balloons and a military band playing the *Calypso* hymn, the song written by John Denver. In a return goodwill gesture, JYC had sent the *Calypso* out to Cape Hatteras to look for the remains of the U.S.S. *Monitor*, the world's first ironclad battleship that sank in 1862, "swallowed by the sea from the rear," as a contemporary report had it. Philippe had been one of eight divers going down to explore and photograph the Civil War relic. It had been a difficult dive. The Gulf Stream current had been exceptionally strong but they had managed to get some footage of the 117-year-old battleship.

Philippe was taking delivery of the reconditioned Catalina. It wasn't always easy, or cheap, to find shops that could repair World War II-vintage planes, but the Portuguese navy yard knew how (and came in with the lowest bids). Philippe told his seven passengers to fasten their seat belts. Landing the PBY was sometimes bumpy, more a test of seamanship than airmanship. You had to approach the water at low speed – the manual said 75 miles per hour for touchdown – maybe make one pass over the water to make sure no sandbanks of anything else could catch the pontoons and flip the plane over, then go back up and around and come down again. Using the "power on" technique, you kind of flew the plane on to the water, quickly switching on the windshield wipers so you could see through the spray your several belly splashes made as you throttled way back and sailed to a stop. Once you learned the power-on trick – jets, too, were *driven* on to the runway not glided down – there was nothing to it. Philippe had done it a hundred times.

He leveled off, skimmed closer and closer to the fleeing surface. As they had filmed him do it with his American copilot Hank Levibach in *The Sleeping Sharks of Yucatán*, he reached up with his left hand and gave a thrust of power. The bottom of the flying boat touched the water with the familiar thud, bounced back up like a skipping stone, and landed again. Then it hit something that flipped it over, tore it apart, and threw them all forward. In a second, everything was deafeningly silent.

The first thing anyone realized was that they were sinking. Somebody pointed to the ripped fuselage and they scrambled out into the muddy waters. Portuguese voices were shouting and one by one they were hoisted aboard small fishing boats. On deck they stood dripping and stunned, discovered minor injuries on themselves, and looked back at the wreckage. The cockpit was gone. Then someone realized Philippe wasn't there.

Captain Cousteau and Simone arrived. Jan, expecting a second child in five months, came from America with Alexandra. Jean-Michel and Dr. Jean-Pierre Cousteau flew in. As Jacques and Simone were friends of the local representative of Air Liquide, they, Jean-Michel, and Jean-Pierre were put up in a sumptuous villa – out of reach of journalists – while Jan stayed with several friends in a hotel. Rescue units began dredging the river.

The atmosphere at the villa was lugubrious. Simone was a walking statue, a knot of held-back emotions. Jacques was less able to hide his feelings. Jean-Pierre went to the hospital to see the copilot, who had a broken arm. Supported by helicopters and a dredging barge, members of the rescue team located the cockpit, which had broken off and sunk that Friday. Saturday, thirty skin divers continued the task. Jean-Pierre was appalled by Jan bringing little Alexandra over, a three-year-old asking, "Where's my Daddy? Why are you crying?"

They were at the table Sunday when Jean-Pierre was called to the phone. Since he was a doctor, it was best that he be the first one to know. Philippe's body had been recovered. It had been heavily mutilated, apparently by one of the plane's engines falling forward into the cockpit. Jean-Pierre returned to the table and simply announced Philippe's body had been found.

Reports from aviation officials and police were conflicting. Some reports said a loose hatch has caused the PBY to flip over and that Philippe was killed instantly by a broken propeller. Other reports said the plane had hit a sandbank; still others that it had struck a submerged object on the landing.

The *Calypso* was in the Caribbean on her way to Martinique and more shipwreck filming when the news reached her. Henri Alliet, who had been Philippe's cameraman on the Nile trip, remembered the shock and disbelief, the demand that the radio report be confirmed. They sailed on toward St. Pierre, the 6,000 population town below Mount Pelée where 26,000 people had lived on May 8, 1902, when the volcano erupted. At the bottom were all the ships that had sunk when the disaster struck.

Jacques and Simone refused all public expressions of grief. The French embassy took charge of the details, but when a few journalists managed to talk to JYC, he spoke

362

in dry emotionless tones. "What was a tragedy for my son was a miracle for his copilot. The propeller that killed Philippe saved the life of the copilot, who was tossed, injured, to the surface. That is fate. We must accept it and go on. I have another problem now. Philippe, of course, was to take over and continue my work when I am gone. There must be someone to run the society. There must be continuity." Philippe had expressed the desire to be buried at sea. While Jean-Michel identified his brother at the morgue, representatives of Air Liquide and the French embassy tried to cut through a ministerial crisis that had paralyzed Portugal to find someone who could authorize a foreigner's burial at sea.

After a brief ceremony at Lisbon's Saint Louis-des-Français church, Portuguese marines carried the coffin, draped in intertwined Portuguese and French flags, aboard the corvette *Baptista de Andrada*. With the family on board, the ship sailed 30 kilometers out into the Atlantic for the ancient rite of lowering the coffin over the stern. When the warship returned to Lisbon, Captain Cousteau told a reporter from *Nice-Matin* that the upcoming mission would proceed as scheduled. "Nothing is changed in our program." A little investigation by

Nice-Matin, however, showed the logistical support the PBY was to have flown for Falco and the diving saucer would be taken over by a surface vessel and the program delayed from mid-July to September.

Jan had to think of herself, Alexandra, and the child she was carrying. Finding out where she stood financially suddenly became urgent to her. Yet to untangle the enmeshed affairs of father and son was not easy. A boy was born that December. Jan named him Philippe Pierre Jacques-Yves. Her relations with her in-laws were strained. She eventually moved to Palm Springs, California, remained a widow, and in 1985 attended, with Alexandra and little Philippe, her father-in-law's seventy-fifth birthday celebration in Washington.

The belief in fate, in the need to live with destiny, ran deep in Cousteau. As a mariner and naval officer, as a poet and free-thinker, he believed freedom and initiative are associated with risk. You had to live with life's punches. The dangers of the sea, the whims and even its treachery, are outweighed by its generosity, by the inner wealth that, he said, a seafarer must learn to deserve. To him love and death are intertwined, but love requires no reciprocal obligation. Needs are not always returned. Tenderness, complicity, the courage to cherish someone can be a father's love for a son, a brother's love for a sister, a love for friends.

Cousteau refused to talk about his son's death. He thought of making a film about Philippe – there were thousands of feet of footage dating back to his own black-and-white film of Jean-Michel and Philippe as boys with their mother at Sanary and Le Mourillon Bay. He thought of abandoning everything – so few things seemed important all of a sudden.

Yet there was salve in plunging forward, in drowning himself in work. If the pace had been feverish before, it now became frantic. Time spent in any one place was telescoped into hours as he flung himself through a jet-set existence that impressed some, scared others. His offices often didn't know where he was. To Susan Schiefelbein, a young writer he had met at *Saturday Review* and put to work on a telefilm to be dedicated to Philippe, he talked of his regrets, the time not spent with the boys. If he had to do it all over again, he wouldn't have married. You couldn't be an adventurer and a bureaucrat at the same time. Simone was a good wife, and despite his life of perpetual motion he had tried to save their relationship, but he could have done better. Schiefelbein met Jan and came away with the impression she was a remarkable woman.

Simone withdrew to the *Calypso*. JYC hurtled through airports. He was a man who throughout his life had stubbornly demanded attention to his priorities, and he continued. He was a celebrity craving attention, and he was someone who made a difference. He knew it – as people kept telling him – and there were moments he almost felt embarrassed at how rich his life had been. What he wanted most, he sometimes said, was to go on, to die in action.

To the members of the Cousteau Society he wrote a letter addressed to Philippe, a letter recalling their best moments together, his own impatience in wanting to show Philippe the Conshelf II habitat, the two of them scubadiving down. Cousteau holding, keeping his son's hand to guide, and feeling strangely proud. "Three years ago, I found myself sitting near you in the cockpit of our Catalina," he continued. "I looked at you my guide in the sky, as I had been your guide in the sea. I saw your shining face, proud to have something to give back to me, and I smiled, because I knew that pursuing rainbows in your plane, you would always seek after the vanishing shapes of a better world."

Jean-Michel had not wanted to go with his father. He was forty-one years old and had come to terms with himself. Also, he was finally making a living as a lecturer. Americans loved celebrities, and sons of famous people could trade on their father's fame. Philippe had rebelled against it. Jean-Michel had learned to make slide shows and minifilms, and to give conferences on the oceans. His surname opened doors to the lucrative lecture circuit, but it hadn't been easy. There were times when he and Anne-Marie had been destitute. By the time of Philippe's death, however, Jean-Michel was doing three speaking engagements a week and was booked six weeks in advance. Jacques didn't particularly like the way Jean-Michel made cut-rate nature films and went on lecture tours saying, "My name is Cousteau." On the other hand, Jean-Michel had felt unwanted and didn't like the way he had been kept away from the center of gravity of his father's organization, and for a while their relationship had been strained.

Father and son met, talked, and discovered that nothing was definitely broken between them. Jean-Michel discovered that if his father had taken Philippe's side, it was also because he had seen Philippe constantly. The two had been in a give-and-take partnership. Now, Jacques offered Jean-Michel Philippe's place, to come home.

Jean-Michel didn't have his late brother's gifts and, as he took over as JYC's right-hand man and vice-president of the Cousteau Society, he said so publicly. "With the death of Philippe we've lost a talent I don't have. Philippe was full of poetry and dreams, he was a beautiful story-teller, a talented filmmaker. His world was in the air. How can we reinstate that perspective? I'm not a balloonist, not a pilot. I'm an ocean person. The society will always be marked by his absence."

A lot of people resented Jean-Michel, finding him arrogant, incompetent, too eager to fill his brother's shoes. The Canadians who put together the *Calypso*'s next big mission, the 1980 St. Lawrence – Great Lakes expedition, felt uncomfortable with the Cousteaus. When he was there, which wasn't often, JYC was at his worst super-star behavior. Jean-Michel tried to take command and ran up against people more knowledgeable than himself. JYC had to intervene, smoothing feathers. Falco was the mission leader, Benard Delemotte chief diver, and Dominique Sumian, a Corsican gentle giant everybody had come to depend on in trying circumstances, was in charge of specific explorations. Crew members felt the tension. Old-timers like sound engineer Guy Jouas, who had been on expeditions since 1969 and was famous for recording the amorous shrieks of mating and elephant seals, cued in the Canadians on JYC's here-today-gone-tomorrow routines. Montreal cameraman Guy Dufaux was still shocked. "When the captain flies in for six hours, it's Hollywood. It's *his* close-ups, *his* second take." The Quebecers didn't appreciate the boot camp for the rest of them. In nearly four months, no one had a single day off.

Karen Brazeau and Paula DiPerna, two new Cousteau Society staff members, had no difficulty finding Canadian scientists and institutions eager to contribute, but the National Film Board felt shortchanged for the money it put up. Even Cousteau enthusiasts felt the resulting three hours of television disappointing. Such St. Lawrence problems as pollution and acid rain were never raised. "It seems Cousteau was content with getting the film board's million dollars, or maybe he was pressured by his U.S. backers," said Jean-Pierre Lefebvre.

The summer expedition took the *Calypso* a distance twice the breadth of the United

States. From Halifax, she sailed around Newfoundland and up the St. Lawrence, through Lakes Ontario, Erie, and Huron to Thunder Bay in western Lake Superior on the Minnesota-Ontario border. Off Newfoundland's Cabaud Island they came upon a baby humpback whale inextricably caught in a fishing net and a mother whale circling and – as Jouas's hastily lowered microphones revealed – talking to the infant. Neither the captain nor Jean-Michel was onboard but Delemotte decided this was an encounter of the photo opportunity kind. He got himself, Mounier, and Dufaux suited up, and with Raymond Coll maneuvering a Zodiac into place, got into the water and in two hours of painstaking net cutting and soothing petting of the baby freed it. Most extraordinarily, mother and 12-ton baby followed the *Calypso* until nightfall, jumping or keeping their baleen mouths just above the surface.

In the St. Lawrence Bay near Saguenay, Quebec, the *Calypso* and crew came upon a gush of nutrients that attracted shoals of fish and hundreds of whales. They filmed scientists taking a census of seabirds in Labrador, and caribou wandering uninhabited Lake Superior islands in search of food and mates, and numerous shipwrecks in the lakes. It was during an investigation of the *Barnes,* a three-masted schooner, near Kingston, Ontario, that thirty-year-old electrician Remy Galliano failed to resurface after a routine thirty-minute dive. A search dive was immediately organized, but the body was not located on the muddy lake bottom until five hours later. The cause of death was embolism. It was theorized that Galliano had misjudged his depth in the turbid water and had started to come up without exhaling, a mistake that had ruptured his lungs, forced air into the bloodstream – thereby reducing the flow of oxygen – and no doubt caused his fatal disorientation.

From the moment he took over the business burdens, Jean-Michel was a forceful deputy. The move in 1979 to Norfolk allowed him to cut back by 20 percent the operational budget and staff of the Cousteau Society. He and Anne-Marie moved to Norfolk and opened the Twenty-first Street headquarters. The Third Avenue office in Manhattan was not closed, however, nor was the Los Angeles office, which moved to a new address on Santa Monica Boulevard. The building of the Cousteau Ocean Center, which had been behind Norfolk's spirited bidding effort, was delayed indefinitely.

Jean-Michel wanted to expand the society's research activities with universities and government agencies. JYC had had a long and fruitful relationship with NASA and NOAA, the National Oceanic and Atmospheric Administration. Since 1972 the *Calypso* had carried American state-of-the-art communications, weather, and facsimile equipment. This allowed her to receive NOAA's extended seventy-two-hour forecasts for the South Pole, for example, when she was in the Antarctica, and to send back oceanographic readings. The NASA cooperation and satellite "uplink," of which Cousteau was proud and freely taked about, raised eyebrows among radical ecologists.

Inside word had it that the *Calypso* was really a CIA spy ship. This rumor started aboard the American Red Cross ship *Hope*, which, for political reasons, could not enter the territorial waters of a number of countries. Apparently, volunteers aboard the *Hope* had seen the *Calypso*, bristling with electronics, blithely sail past them into forbidden waters.

To boost revenues, Jean-Michel organized treasure hunts and tours for wealthy amateurs to join marine scientists in the Caribbean and the Pacific. Called Project

Ocean Search, the program had him as tour guide for 1,500 guests, ranging from veteran scuba divers to people who had never seen a boat deck, to explore the Devil's Elbow Island in South Carolina, Mosquito Island in the British Virgin Islands, or Maupiti in French Polynesia, described as an underdeveloped Bora Bora with virtually no hotels or restaurants but a coral atoll rich in marine life. "We get some college students, some older people, some world travelers, some who've never been out of their home state," he told *Esquire* in 1982. "Put all that in a blender, and it really works well. They learn from one another. When we first meet, we tell them, 'Rich or poor, here we don't care, because there is no place to spend money on these islands. Beautiful or ugly, we are all going to look the same in a few days, full of mosquito bites, wearing T-shirts and diving in the same wet suits.'" Prices ranged from $825 to $3,500, depending on length and location.

The two-hour Nile film, broadcast four months after Philippe's death, and the Cousteau *Almanac*, published in 1980, were dedicated to Philippe. So was *The Warm-Blooded Sea: Mammals of the Deep*.

It was perhaps typical that Cousteau would pour his heart out in a film, his chosen medium since adolescence, that he would express his innermost convictions to the accompaniment of old clips and outtakes and turn *The Warm-Blooded Sea* into his most profound, most melancholy warning to humanity. Over opening shots of a rising rocket, Cousteau says infinity beckons humanity, that we who hunger for companionship reach for distant planets, search for even one drop of water because it is a sign of life, only to find desolation and dust while we disinherit ourselves from life on earth. The sea is the womb of life. It is in the sea that the first cell took shape, that, with the DNA genetic code implanted like a seed within, endowed their improvements to the future. Landmarks of time – nerves, jaws, vertebrae – were formed, and after billions of years, life crawled up on land. Creatures now developed new traits to help them master terrestrial gravity.

John Soh did the editing, pulling together sequences from as far back as 1972 with shots of Canadian seals and their pups. Susan Schiefelbein was brought in once the rough cut was ready, and the actor Robert Wagner did the narration. "The words were mine, the sentiments his," Schiefelbein said of her collaboration with Cousteau. *The Warm-Blooded Sea* was about the mammals that, some 45 million years ago, had returned to the primordial ocean and evolved into whales, dolphins, and seals – animals whose behavior mystifies humans. "Their capabilities bewilder us, their intricate sounds, their elaborate brains, the bonds they make with their young, the bonds they seem to seek with us. All are ancient riddles that still confound the modern mind."

The TV hour showed Jean-Michel in South Carolina watching dolphins chasing tiny fish up a mud bank, Philippe with the tamed dolphin that lived with a Miami family. It showed Japanese fishermen slaughtering dolphins for interfering with their tuna nets, and asked why man always needs scapegoats. "Why can we only point accusing fingers and never hold up a mirror?" It showed the seals of Guadalupe Islands, once down to a hundred animals, increased again to careless, degenerate opulence. It quoted Teilhard de Chardin and ended with the seals of Labrador, cutting between an aproaching sealing vessel and the big-eyed pups on the ice. If time is running out for the pup, says Cousteau, time is running out for humankind as well. The story of marine mammals is our story as well. "The death ship waits," he intones. As the camera comes in close on the pup's face, he adds that mammals that may be gifted with senses we have lost or never attained are not our brethren, are not our underlings, but other nations caught with us in the net of life and time.

Before classical music swells and we look into the pup's eyes, Cousteau's voice comes back one more time: "Perhaps the mammal that is most unpredictable, incomprehensible, and inexplicable is the human being."

17
WONDERMENT

The thought sent a shiver down his spine. He was sitting in a stilled Zodiac in one of the Amazon River's tributaries and sensed what our primal ancestors must have sensed. He felt the river, the heat, the forest, and the dangers with *their* sharpened senses. For the instant of a frisson, he knew the chasm that separates us from them. In a grasp of mind and senses, he *was* one of them. He knew the forest had more eyes than leaves.

The continent was propitious for magical insights, imperishable voices, ancient silence, and time taut with terror and fantasy.

Jacques Cousteau was overwhelmed by the sheer size of it all, by the exuberant vitality and awesome alchemy of the jungle. The most extraordinary aspect of the largest, widest, and oldest river whose drainage area includes parts of nine nations, he would discover, is in obscurity. "Too dense and vast to be easily penetrated by human enterprise, rife with disease-carrying insects and fraught with legends of vicious and venomous creatures, bathing in steamy heat, the Amazon remains one of the last and least-known earthly secrets," he would write at the end of the biggest-ever Cousteau expedition."

Everything was big. The Amazon is the largest river in the world in volume and in the area of its basin. Its overflow is twelve times that of the Mississippi; the volume of water discharged into the Atlantic 7,025 kilometers from the Auprymac beginnings could fill Lake Ontario in three hours. The immensity of this flood that rises in a chain of glacier-fed lakes on the western edges of the Andes carries nearly one-fifth of all freshwater runoff on earth and, in the rainy season, creates a plume of brown water in the Atlantic extending a tenth of the way to Africa. It is navigable for oceangoing vessels nearly across the continent to Iquitos, at the eastern edge of the Andes. A single island at the river's mouth, Marajó, is as large as Switzerland, and the dense jungle of its entire basin would barely fit within the contiguous United States.

The Amazon has more species of fish than the Atlantic Ocean – five hundred species of catfish, including one so large that river people claim it has swallowed children. Among the bewildering assemblage of plant life – flowers that survive in tree tops and never touch soil, strangling plants that wrap themselves around huge trees and kill them – are spiders so large they catch birds, nearly half of the world's total bird species, the largest parrots, rodents and ants, the longest snakes, more species of bats and monkeys than anywhere, freshwater dolphins, and the world's largest otter. When the Brazilian government began aerial photo and radar mapping in 1971, scientists discovered a 600-kilometer river whose existence had never been suspected. Perhaps only half the vegetable and animal species of Amazonia are known. Some remote human tribes, only decades from the stone age and yet on the brink of extinction, are rarely visited. It is widely assumed that undiscovered tribes survive in the deepest reaches of the jungle.

To sit in the debilitating humidity and

378

sense ancestral bonds in the tangled greenness and rain forest murmur, Cousteau had committed his energy and talents on a dozen fronts in 1981. To finance this massive expedition, he had needed big money – $5 million was an early estimate – and had turned to an old friend, Bud Rifkin.

As in 1966, Rifkin had gone to the nertworks and found both new executive fans and objections. Grant Tinker, NBC's bracing chairman, loved the idea. Rifkin had JYC fly to L.A. for meetings, but Brandon Tartikoff, the network's president and programming chief, thought underwater TV was dull. Cousteau and Rifkin signed a contract that made Rifkin co-executive producer of the planned Amazon series. But while Rifkin went to others, JYC made his own deal with cable TV maverick Ted Turner. "It was love at first sight," said Rifkin, who was included in the overall package.

John Denver, the singer and Cousteau Society stalwart, introduced Cousteau to Turner. The flamboyant forty-three-year-old broadcaster, America's Cup racer, and baseball and basketball club owner had not yet attempted a hostile takeover of CBS, but through years of hard work and innovative thinking he had transformed the cable TV industry with his Atlanta "superstation" WTBS and his Cable News Network (CNN) to become a credible challenge to the networks' news organizations.

A man of complex character, "Terrible Ted" often talked hardline conservatism, but was also concerned with "liberal" issues such as world hunger and overpopulation, nuclear proliferation and improving the environment. "God bless you, Captain Cousteau, you have been a great inspiration to me," he would say in public. In private, Turner simply asked how much money JYC needed. Cousteau mentioned $6 million. "You've got it," Terrible Ted grinned. "Go to work!"

In the spring of 1982, JYC, Jean-Michel, and the Cousteau Society mounted an expedition that featured more people and more equipment than ever before. The polyglot team that at all times averaged fifty men – and, at strategic points, women – spent fifteen months first gaining a general understanding of the almost inconceivably vast subject and, in a narrowing focus, concentrating on how man's presence is changing Amazonia.

The first job for Cousteau himself in Brazil was to stroke the national ego. To the assurances he heard in government offices that to retain the Amazon's exuberance large regions would indeed be made off-limits to human exploitation were added prickly concerns for Brazilian sovereignty and Brazilian solutions. In return, JYC had to reassure Henrique Bergamin Filho, president of the National Institute for Research on Amazonia, that Brazilian scientists would be part of it all and that the *Calypso*'s satellite communications system would not be used to send vital information out of the country. To dilute the Brazilian presence, Cousteau invited scientists from Peru, Venezuela, Guyana, Suriname, and Ecuador. When the teams of divers, scientists, film and support people actually got under way, the old core of collaborators was augmented by American, Canadian, Brazilian, and Italian crew members and a hefty contingent of Peruvian, Argentine, Brazilian, and American scientists. There were a Martinique doctor specializing in tropical diseases, Canadian bush pilots, Peruvian mountaineers, and Argentine drivers.

There were old-timers like Raymond Coll and Albert Falco as well as newcomers like divers Xavier Desmier and Bruno Vidal, who hadn't been born when Coll and Falco went "vacuum cleaning" at the Grand Congloué. And there was Jacques Ertaud, who had taken the stunning pictures of the Red Sea coral reef on the first expedition in 1951, now a second-unit director on the land team that started from the Amazon's cold birthplace in the Andean snows.

And there were the women: daughter-in-law Anne-Marie, still photographer on Jean-Michel's land team and negotiator of access to Tzukahamei Indians; Susan Schiefelbein, brought down from New York to coauthor the telescripts; Paula DiPerna, advance person, diplomat, procurement officer who handled navigation, customs, weather and radio frequencies, medical precautions, airlifts, and helicopter rentals from a hotel room in Manaus; and, in Lima, Karen Brazeau handling the chores for Jean-Michel's land and raft travel down to a Stanley-and-Livingstone rendezvous with JYC, Simone, and the *Calypso* team at the confluence of the Marañón and Ucayali rivers in Peru, nearly 4,000 kilometers upstream from the Amazon's mouth. The land team transported itself and its rafts on a pair of much-filmed six-wheel-drive yellow amphibian Iveco trucks.

"Nowhere on earth have the same conditions prevailed on such a scale for such a long time and created such an elaborate, awesome forest and river," Cousteau said. Jacques Constans, the exacting science coordinator, was struck by the similarities of Amazonia and coral reefs. Both were among the oldest and most complex systems on earth, and both contained the most extraordinary, most colorful, most beautiful organisms. Both were tropical, both survived in relatively nutrient-poor environments, both covered immense territories but were among the most fragile of all living systems. The removal of rain forest in order to plant crops, graze cattle, sell timber, or mine minerals eradicated the leaf ceiling that protected the jungle vitality. The exposed soil was quickly baked by the sun and washed away by thunderstorms.

To film wildlife, study the fate of animal species barely documented, and get a handle on the consequences of the handful of grandiose development projects, the group split up in several teams. With JYC shuttling by plane between the various missions, Raymond Coll and Dominique Sumian headed camera teams on aerial expeditions to undisturbed regions along remote tributaries, Albert Falco set up a station to swim with river dolphins and otters while Jean-Michel's party looked at the impact of poaching, the balance of life in river and forest, and the plight of the surviving Indians.

Brazilians may have been more than neglectful toward the 180,000 surviving Indians, but all contact had to be handled by FUNAI, the Indian affairs agency. Coming with the FUNAI stamp of approval was both an advantage and a drawback. Without the presence and guidance of the FUNAI *sertanista,* or jungle Indian contact man, in remotest Serra Tapirapecó mountains straddling the Brazil-Venezuela border, any encounter with the Yanomamo Indians could have been deadly. The Yanomamos, who warn missionaries to stay clear of their lands, never showed themselves, but according to the *sertanista,* were watching the helicoptered-in "flying team." The Kumaiura Indians in the southern High Xingu jungles did not want the Cousteau truck team to scubadive into a sacred lake for relics of long ago cultures. To get his way, JYC had a FUNAI bureaucrat fly in to coax the Kumaiuras. Their answer, according to filmmaker John Boorman who was preparing his *Emerald Forest* shoot in the region, was to kidnap the FUNAI man. When he was allowed to leave ten days later, his bush plane was covered with war paint and a list of threatening demands was stuffed into his shirt pocket. The Cousteau team never dredged the mysterious waters.

Death came closest when Jean-Michel decided to follow up on Peruvian river people's very broad hints that the *Calypso* and the entire expedition amounted to one huge cover for hauling out some hefty loads of cocaine. "We were told, for example, that plastic bags of coca paste, to be refined elsewhere, could be nailed to the hull," Jean-Michel reported.

The Cousteaus and Mose Richards decided it was a subject they couldn't pass up. With Jean-Paul Cornu filming, they profiled poor Peruvians and Bolivians smuggling the coca paste and going to prison for it, hopeless cocaine junkies, and government officials burning sacks of coke headed for the most part for the United States. One Peruvian stated on camera that as long as the United States exported imperialism to South America, Peru might as well retaliate with cocaine. But the profiteers remained in the shadows. Jean-Michel met people who maintained the Sendero Luminoso, the "Shining Path" Maoist guerrillas attacking Indian villages in the Andes in an effort to overthrow Peru's fragile democracy, were in on the trade and exported via Cuba. Rifkin told Jean-Michel to back off and after threats that the Cousteaus took very seriously, they did. Still, they made *Snowstorm in the Jungle,* narrated by Orson Welles, the seventh and concluding hour of the *Cousteau/Amazon* teleseries. JYC was convinced that cocaine was becoming a weapon in the extreme left's arsenal, a means of attacking the moral foundations of the United States.

But more hypnotic than the lust behind the cocaine trade was the sight of 45,000 men hacking for gold on one small knoll rising in the jungle called Serra Pelada, or Naked Mountain, at the end of a dirt-road spur to the Trans-Amazon Highway. The sight was something out of Babylon or Pharoah's Egypt or the world of insects. Tens of thousands of men, their bodies coated with dust and mud – no women were allowed at Serra Pelada – were hacking two-by-three-meter plots of brown earth and carrying away the mountain in baskets on their shoulders, their minds riveted on the stories of phenomenal nuggets clawed from the earth.

With Coll and cameraman Louis Prezelin, who had nearly drowned filming the raft team white-water rafting on the Apurímac, Jean-Michel spent ten days in this eerie fantasy land where men shoveled in their assigned cubes and built canals to divert springs coming out of cliff walks, and their hired carriers passed baskets of sifted, worthless earth up rickety ladders called "mama mias." Jean-Michel talked to one man who with his carriers had found 1.28 kilos of gold worth $2 million in one year. Each miner could claim a two-by-three-meter plot and keep 75 percent of the gold he found; the government kept the rest. If a plot was abandoned for seventy-two hours, it was redistributed. Because the square plots were being dug at different speeds and none were at the same level, mud slides and cave-ins were frequent. Thirty diggers had died in collapsing holes. Men without claims worked as bag carriers and shovelers. Some carriers were paid 40 cents a bag and made sixty trips a day up the mama mias. If their prospector-employers didn't hit pay dirt fast enough, carriers became percentage owners in the stakes.

From a distance Serra Pelada looked like a gigantic bowl of dirty sugar cubes. It was guarded by militiamen who told Coll not to believe everything. The stories were as feverish as the $800 million worth of gold hacked from the hold during the first three years after the 1980 discovery (itself a story of someone passing a tree felled by a violent storm and in the gaping hole beneath the tangled roots seeing rocks of gold). The main gathering place was called Plaza of Lies, but the stories of Brazil's poor-turned-gold diggers all had in common the dream of respect, of winning with class.

It was the infinities that haunted Jacques Cousteau, the global significance of this rain forest and river, Amazonia's immense storage and transfer of vitality to the atmosphere and the Atlantic that sustains every living thing on the planet. It was the infinitely small. Frogs as tiny as a human fingernail existed, as did Marmoset monkeys weighing a little more than an egg. He came to realize that this was a kingdom of small beings – insects, birds, spiders, rodents, butterflies, lizards, bats – and of solitary living. Except for monkey troops, peccary herds, and families of capybaras, most animals appeared to be single hunters, rarely seen in their travels and commonly nocturnal. "We are fascinated by the phenomenon and eager to solve the mystery in our minds: why is such a vast, verdant environment principally an empire for the small?" he noted at the beginning of the expedition.

He was most impressed by the mood of the forest. "It is the presence of biological antiquity, powered by the solar energy of the tropics, quickened by the serum of life – water – which pervades, dripping from the canopy above, coursing through the blood-streams and leafstalks, clouding the air, flushing ground nutrients toward taproots below and ocean-bound rivers beyond," he would write. "I feel here a caress of the life force, of somber energies and a deep jungle intelligence in fundamental matters of life, death, blood, breath."

His final verdict was cautiously optimistic. When modern man carved in the jungle from the edges and industrialized it with high-tech logging and agriculture, the exuberant yet shallow, fragile jungle lost. When man started in the middle with a clearing, the forest won, overpowering intruders with disease, madness, and overgrowth. The team saw both the Jari paper pulp plantation the size of Connecticut and the Carajas iron mines, as well as the ruins of railways never finished and riverside settlements reclaimed by the jungle. "Though inexorable forces are at work to alter it, huge areas remain vibrant and little changed," Cousteau would sum up. "We have flown for hours over vast unbroken sheets of tree cover still beyond the heavy machinery of human trespassers, and our samplings of the river have revealed only scattered signs of pollution." He quoted Breno Dos Santos, the geologist whose forced landing on a jungle mountain led to the discovery of the vast Carajas iron deposits, as saying that in the past man has always gone into virgin regions destroying the land and killing other men, that Amazonia is our last chance to go in using our heads, the last chance to show whether we are congenitally hopeless or *can* grow up.

While in Paris John Soh and Hedwige Bienvenue trimmed two hundred hours of film into seven television programs, Cousteau kept up his frantic pace. He took part in the *Calypso*'s most intellectual expedition, a survey of the Mississippi River. He tried out "windships," greeted the millionth visitor to the Monaco Oceanographic Museum (a young Italian tourist and her husband), and for the late 1980's, prepared a *Calypso* mission to the only shores she had never seen: Australia, Indonesia, and China.

There was one legal disappointment. France's highest administrative court ruled against Cousteau and his CEMA company in the 1971 cancellation of the Argyronète deep-sea exploration submersible. The French government was not liable when François Ortoli, as minister of Industrial and Scientific Development, canceled the Argyronète program.

Six doors down from the Cousteau

apartment-turned-cutting room, a design team finished work on the first prototype of a ship harnessing the wind with a super-efficient system using so-called turbosails. The renaissance of sailing ships was an old Cousteau dream that concerns for the ecology and the rising oil prices made viable. The Organization of Petroleum Exporting Countries' 1981 benchmark was $32 a barrel (Libya and Nigeria asked for $41), and oil experts all agreed the price of a barrel of oil by the end of the decade would hover around $80. At 1982 prices, fuel represented between 30 and 50 percent of a cargo vessel's operating costs.

Japanese, British, German, and American shipbuilders were rethinking the potential of commercial wind power. With financial backing from Pechiney, the French aluminum multinational, Cousteau and Lucien Malavard, an aerodynamics expert who had worked on the Concorde and Aribus designs, modified the concept of Anton Flettner, a German builder who crossed the Atlantic in 1924 in an odd-looking "rotorship" driven by two large cylinders turning at 100 to 150 revolutions per minute. Air flowing in the direction of the rotation created a pressure on one side of the smokestack-looking cylinders which produced a low-pressure lift, pulling the ship forward at a right angle to the wind.

While a 22-meter catamaran was outfitted with a fixed but hollow aluminum mast designed to create thrust with the airflow from inside the shaft cavity, JYC, Jean-Michel, and a *Calypso* team headed by Richard Murphy, the Cousteau Society's vice-president for science and education, surveyed the Mississippi River. The Cousteau's lack of concern for the St. Lawrence – Great Lakes contaminants that had angered Canadian ecologists three years earlier was not repeated here. From the headwaters of Lake Itasca, Minnesota, to the Gulf of Mexico, the Mississippi was sampled for toxics, from herbicides and heavy metals to plasticizers, alkylbenzenes, halogenated organics, saturated hydrocarbons, and a bevy of other pollutants. But more than a health checkup, the 1983 Mississippi run became an exploration of new frontiers of economics and ecology, two disciplines that Cousteau felt were not mutually exclusive.

A shallow river meandering through a broad floodplain, the Mississippi, which drains 40 percent of the United States, was difficult to navigate and inhospitable to early settlers. During the last century, the river was therefore engineered into a transportation system. Its course was altered in places, its floods controlled, sandbars and logjams were eliminated, and channels, dikes, levees, and a system of locks and dams built. The river, in short, was tamed, developed, and controlled. At what price? Or, as Murphy put it, Are the benefits we now derive any greater than before we began engineering it? Benefits imply economics, but the current state of the so-callecd dismal science, economics, is totally "anthro-pocentric" – that is, it only calculates what benefits humans. Economists do not know yet how to put figures on clean air, clean water, soil, nutrients, other species, kelp beds, wetlands, etc., partly because scientists don't fully understand or appreciate the services provided by natural ecosystems. Since we cannot yet compute the "value" of ecosystems, we are entitled to wonder whether it is in our long-term interest to develop natural resources at all.

These considerations led Eugene Odum and Mark Brown, a pair of Georgia scientists and Cousteau Society members, to use energy analysis to calculate costs, benefits, and losses in human as well as natural systems. In 1978, Odum had figured the economic value of an acre of marshland to be $100 if used for commercial and sports fishing; $2,500 as a waste treatment site; and, because of its ability to absorb carbon dioxide, produce oxygen, harbor wildlife, and provide storm protection, $4,100 if left alone. Based on the premise that micro-organisms, fish, humans, cars, cities, and the entire biosphere all use energy, Odum and Brown concluded that since the universe evolves toward the ever more complex, evolution in a sense favors greater concentration of energy. Grasslands becoming forests concentrate greater energy in the biomass of trees than in the grasses hunter-gatherer groups evolve into farming communities that evolve into massive civilizations according to their ability to maximize their use of energy.

Applied to the Mississippi, this analysis showed that the embodied energy of the river system's nonrenewable resources – its nutrients in the soil, topsoil, organic matter, and such exported resources as fuel (gas, coal), products (grain, goods, meats), and services – far exceeds the renewable resources – sun, rain, tides, and the downstream movement of the river itself. If the economic principle that a positive balance of payment between imports and exports is necessary to stimulate growth is applied to energy resources, it could be said that the Mississippi was being used to stimulate growth elsewhere in the United States and the world. "This," Murphy observed, "may be good from a national point of view, but we as a society should be aware of what is taking place."

This analysis also magnified the contrast between the essentially "wild" Amazon and the developed Mississippi. Most of the Amazon's poor "river people" depend on the renewable resources and therefore live in relative immunity from depleting their resources or world market fluctuations. For the moment, the people of the Mississippi basin derive great benefits from it, but they are in fact using up their nonrenewable wealth. Should demands for their exportable wealth begin to fall, they will suffer more than their Brazilian counterparts. Once nonrenewable resources decline or are used up, it seems, people who know how to husband their renewable resources will be the winners. Future societies will no doubt place great importance on maintaining the integrity and productivity of their natural resources.

In November 1983, JYC, Jean-Michel, and a five-man crew left the coast of Morocco for the New World in a boat totally driven by renewable energy. The craft was the experimental catamaran windship, christened the *Moulin à Vent* – French for windmill and the name of JYC's favorite Beaujolais. Tailed for a day by the *Calypso* – Simone had no intention of venturing aboard a sailboat with no sail – the *Moulin à Vent* reached speeds of 10.5 knots, but also slowed maddeningly in persistent doldrums on the way to Bermuda and Norfolk. Prezelin was reduced to cranking domestic scenes of passing dolphins and of JYC vacuuming the sleeping quarters. After two weeks of little wind, a storm caused the first damage, and as an emergency measure, wires were used to strengthen the 14-meter turbosail. It didn't look good, however. Jean-Michel radioed his mother to have the *Calypso* pull alongside so a crew member with knowledge of the tricky aluminum welding could be transferred to the *Moulin à Vent*. New welds seemed to stabilize the cylinder.

They were near the American coast when, on JYC's night watch, the turbosail began to topple. He was fast enough to veer so the aluminum mast fell forward into the sea and not on the aft cabin and his sleeping men.

Eighteen months later they were a twelve-man crew aboard an all-automated, computerized, push-button windship called the *Alcyone* after the goddess who gave her favors to Neptune. Built entirely of aluminum in La Rochelle with Common Market funds, French government grants, and Pechiney investments, the broad-beamed 30-meter *Alcyone* featured two turbosails and, for a combination sail-motor tryout, a diesel engine. A pair of computers constantly shifted the angle of the turbosails and the diesel engine's output for maximum performance. Pechiney, which acquired the turbosail license, estimated that a 30,000-ton turbosail cargo ship spending 300 days a year at sea could make annual savings (at pre-oil glut prices) of $300,000.

The summer 1985 voyage from La Rochelle to New York was an all-encompassing public relations trip. The crew included a CNN correspondent and a Soviet journalist who made daily radio progress reports. Followed by the *Calypso* and Simone, the first leg of the maiden voyage was propitious, but after the Azores the ocean remained hopelessly flat. On moonless nights JYC stood on the deck watching the luminescence created in the ship's wake by a zillion plankton. By day, Prezelin was again reduced to filming passing dolphin schools, solitary finback whales, or diving into the sargassum seaweed. After Bermuda, wind and sea picked up, allowing a series of precise wind trials. With 25- to 30-knot crosswinds, the *Alcyone* attained speeds of 10 knots without the use of diesel power, meaning fuel savings of 50 to 60 percent had she been a conventionally powered vessel.

While the *Alcyone* went through her paces, the *Calypso* took Jacques, Simone, Jean-Michel, and a number of the veteran crew members up the Chesapeake Bay and Potomac River to a birthday party at Mount Vernon and a White House reception. Monday, June 10 was Cousteau's seventy-fifth birthday.

It was a festive, if muggy, Sunday afternoon. YC was dressed all in white. Simone in a navy blue and white dress. Jazz and calypso music wafted across the verdant lawns of George Washington's home. The organizers from Turner Broadcasting and the Cousteau Society had made sure everybody was there, and it took the size of a circus big top to accommodate the eight hundred buffet dinner guests. John Denver led the guests in his 1975 paean, "Aye, Calypso," and "Happy Birthday." Ted Turner, in open shirt and seersucker slacks, said, "God bless you, Captain Cousteau," and Jean-Michel had the cameras cut to Simone as he wondered "if the real captain

398

behind the scene is not '*la bergère,*' my mother." She saluted him like a sailor, nervous at being in the spotlight.

Simone was, at sixty-seven, a dauntless, handsome woman with a strong direct gaze and a somewhat stern mien under a curly crop of gray hair. Surprisingly small when seen next to her gangly husband, she was perhaps more rock of certainty than power behind the throne, as it implies artful manipulation. Simone was no juggler. She had followed Jacques's career without losing her own personality, and if she had remained in the shadow so much that people were surprised to learn of her existence, she had done so out of her own accord. She never appeared in the films, she never gave interviews, never wrote anything, yet she was, as her son told the Washington gathering, "the permanent and original source of *Calypso*'s spirit." She was happiest when aboard the *Calypso*.

Raymond Coll was there, uncomfortable in tie and jacket. Harold Edgerton and Luis Marden were there as were Jean-Michel and Ann-Marie's children. Jan was there with her and Philippe's chilodren, sitting at a table with Perry Miller Adato. A *People* magazine photographer snapped Cousteau hugging his granddaughter Alexandra. At one point he looked across his shoulder and caught Perry's eyes. "He came over without saying a word," she recalled. "We just embraced and I knew what he was thinking – Philippe."

When it was the birthday celebrant's turn to speak, he downplayed the occasion. "It's entirely artificial," he said. "Nature doesn't count days. Monkeys and mosquitos don't have birthdays." But he also looked forward and expressed the hope that even if he couldn't count on a second seventy-fifth birthday, the Cousteau Society would live much longer than that.

The White House ceremony was brief. President Reagan awarded Cousteau the Medal of Freedom, the highest civilian honor of the United States, for having done more than any other individual to reveal the mysteries of the oceans. "It is therefore likely that he will be remembered not only as a pioneer in his time but as a dominant figure in world history," the President concluded. Nearly twenty-five years earlier, Jacques and Simone had stood in the White House Rose Garden and seen John F.Kennedy bestow the National Geographic's gold medal on JYC for "having opened up the ocean floor to man and science."

The arrival of the *Alcyone* and *Calypso* in New York a week later was carefully

400

orchestrated. Turner and other VIP's helicoptered out to the ships for the last mile in past the scaffold-covered Statue of Liberty and saluting fireboats to the renovated South Street Seaport docking. An army band struck up, balloons flew into the wind, and Cousteau and his men stood on deck in snappy white overalls as they slid to the dock. Mayor Edward Koch called JYC "Admiral Cousteau" as television choppers hovered overhead and more balloons were released. The *Alcyone*, said the admiral-for-a-day, "is just like woman, difficult to understand. But once you succeed, it's worthwhile."

Nothing could be more out of tune with what, in the public imagination, Jacques Cousteau stood for than this Lower Manhattan Disneyland media event – and *The Riders of the Wind*, the Turner Broadcasting TV hour on the two windships' crossings, produced by Soh, written by Mose Richards, and narrated, with gushing interludes of Gregorian chant, by Peter Ustinov.

The reaction was often severe. Family members, old collaborators and friends, scientists, and ecologists were both disturbed and baffled. They were still in love with "what Cousteau quote stands for unquote," they said, as if to mark their awareness of

401

how the world's most famous living explorer had strayed from their ideal of the world's most famous living explorer.

Jean-Pierre saw the chasm: the smiles on his cardiac patients' faces when he confirmed that Jacques Cousteau was his uncle, and the media star he had lunch with whenever Jacques was in Paris, the public figure beyond criticism who no longer had time or taste for impassioned discussions. Rifkin came away rankled from the *Cousteau/Amazon* series. He had found JYC changed, making commitments he couldn't fulfill, concentrating on the bottom line. Scientists at San Diego's Scripps Institution of Oceanography called Cousteau an uninvited person because to them he wasn't much of an oceanographer anymore. If the French government cancelled the Argyronete, it was also because experts found the diving habitat more showpiece than practical instrument for ocean exploration. Cousteau is to oceanography what French cancan is to *Swan Lake,* the Paris newsmagazine *L'Exprès,* quoted a French savant as saying.

European ecologists, struggling in perpetual underfunded misery, wondered what to make of $6 million TV documentaries featuring amphibious trucks, white-water

402

rafting, and visionary boats. French and British environmentalists thought the torch had passed to the likes of David McTaggart and his loose coalition of fifteen national chapters of Greenpeace. Cousteau talked of the nuclear threats hanging over future generations but admitted he didn't use the White House occasion to give Reagan an earful, to create a scandal if necessary. The basis of support for Greenpeace was parents wanting a better world for their children, said the fifty-year-old Canadian ski resort millionaire. His zealous activists protested the nuclear arms race in both Seattle and Leningrad, put their lives in jeopardy in Zodiacs alongside ships dumping nuclear waste drums in the North Sea, or positioned themselves between Japanese whalers' harpoons and Pacific gray whales. They also produced mock commercials of fashion models splattered by the blood of the animals whose fur they were modeling.

French ecologists appreciated Cousteau's antinuclear stand and the value of the *Calypso* in sensitizing public opinion to environmental isues, but resented the trumpeting of the Cousteau name and face. Dominique Martin felt that *Cousteau/Amazon* supported Brazilian government positions and tiptoed around the Indian problem, and that Jean-

Michel had been much more biting with the Serra Pelada gold rush. When she interviewed JYC he refused to talk about the Amazon Indians. A minor but typical irritant she encountered at the Cousteau Foundation on Avenue Wagram was that no Amazon photos would be available for Les Amis de la Terre unless Cousteau was mentioned. Across the Channel, activists thought he was a nice eccentric who had to be admired.

But to Raymond Vaissière, who was always looking for "a young Cousteau" in his oceanographic and marine ecology classes at Nice University, the thinking among utopian environmentalists was deeply flawed insofar as it failed to take into account the forces that made humans competitive, the biological urges that were identical whether observed in Xingu tribesmen or the superpowers. While it was suicidal to go on polluting the environment, innate human dynamics dictated that some people produce and others consume. "Whether it is for economic reasons, or profound innate reasons that have to do with traditions, religious or otherwise, there are those who want to dominate others, yet a kind of equilibrium tends to take place. We are forced to maintain a balance, and in order to do so we are forced to manipulate things that are dangerous." To primitive man, fire was mortally dangerous: in war or by accident, whole forests must have been torched. Ever-sharper knives were literally two-edged swords. The dangerous things we were manipulating today could, of course, become permanent poisons, but there, too, we were, perhaps unconsciously, reaching equilibrium.

Cousteau himself was not afraid of proposing utopian solutions to that most dismal of equilibriums – the nuclear balance of terror. Since the nuclear arms race threatened future generations, the solution was to make children pawns, and therefore guarantors, of peace.

After many brainstorming sessions with Simone, Jean-Michel and Anne-Marie, with friends aboard the *Calypso* and around the world – JYC and Arthur C. Clarke pecked out messages to each other on newfangled word processor hookups – he decided nuclear annihilation could be averted through the compulsory exchange of children at a relatively young age, seven to eight, to live for one year with a family in an enemy country. Compulsory, he said in 1985, meant everybody. "Millions and millions. I mean all the children from seven to eight. I don't see how a nation could press the button on those terrible things when they know that three million of their children are over there. I mean, the mothers would not tolerate that. We still need to work this project out much better with specialists, with psychologists, with child specialists, but I have decided to spend the rest of my life on the project. It is my number-one priority."

Did he honestly expect to see this happen in his lifetime? journalists asked.

"I don't care." He smiled. "The important thing is to act according to your conscience – and whether it's going to be sucessful or not, I do not care. I believe in this."

Elaborating on the children exchange project, he admitted it was the most utopian undertaking of his life. What he would like to see, however, was one percent of the superpowers' military budgets financing the idea. "Imagine a world where all the children from seven to eight, for example, would have to spend a year on the other side of the fence. From an educational standpoint it would be a great opening of the mind. It is because of the hope that I have in the future of mankind that I want to join forces and forge a better world for future generations."

"I believe in children. I live for children. Whenever I have time, I go to schools and talk to them, answer questions. I find more sense in them than in adults. When we have a plan, the adults will say, 'Oh, but that is utopian.' With that they mean, Forget it. Children accept utopias; for them all is possible. They say, 'Let's do it.' Children are the only hope we have. I may be wrong, but please, let's assume they are the solution, for we have no other. I trust our children."

In Paris, he liked to take skeptical journalists away from the Avenue Wagram headquarters, with its bewildering output of calendars, almanacs, filmstrips, and tapes for school use, to a nearby schoolyard to show how simple it could all be, to show children's drawings. A drawing of a penguin would make him smile and say he trusted penguins, too. "Penguins are truly monogamous for life," he told a couple of journalists in the schoolyard. "For seven months of the year, penguins go fishing far away from one another. Then they go back to their rookeries. The one who gets there first waits for his or her mate. The joy when they meet is one of the loveliest things you can ever see."

18
SERENITY, NOT QUITE

If there was going to be any sailing into the sunset, he would be at the helm himself, at least most of the time. The five-year odyssey that started in the fall of 1985 was taking the much rebuilt, nearly fifty-year-old *Calypso* and the new *Alcyone* through a lead and catch-up course through the South Atlantic and Mexico's Sea of Cortés to New Zealand, Australia, and New Guinea; to China, perhaps with a trip up the Yangtze, the world's fourth largest river, Indonesia and, in Africa, an expedition on the fifth largest river, the Congo. The favorite body of water, said the tireless explorer, was "the only one I've never been to."

The plan was to slowly "depersonalize" the twenty television hours the expedition was contracted for, to gradually shift the focus from Captain Cousteau to the Cousteau Society and to make himself and Jean-Michel Cousteau "interchangeable." Following a book about the environment, nuclear danger, and Third World problems,

Jacques Cousteau would begin to write his memoirs, "to be published, if God gives me life, in 1990 or before."

Reality, as usual, was more perverse. However much he wanted to do a graceful fadeout and write his life story, his stardom played tricks with him. Television audiences didn't tune in to see a non-profit organization or the explorer's son. Cousteau on television was no National Geographic special, no marine series featuring well-meaning unknowns. It was the ongoing saga of Neptune's modern descendant that a generation had grown up with, the adventures of one seal-sleek man whose craggy face, beaked nose, and lilting voice hundreds of millions knew, one mariner who with his friends had helped open a new world.

There were moments of profound lassitude, moments of revolt against the financial millstone that forced him to accelerate instead of slowing his pace, but for which, ultimately, he had only himself to blame. In public he spoke of the good old days when he could spend eight months of the year aboard the *Calypso* whereas now the tooth-and-nail fight for funds allowed him, at most, four months at sea. "And the sea is my best friend, it has never betrayed me. I hope I'll never have to give up sailing."

The figures said it all. To keep ship, crew, and postproduction afloat, the Cousteau Foundation, the corporate producer of the *Rediscovery of the World* series, had to complete four episodes annually at an average cost of $1 million each. Turner Broadcasting paid $15 million for all twenty, leaving a shortfall of $250,000 per episode, or a million dollars a year. As Cousteau never ceased to repeat when soliciting funds, he couldn't create his telefilms in a controlled studio setting, where the costs could be calculated in advance. To probe nature's secrets and the spectacle of life would always be an expensive proposition.

Building tourist facilities kept him busy on several continents. The first of the Cousteau Ocean Centers was to open in Paris' renovated Forum des Halles in 1988, followed by similar mixed-media museum-theme parks in Huntingdon Beach, California, Brazil and Japan. At the Parisian Centre Cousteau would feature a life-sized replica of a whale and video satellite hookups allowing visitors to talk to the *Calypso* at sea and to actually take over the wheel of the *Alcyone*. Conceived by JYC and Jean-Michel and executed by the people who built Disneyland's Pirates Cove, the tour would take visitors in suspended gondolas into a simulated ocean depth with audio and visual effects of undersea life and shipwrecks. The much-delayed original Hampton Roads Cousteau Ocean Center designed by Jean-Michel seemed destined to be the last to open. With the city of Norfolk, however, he took on fund-raising chores for a possible 1989 ground-breaking ceremony.

The Cousteau Foundation, whose world-wide membership in the late 1980's surpassed 250,000 (including the 183,000 Cousteau Society members), constantly had to ask him to raise money – in 1986 there was a sudden urgent appeal to all members for $165,000 to replace the *Calypso*'s aging power plant. His star status was its only bankable asset. In return, his indispensability gave him clout with the society, with Turner Broadcasting System (TBS), with everybody in the entourage. "What JYC wants goes," said Tom Blanchard of the Greater Norfolk Corporation, joint fund-raiser with the Cousteau Society of $3 million for the Virginia center.

Jean-Michel's plans were to carry on the legacy. If he couldn't fill his father's metaphysical shoes yet, he could be the deputy, the stand-in, the crown prince, on occasion more daring than JYC in ruffling bureaucratic feathers. "He beats me in one

411

thing, he's a good administrator," the elder Cousteau admitted.

Approaching fifty and with streaks of gray in his luxuriant outdoorsman's beard, Jean-Michel was the tireless supervisor, manager, scheduler, and troubleshooter of organizations and events. Less than ten years after Philippe's death, he was in charge of the all-encompassing and, for tax purposes, all-enfolding society. Wherever he could, he added revenue-enhancing endeavors. After fifteen years of taking paying guests on "hand-on tours" of tropical waters (averaging $2,000 for ten days, transportation to and from warm-water startoff points not included), his aquatic Club Med-style program was expanded to include lecture tours aboard cruise ships. After the *Alcyone* trials, he was at trade shows introducing new diving equipment – steel-titanium alloy backpacks allowing for higher compressed air, helmets featuring headphones and, inserted into the regulator mouthpieces, microphones, lightweight scooters, and, in keeping with the look of space-age technology, wetsuits in silver with black striping instead of the familiar black-and-yellow Cousteau team suits. His wife took over the visual arts documentation. Anne-Marie organized a Porte de Versailles retrospective

412

of Captain Cousteau photos in Paris and a touring *Cousteau/Amazon* exhibit in Brazil.

The society's monthly publications in French and English reflected the general reassessment of goals, methods and structure that environmental groups were going through in trying to remain relevant to an increasingly pragmatic mainstream. To go through *Calypso Log* and *Calypso Dispatch* issues was to leaf through an eclectic mix of articles on involvement in ecology and Third World development dilemmas with forewords by Jacques Cousteau, interviews with influential newsmakers and environmentalists, *Calypso* travel pieces, plugs for new Project Ocean Search tours, and, in the back of the American editions, order forms for Cousteau Society almanacs, belts, books, jackets, *Calypso* model kits, posters, records, sticker, T-shirts, and tote bags.

The television postproduction, meanwhile, was moved from Los Angeles to Paris. In 1985, JYC decreed no more Hollywood script rewriting, rough cutting, editing, and scoring. All postproduction would henceforth be done in his own Paris apartment. The reason: After twenty years of working with 16mm film, he "recycled" to videotape. Whatever infinite superiority in resolution was lost in abandoning 16mm film stock for electronic images was compensated by the versatility and speed of video, but he wanted the best, the high-resolution PAL system, not the 525 lines-per-frame TV system in use in the Americas and Japan."

JYC was aware that Ted Turner was controversial and had enemies, "but this man places his money and his actions where his heart is. So even if he is a little rough outside, he is the most sincere man I've ever met. I believe in what he says." To show his solidarity for Turner and quality programming, he took a great deal of his savings and bought $50,0000 of CBS stock in 1985 when Terrible Ted made an unsuccessful bid for CBS Inc.

When he signed with Turner for the Amazon series in 1981, the switch to cable and satellite television had perhaps been a little premature, he conceded, but he had always been a pioneer and was happy to have been sooner rather than later. There was also a residual bitterness against the American networks behind the move. In the how-low-can-you-get category was NBC's *Ocean-Quest*, a five-part underwater series. Brandon Tartikoff, who had turned down Bud Rifkin's Amazon series pitch saying underwater television was a bore, not only scheduled but ordered the producers to expand this aqualung and bathing suit docudrama. Before the 1985 indignity of *OceanQuest* – lows ratings and critics' howls killed the prime-time show – JYC had raged against the quality of network programming, particularly ABC's cancellation of *The Undersea World* in 1976.

Since it was easier to work down from PAL to lower definition TV than up to higher standards, crews got the newest PAL minicams and the Faubourg St. Honoré apartment was invaded by state-of-the-art equipment. Bent over word processors, TV monitors, and whirring Kem tables, a handful of writers and editors blocked out rough cuts in several languages, and always looked startled, it seemed, when the chief bounced in for hours of concentrated review on the monitors before whizzing off again. "I learned to construct my films from American television," he told visitors. "The numerous commercial breaks have forced me to build in four acts. I'd even say publicity can help you become creative."

To enter the apartment was to burrow into the explorer's secret lair. In snatched moments here, Cousteau painted pictures he would not let anyone see and, under the

415

loggia jutting out over the living room, played and composed on his piano, finally taking up the challenge of writing the score for one of the telefilms that were approaching number 100. "The piano is a relaxation," he smiled, explaining that, because of the huge rubber plant by the stairs, he could play only classical music. "To play jazz puts its life in jeopardy. I have to be very careful."

Behind a sand-colored Scandinavian sofa with red throw pillows, a small selection of awards lined a mantelpiece next to a black bronze replica of a bearded Neptune. Awards no longer meant much, he said, and the seventeen Emmies had remained in New York. The Oscars and the Sept d'Or, the French Emmies, were on the mantelpiece. The long modern desk with its multiline telephone was graced by a gorgeous replica of the *Calypso*, complete with miniature helicopter and aft hydraulic crane.

He reached for a piece of black coral, polished and flawless, and told how he had given Picasso a bigger piece like that. "After his death I met his wife, who told me Picasso had the coral in his hand when he died. He liked to touch it, to feel its smoothness with his fingers. That was moving for me."

Talk of life and its caprices evoked family statistics and mentions of health habits. "My

416

father died when he was ninety-three, my mother at sixty-four. My brother died of cancer when he was fifty-two. Simone was seventeen, I was twenty-five when I met her at a friend's cocktail party. In July 1987 we will celebrate our golden anniversary."

The death of old collaborators and fellow explorers, even if he didn't know them, affected him more than contemplations on his own demise. The passing of Alexis Sivirine, the engineer who since the Grand Congloué days had been involved in the endless refittings of the *Calypso*, made Cousteau fly the vessel's flag at half mast and say the ship had lost her guardian angel. After the 1986 *Challenger* shuttle disaster he sent a telegram to President Reagan offering, as a token of his solidarity, to take part in one of the next shuttle missions. Said his telegram: "It is difficult for me to express the many feelings that storm my heart – deep sorrow when I think of the victims' families, pride on behalf of humankind that produced such heroes, faith in the future of the shuttles, of the planned orbiting station and of space explorations for the benefit of all."

As for his own death, even the prospect of the most dreaded disease left him unmoved. "If I have cancer so what? That's a way to finish your life. It's one more sickness. It's nothing terrible. I mean, yes, it's terrible, but death is terrible in itself. But I have made friends with death. I mean I have accepted it not only as inevitable but also as constructive. If we didn't die, we would not appreciate life as we do. So it's a constructive force."

During sedentary periods in Paris or Monaco, he used dumbbells and tensile stress exercisers. On expedition, he was up half an hour before everybody else for twenty minutes of running in place and twenty minutes of calisthenics, followed invariably by dry toast with orange marmalade. He took vitamins and eliminated all fat, butter, milk, and cheese from his diet, but kept no schedule for eating and sleeping, often working through the night. "I have a very irregular life. I think a regular life is a step to the tomb."

On another occasion he said he liked to live like an animal. "When an animal is hungry, he will hunt several weeks without sleep, and when he has eaten he will sleep for three days, and that's the way I go."

Would that mean the majority of humanity lived all wrong? Oh, absolutely. When I look at those people who claim that they have insomnia – it doesn't exist. If two or three times a year I have difficulty going to sleep, well you know what I do? I go running a little bit, even at night, for fifteen to twenty minutes. When I come back panting I take a shower and go to bed and sleep like a stone."

He came to appreciate Thai food for its flavor and lightness. "I like a wine that smacks of the soil, but I don't mind a good Burgundy. Did you know a cousin of mine is a Bordeaux grower? She makes a Pomerol, rich with that special undertaste experts call a 'truffle taste.' My affection for tea is as great as for wine. I had a long-leaf Hou Long at Chez Edgar. It's an expensive tea, tastes like water, but afterward you have a delicious flavor in your mouth."

He never saw any of the two-hour retrospective *Cousteau; The First 75 Years* that Mose Richards and Jean-Michel put together for TBS, but simply gave them access to his film archives and consented to have Jean-Paul Cornu follow him around for a month before filming the Mount Vernon birthday party. The fact that the French TV version was only sixty minutes long, he told *France-Soir*, could only be an improvement.

The French and Monegasque celebrations were subdued. "They could have waited till I was eighty," he told Parisian friends. In Monaco, he was handed a specially engraved plaque at the Oceanography Museum, and a box of the frightful black Indian cigars he was fond of. With a pirouette, he told the gathered personnel that if he wasn't often there, it was because the museum was in capable hands.

The apartment on Monaco's Boulevard de Belgique was another refuge. Overlooking the ocean, it resembled a gift shop, crowded with carved fish, polished stones,and other souvenirs of countless journeys. An old-fashioned diver's helmet peered at the panoramic harbor view. If he never took vacations, he explained, it was because vacations implied a change of activity, "and that is something I'm always doing."

He joined the *Calypso* and Simone after the Monaco homage for a Turner-inspired visit to Cuba en route to Haiti. To help quench the smoldering hostilities of a quarter century of U.S.-Cuban animosity, JYC's nautical diplomacy included filming a TBS special and arranging a meeting with Fidel Castro, which turned to a talk about cigars. Castro's doctor had just told him to stop smoking. "I met Castro in Havana," he said with a shrug, "as I met Reagan in Washington. In turn they visited the *Calypso*. I'm pretty good with presidents."

Haiti, the Western Hemisphere's poorest

country, was infinitely more significant for humanity than the drawn-out cold war squabbles between Washington and Havana. The pressures of overpopulation – with six million inhabitants Haiti has a population density worse than India's – was dragging down everything. JYC had first denounced "preposterous birthrates" in 1963, but the two months he, Jean-Michel, Albert Falco, Mose Richards, Cornu, Guy Jouas, and Paula DiPerna spent in Haiti during the waning days of the Duvalier regime was a preview of the ultimate standing-room-only nightmare. And it was all the more unbearable as it was happening to a gentle, spirited, and hopeful people who dreamed of winning the lottery – the only infinitesimal chance of escape – and in the meantime wrapped themselves in the most colorful garb and put their trust in voodoo.

Illiteracy was 75 percent, reaching as high as 96 percent among rural women and 99 percent among rural men; malnourishment was chronic among 60 percent of adults and 30 percent of children. Infant mortality was the highest for all developing countries, and malaria, AIDS, tuberculosis, polio, parasitic diseases, dysentery, and vitamin deficiencies took a regular toll. Cornu filmed people bathing in a fetid stream cutting through

Port-au-Prince. The odors of the market were overwhelming, coming from heaps of green-tinged meat and decaying small fish. Everywhere young boys sold water from steel tubs balanced on their heads. Only one in five Haitians has access to safe drinking water. In places, land was as raw as skinned knees, and patches of erosion grew seemingly overnight. Two-thirds of the watersheds were partially or totally deforested. A dam that provided electricity for Port-au-Prince would be silted up in thirty years. The pressure on the land had an impact on the surrounding Caribbean. Without tropical forest to retain rainwater, Haiti was "bleeding" earth through the veins of its rivers, spreading fertile, eroded soil over the ocean bottom and suffocating the coral reefs, destroying habitat for fish. When Columbus discovered the island in 1492 it was 80 percent covered with tropical forest; now less than 7 percent was still forested.

Could the rediscovery voyage be considered a summing up, a recapitulation?

"No, nothing is finished for me."

A turning point?

"No, I keep going straight."

A stage in life?

"I don't stop."

The rediscovery expedition was new

because it tried to introduce the human factor in the research – to factor in human destruction and, sometimes, protection of the marine environment. The voyage would also try to look at the aquatic whole – oceans, rivers, rain, ice, and snow. The TV films should provide revelations about the links between natural ecosystems and humanity, about the present and future consequences for all life if these interdependencies were ignored. "We are going to examine marine life in the Sea of Cortés, the effects of atomic tests at Bikini, Eniwetok and Mururoa atolls, earthquakes and volcanoes in the Pacific, the fate of Australia's Great Barrier Reef, the Andaman islands in the Bay of Bengal stretching from the western tip of Indonesia up toward Burma."

If asked to what he attributed his enormous success, he had short and long answers that were intertwined and had to do with his filmmaker's ability to hold, inform, and entertain an audience and to put across a message. "If *The Silent World* was such a success when it came out, it was, of course, because people were beginning to have a feeling for their surroundings and a curiosity about the sea depth that no one had seen before, but it was also because I knew how to make a movie."

He believed he was one of those who had pointed out the cause and effect of people and environment. Too many people, for example, impoverished the environment. He would wish everybody a life as fulfilling and interesting as his, but quality of life implied a variety of choices and that, in an ever more crowded world, was becoming difficult. If you didn't know what to value, how could you have a richly satisfying life? Urban children had never seen a wild animal, he said. "They don't know what it is. And that is a thought that makes me shudder. In order to want to protect something, you must know what it is. If most kids have never experienced wild animals, how can they learn to love them, and come to see them as life that enriches their own, as an incomparable asset?"

Humanity will have to learn to think in eons and to establish rank and order in its needs. "The earth is probably two-and-a-half billion years old, and we know that in about five billion years life will be impossible on earth because the sun is going to expand and burn everything. So we're about a third of the way in the life of the earth, which means that if we take care of it, humans can plan for several billion years on this wonderful planet. Things do change, of course. The world is not what it was. We must plan long-term. Accordingly, to save it for our distant children, we must establish four priorities. The first one is peace. We know it is difficult, but there must be ways to live in peace other than leaving it in the hands of governments."

The second priority is limiting our own number. "Today the rich nations are getting richer and the poor poorer. The rich nations have stable populations, the poor nations are a time bomb. We must find a solution even if this is not something we can resolve immediately. The third problem is education. Because if we want to do something for peace and population, for the Third world and the environment, we have to demonstrate the problem.

"The fourth priority is the environment. If I let my reason speak I am not optimistic. I don't see any possibility to change people, the people who make the decisions. However, I believe that by action, faith, and hope we can achieve something. Each one of us must do something to fight for peace, for better cooperation among people, for education and the environment."

The urge to inform and to alert was behind his keen interest in satellite broadcasting. The 1985 debut of TDF-1 and SES-1 direct broadcasting, giving Europeans their first

425

chance to pick up programs from individual dish antennas, had him negotiate with the French deregulated broadcast industry before anybody was on the air. Jean-Michel joined former President Jimmy Carter, Worldwatch Institute's Lester Brown, and U.N. Undersecretary General Yasushi Akashi on the board of a Turner-inspired Better World Society, to produce global programming on the environment, nuclear arms control, and overpopulation.

If the Cousteau Society had a mission, its founder believed, it was to make information – educational video, filmstrips, print – available on a worldwide basis. "I am very proud that the society is possibly the only existing organization that (1) is interested in global aspects of the environment – we are not really interested in local problems – and (2) is not negative. We try never to say no, but to offer alternatives, even though counterproposals require a tremendous amount of manpower and work."

Here again he was in the vanguard. Virtually all leaders of the environmental movement agreed that more time, effort, and money would have to be spent on international and global issues in coming years, that people would be fooling themselves if

426

they believed it was enough to solve local or national problems.

To offer help meant to listen first. Cousteau found wisdom among the most desperate people. In Haiti's Baradères peninsula, a subsistence farmer told him he was fully aware that he couldn't cut an entire mangrove tree for firewood to cook his family's food, that he could cut one big branch one year, another branch the next, to make the tree last. The man said he wished he didn't have to cut it at all. A few years earlier in Jamaica, Cousteau met an old man who knew he was overfishing, that by using a too fine mesh net he was eliminating the young fish and compromising his children's future substenance. The man had tears in his eyes. He knew what he was doing, but he had to eat.

In Haiti, the Cousteau Society suggested temporary alternatives while trees got a chance to grow back – donated supplies of charcoal, individual solar stoves – to make the dispossessed stop trading today for tomorrow. What excuse did the industrial world have for refusing to purify emissions or cut down on chemicals in farming, when we knew our children would have to deal with these problems? With a smile, JYC brushed his only cloudy objections away.

Human beings, fortunately, were endowed with a knack for assessing danger and an ability to imagine ingenious solutions to the most complex puzzles.

"We don't ring ecological alarm bells. We don't say things are desperate when we aren't sure. For example, the ozone layer is not noticeably diminished. The Atomic Energy Agency in Vienna runs a marine laboratory, the only one, and it's in Monaco, and I am one of the four people controlling it. For the moment there is no increase in the radioactivity of the oceans."

The breadth of his globalism sometimes saved him from parochial holier-than-thou indignation. There is something ridiculous for Europeans, living on a virtually ruined continent, to flay away at Brazil's rapid industrialization, or for Americans, who had exterminated their own continent's native peoples, to try to pick apart the FUNAI program. The violence toward the Amazon Indians had ended, he believed, although their culture was dying and their knowledge of the forest was being lost.

There were blind spots, residuial hang-overs of the white man's burden and explorer's interest in the exotic, that jarred with the universal egalitarian ideals of a global humanism. Strange tales of strange people fascinate, whether told by the village shaman about the creatures over the next hillock or by TV cameras in Antartica. Jean-Michel could mount a heroic public relations appeal to bring a Jivaro chieftain of the threatened uplands of the Amazon to meet the president of Peru. He could report on Yakunda tribesmen in the Colombian jungle stoned out of their minds on cocaine as their elders sang for hours of God's award of coca to those who "will use it properly." But would he film – and we be interested in – the "contamination" from the outside world of our local exurbia, or give anthropological dignity to local cocaine junkies? Twenty-five years ago you could meet old people in the Vallée de Chevreuse who had never been to Paris. Today, the Valée is a dormitory suburb of Paris. Changes of seismic proportions must have happened between the milking of the last cow and the gangs of *loubards* snatching purses among the high-rise projects. Current American and Canadian policy toward the continent's remaining native people, he admitted, was not only schizoid but perhaps the greatest hinderance to their reaching dignity and the mainstream. Funds were voted to well-meaning scholars who could help Eskimos keep, and on occasion relearn, native folklore and speech, while cuts in education budgets in Los Angeles and Vancouver forced the children of Asian immigrants into swim-or-sink assimilation.

Cousteau could get sentimental in good company. When old faces assembled and a good bottle circulated, he remembered other times around the long table in the mess – Christmas in Antarctica, the successful end to the first Conshelf. All questions about his personal life appalled him. He was not interested in the concept of accomplishment. He was merely doing what he thought was right, and in any case, the more disinterested a person was, the more sensitive he or she became to the shimmering instances that mattered, to the deep undertow of life's meaning. The joy of living was to expand oneself, to extend one's reach. One of his fascinations is to try to assess the real value of truth. "When I reason, when people reason, they come most of them to logical absurdities. I find poets closer to the truth than mathematicians or politicians. They have visions that are not only fantasy. They are visions that are, for some reason they cannot explain, an inspiration that guides them and brings them by the hand, or by the pen, closer to the truth than anybody else. I believe we should follow the poets more than anybody else in life. It's the light. It's the star we should be guided by. Poetry, and poetry under all its forms. Poetry in anything you are doing. The only remedies to the logical absurdities are utopias, reasonable utopias."

Questions about the past could elicit sharp retorts. From the hindsight of fifty years, he said, his training at the Naval Academy was nothing more than brainwashing "to teach me to be a better killer." Perhaps the navy also had its doubts about this gunnery officer who caressed dolphins and believed humans were just one more animal. "If there is a God and He's interested in life, He's just as interested in a French poodle as in you."

Cousteau's love of animals translated into a commitment to all manner of beasts and to a belief that animals were a measure of human sensitivity. It had always depressed him to see animals in captivity and he created an incident in 1973 by refusing to pose for photographers with the penguins in the Detroit Zoo. Perhaps the most intense three days aboard the *Calypso* had to do with the rescue attempt in 1970 of a grounded baby whale in a Baja California bay. The two-ton calf was brought on board in a net litter and expert Ted Walker, Philippe, Jacques Renoir, and the rest of the crew tried to save it. Some crew members were overly emotional, some pretended indifference but sneaked peeks to see if the baby was still breathing, while the coolest man came up with the most ingenious and effective suggestions. Nothing moved the thirty men more than the slow agony of the calf they wanted to give life. The sea was unforgiving and Cousteau and his men had seen death before, yet they remained in a trancelike state of fascination until the baby's death. Cousteau felt that death was especially impressive when embodied in these giants, not built on a human scale yet breathing, loving, and suffering like us; though different, their lives and ours were finally not distinct. Swimming with big groupers he had wondered if they didn't know more about us than we do about them. It was only when we began to admit that severely retarded humans had rights that we understood we had a moral obligation to treat them. When would we begin to bestow a moral rank on animals?

"We're absolutely opposed to the exploitation of dolphins turned into circus clowns, to zoos where animals turn and turn in cages, but we're for parks and reservations." He used the first-person plural to include himself, the society, and conservationists who were beginning to stress the economic rather than the moral imperatives for saving species. Rare animals had the irritating habit of living in poor countries, so the people in those countries must somehow be given a vested interest in seeing wildlife preserved. "We're for ranching. Papua New Guinea has got the right idea regarding the $100 million worldwide trade in exotic butterflies such as the huge swallowtail butterflies. Ranching means the animals spend some of their lives in the wild, as opposed to farming where they were totally under human control. Instead of being hunters of swallowtails, the Papuans can become ranchers, setting a few acres aside where they cultivate plants that attract the butterflies to come and feed and lay their eggs. Their caterpillars grow on the cultivated plants and are collected, as chrysalises, by the villagers while others are allowed to escape. In the oceans let's go for pisciculture, fish farming, instead of the kind of blind fishing that slowly empties the seas. If one day humans will have to eat dolphins, all right, let's go for ranching dolphins."

He was persuaded that the future belonged to sunny lands. He would not be against nuclear power if the problem of waste was solved, but in the long run solar energy was the logical solution. "Look at the English. Its wealth was coal, but coal is finished. The United States has oil, and its reserves are running down. We're drawing down everything on the planet. One day only solar energy will be seen as truly inexhaustible and sun-drenched semi-tropical and tropical countries will be rich."

Cousteau spent a third of his time in the United States, a third in France, and a third aboard the *Calypso* or *Alcyone*, he said, making it all sound easy. While most people needed days to recover from polar flights, he ignored time changes and spent airborne hours sipping endless cups of tea and tearing through stacks of magazines and books, ripping out what he could use. He tried to keep up with politics and engineering, films and plays (which he never went to see but wanted to know the critics' opinion), and said the fascinating thing about our time was that despite the alleged overspecialization, it was much easier to know about everything that was going on than it was in Leonardo da Vinci's time. He claimed he never read novels and considered fiction little more than a sickly display of the self, but could quote Victor Hugo and Alexander Pope.

While he believed in popular groundswells and in people's innate sense of self-preservation, he had no faith in politics. All too often he had seen political leaders back away from environmental problems deeply inherent in our system of production, such as the continued use of pesticides and chemical fertilizers. Intimates called him politically unsuspecting and guileless, a naîf who had a knack for landing just right in a political minefield. He had little use for the politicians' handmaidens, the technocrats. Every time an accident occurred in the nuclear industry, and before anybody had any clear idea of the consequences, technocrats announced *urbi et orbi* that there was absolutely no danger.

There was a measure of irony in the fact that environmental groups were seeking the middle ground he so naturally occupied and, still more astounding, were beginning to agree that scientific and technological solutions were perhaps the only answers to the exponential and catastrophic destruction of our environment that science and technology had wrought. Aplying economic theory to nature – *Cousteau/Mississippi* won a 1985 Emmy as "outstanding information special" – was part of the "deep ecology" which held that all things – animals, insects, and plants – had intrinsic value and a right to existence for their

435

own sake, not because of their value to humans.

Europe's committed ecologists, known as the "greens," talked increasingly of "decoupling" their movements from left-of-center politics. A person should be able to love the forest without having to join antinuclear rallies. American environmentalists, who saw virtually no chance of a Green party emerging in the United States, believed their future was in veering away from single issues toward programs that joined economic and social needs with environmental concerns. Even if it meant that some of the passion and inspired amateurism would be lost, ecologists leaders saw a need to upgrade theprofessionalism of their organizations, to have more scientists and engineers join their ranks. Focusing on the leak of the day was not going to tame the process that created 1,000 new chemicals a year – the "toxic tornado," as the National Audobon Society called it – nor come up with answers to the sophisticated arguments of the industry lobby that concerns for the environment were exaggerated or had already been taken care of. Next on the ecology agenda, its leaders said, was the need to address the underlying issue of such hazards as toxic waste, for example, to discuss ownership and equity and who should make the decisions. Fearless ecologists could even see the role of capital in our society come up for environmental review.

Jacques Cousteau is a poet of sight – and second sight – and has a gift for exploring the universal, instinctive drive deeply ingrained in all living beings. He is a poet who is good at summarizing scientific information and at focusing on the vitality of wildlife, the delights of a blue planet. As an explorer his love of life transcends the boundaries of species. Cousteau is fascinated by the idea, now back in vogue among scientists, that our nearer relatives among the mammals have an operative intelligence. He is a filmmaker of lilting mediation, a storyteller with an eye for the mysteries within, who knows how to pull at us in unexpected ways.

He is an explorer who cannot wait to get up in the morning. The focus of his observations, empathy, and wonder is the instincts of creatures big and small, the instincts to live – to love, to adapt, to survive. Humans tend to forget, to avert their eyes from their own cosmic solitude, their coming into the world and dying alone. Cousteau can marvel at the joy of penguin couples finding each other on an arctic rock after a long separation, or the love duet of a mother whale and her calf, and he can suggest humans fool themselves with love and friendship in order to escape loneliness. He doesn't mind his own contradictions, but cannot see why utopian goals shouldn't be pursued.

His lasting love is the sea, which he hopes he will never have to give up, the ocean that has never betrayed him. His long life gives him perspective and depth of vision. Cousteau has established ties with marine life whose existence, before him, was barely suspected, and with the camera he first fell in love with as an adolescent, has shown up the prodigious means of life in the sea.

Although he is not a scientist, he is what scientists need most, a popularizer who not only speaks their jargon and knows how to make it accessible, but can convey the sense of adventure and the vision that inspires. He is not easy to replicate. A young Cousteau, as Raymond Vaissière says, is not easy to conceive because people endowed with an understanding of both the details and their sum are a rarity. Few people have his gift of vision – with provocative excesses at times – his ardent and vast intelligence.

As he sails toward new austral horizons, we must imagine him fulfilled, ready to die standing up, as he has said, meaning no doubt at the helm of the beloved *Calypso*. With his deep blue eyes behind the granny glasses, the wispy white hair, skin weathered and brown against the turtleneck, the haughty beak and chiseled profile known to hundreds of millions, he is the man who taught us that it is our responsibility to learn a bit more about the world.

His world as a unique witness to our time makes us understand a number of bedrock puzzles and see the bigger questions facing the family of man. His ardent wish is that we will finally learn to use our intelligence and to see ourselves as a part of a whole as he has done.

APPENDIX

BOOKS BY JACQUES-YVES COUSTEAU

All original French titles were published in Paris. Unless otherwise indicated, all English-language versions are published in New York.

Par dix-huit mètres de fond: Histoire d'un film. Durel, 1946.

La plongée en scaphandre. Elsevir, 1950.

Le monde du silence (with Frédéric Dumas). Hachette, 1953; *The Silent World;* Harper Bros., 1953.

La Mer (with Jacques Bourcart). Larousse, 1953.

Book of Fishes. Washington, D.C.: National Geographic Society, 1958.

Captain Cousteau's Underwater Treasury (with James Dugan). Harper, 1959.

The Living Sea (with James Dugan). Harper & Row, 1962.

Bibliographie de la sismique marine. Monaco: Oceanographic Institute, 1964.

Le monde sans soleil. Hachette, 1964; *World Without Sun* (ed. James Dugan), Harper & Row, 1965.

Les requins (with Philippe Cousteau). Flammarion, 1970; *The Shark: Splendid Savage of the Sea,* Garden City, N.Y., Doubleday, 1970.

La vie et la mort des coraux (with Philippe Diolé). Flammarion, 1971; *Life and Death in a Coral Sea,* Doubleday, 1971.

440

Un trésor englouti (with Philippe Diolé). Flammarion, 1971.

Diving for Sunken Treasure, Doubleday, 1972.

Nos amies les baleines (with Philippe Diolé). Flammarion, 1972; *The Whale: Mighty Monarch of the Sea*, Doubleday, 1972.

Pieuvres, la fin d'un malentendu (with Philippe Diolé). Flammarion, 1973; *Octopus and Squid: The Soft Intelligence*, Doubleday, 1973.

Trois aventures de la Calypso (with Philippe Diolé). Flammarion, 1973; *Three Adventures: Galápagos, Titicaca, the Blue Holes*, Doubleday, 1973.

Encyclopédie Cousteau, le monde des oceans, Robert Laffont, 20 vol. *The Ocean World*, vols. 1–7, World Publishing; vols. 8–20, Abrams. English titles: (1) *Oasis in Space;* (2) *The Act of Life;* (3) *Quest for Food;* (4) *Window in the Sea;* (5) *The Art of Motion;* (6) *Attack and Defense;* (7) *Invisible Messages;* (8) *Instinct and Intelligence;* (9) *Pharoahs of the Sea;* (10) *Mammals of the Sea;* (11) *Provinces of the Sea;* (12) *Man Reenters the Sea;* (13) *A Sea of Legends; Inspirations from the Sea;* (14) *The Adventure of Life;* (15) *Outer and Inner Space;* (16) *The White Caps;* (17) *Riches of the Sea;* (18) *Challenges of the Sea;* (19) *The Sea in Danger;* (20) *Guide to the Sea and Index.*

Compagnons de plongée (with Philippe Diolé). Flammarion, 1974; *Diving companions: Sea Lion, Elephant Seal, Walrus*, Doubleday, 1974.

Les dauphins et la liberté (with Philippe Diolé). Flammarion, 1975; *Dolphins*, Doubleday, 1975.

Saumons, castors et loutres (with Yves Paccalet). Flammarion, 1978.

Calypso, 26 ans d'exploration scientifique des mers (with

441

Alexis Sivirine). Laffont, 1978; *Cousteau's Calypso,* Abrams, 1980.

La vie au bout du monde (with Yves Paccalet). Flammarion, 1979.

Les surprises de la mer (with Yves Paccalet). Flammarion, 1980.

A Bill of Rights for Future Generations. Myrin Institute, 1980.

Almanach Cousteau de l'environnement (with Cousteau Society staff). Laffont, 1981; *The Cousteau Almanac of the Environment: An Inventory of Life on a Water Planet,* Doubleday, 1981.

Français on a volé ta mer (with J. Jacquier). Laffont, 1981.

Le destin du Nil (with Yves Paccalet). Flammarion, 1982.

La Planète océan, Encyclopédie science et exploration. Laffont, 1982; *The Ocean World,* Abrams, 1979.

Fortunes de mer (with Yves Paccalet). Flammarion, 1983.

Cousteau's Amazon Journey (with Mose Richards). Abrams, 1984.

NATIONAL GEOGRAPHIC
ARTICLES BY JACQUES-YVES COUSTEAU

Fish Men Discover a New World Undersea" October 1952.

"Fish Men Discover a 2,200-year-old Greek Ship," January 1954.

"To the Depths of the Sea of Bathyscaph," July 1954.

"Diving Through an Undersea Avalanche," April 1955.

"*Calypso* Explores for Underwater Oil," August 1955.

"*Calypso* Explores an Undersea Canyon" (Romanche trench), March 1958.

"Dilving Saucer Takes to the Deep," April 1960.

"Inflatable Ship [*Amphitrite*] Opens Era of Airborne Undersea Expeditions," July 1961.

"At Home in the Sea," April 1964.

"The World of Jacques-Yves Cousteau," April 1966.

"Working for Weeks on the Sea Floor," April 1966.

"The Ocean," December, 1981.

FILMS BY JACQUES-YVES COUSTEAU

Shorts

Par dix-huit mètres de fond, 1942; *Epaves,* 1943; *Paysages du Silence,* 1944; *Les phoques du Sahara,* 1948; *Une Plongée du "Rubis"; Autor d'un récif; Carnet de plongées,* 1949; *Station 307,* 1955; *La Fontaine de Vaucluse; La galère engloutie,* 1957; *Vitrines sous la mer; Histoire d'un poisson rouge,* 1958; Expérience Précontinent I: *La Maison au fond de la mer; Les Océanautes,* 1962.

Full-length Features

Le monde du silence (The World of Silence), 1956; *Le monde sans soleil (World Without Sun),* 1965; *The World of Jacques-Yves Cousteau (Expérience Précontinent III),* 1965; *Voyage au bout du monde (Voyage to the Edge of the World)* (Antarctica), 1975.

Films made for Television

The unvaried French overall title, *L'Odyssée sous-marine de l'Equipe Cousteau* comprised 60 titles in 1986.

On U.S. television, they break down into the ABC, PBS, and TBS series: the 36 titles of *The Undersea World of Jacques-Yves Cousteau* (ABC); 12 episodes in the *Oasis in Space* and *Cousteau Odyssey* series that also include four films coproduced with Canada's National Film Board (PBS and TBS) and, following the *Cousteau/Amazon* quartet (TBS), *Rediscovery of the World* (TBS).

With English titles in parenthesis when applicable, the telefilms are (1) *Les requins (Sharks);* (2) *La jungle du corail (The Savage World of the Coral Jungle);* (3) *Les tortues d'Europa;* (4) *Rorquals et cachalots (Whales);* (5) *Pepito et Cristobal (The Unexpected Voyage of Pepito and Cristobal);* (6) *Le trésor englouti (Sunken Treasure);* (7) *Les mystéres du lac Titicaca (The Legend of Lake Titicaca);* (8) *Les baleines du désert (The Desert Whales);* (9) *La nuit des calmars (The Night of the Squid);* (10) *Le retour des éléphants de mer (The Return of the Sea Elephants)* (11) *Ces incroyables machines plongeantes (Those Incredible Diving Machines);* (12) *La mer vivante (The Water Planet);* (13) *La tragédie des saumons rouges (The Tragedy of the Red Salmon);* (14) *Le lagon des navires perdus (Lagoon of the Lost Ships);* (15) *Les dragons des Galápagos (The Dragons of Galápagos;* (16) *Cavernes englouties (Secrets of the Sunken Cave);* (17) *Le sort des loutres de mer (The Unsinkable Sea Otter);* (18) *Les dernières sirenes (The Forgotten Mermaids);* (19) *Pieuvres, petites pieuvres (Octopus);* (20) *Le chant des dauphins (The Sound of Dolphins);* (21) *500 millions d'années sous les mers (500 Million Years Beneath the Sea);* (22) *Le sourire du morse (The Smile of the Walrus);* (23) *Hippo, hippo (Hippo!);* (24) *La baleine qui chante (The Singing Whale);* (25) *La glace et le feu (South to Fire and Ice);* (26) *Le vol du pingouin (The Flight of*

444

Penguins); (27) *La vie sous un océan de glace (Beneath the Frozen World);* (28) *Blizzard à Esperanza (Blizzard at Hope Bay);* (29) *La vie au bout du monde (Life at the End of the World);* (30) *L'hiver des castors (Beavers of the North Country);* (31) *Les fous du corail (The Coral Divers of Corsica);* (32) *Les requins dormeurs du Yucatán (The Sleeping Sharks of Yucatán);* (33) *Coups d'ailes sous la mer;* (34) *Au coeur des récifs des Caraibes (Mysteries of the Hidden Reef);* (35) *Le poisson qui a gobé Jonah? (The Fish That Swallowed Jonah);* (36) *La marche des langoustes (The Incredible March of the Spiny Lobsters);* (37) *L'énigme du Britannic (Calypso's Search for the Britannic);* (38) *Le butin de Pergame sauvé des eaux;* (39) *A la recherche de l'Atlantide I (Calypso's Search for Atlantis, Part I);* (40) *A la recherche de l'Atlantide II (Calypso's Search for Atlantis, Part II);* (41) *Le testament de l'île de Paques (Blind Prophets of Easter Island);* (42) *Ultimatum sous la mer (Coral Sea and Pollution);* (43) *Le sang de la mer;* (44) *Le Nil I (the Nile, Part I);* (45) *Le Nil II (The Nile, Part II);* (46) *Fortunes de mer;* (47) *Clipperton: Ile de la solitude (Clipperton Island);* (48) *Sang chaud dans la mer (The Warm-Blooded Sea);* (49) *Les pièges de la mer;* (50) *Du grand large aux grands lacs (St. Lawrence);* (51) *Au pays des mille rivières;* (52) *La rivière enchantée;* (53) *Message d'un monde perdu;* (54) *Ombres fuyantes;* (55) *Le fleuve de l'or (Cousteau/Amazon I);* (56) *Un avenir pour l'Amazonie (Cousteau/Amazon II);* (57) *Tempête de neige sur la jungle (Snowstorm in the Jungle);* (58) *Cousteau/Mississippi* (two hours); (59) *Riders of the Wind;* (60) *Mes premiers soixante-quinze ans (Cousteau: The First 75 Years);* (61) *Haiti (Haiti).*

445

MEDALS AWARDED IN FRANCE AND ABROAD

France

Croix de Guerre avec palmes, 2 citations

1946   Chevalier de la Légion d'honneur, au titre de la Résistance

1953   Chevalier du Mérite agricole

1958   Commandeur du Mérite sportif

1959   Commandeur de l'Ordre du Mérite pour la recherche et l'invention

1960   Officier dans l'Ordre des Arts et des lettres

1963   Mérite civique

1964   Officier de la Légion d'honneur, au titre de la recherche scientifique

1966   Officier du Mérite maritime

1967   Chevalier dans l'Ordre des Palmes académiques

1972   Commandeur de la Légion d'honneur

1978   Commandeur de l'Ordre des Arts et des lettres

1979   Grand Officier de l'Ordre National du Mérite

1985   Grand Croix dans l'Ordre National du Mérite

Foreign

1960   Officier de l'Ordre de Saint-Charles (Monaco)

Officier de l'Ordre de Léopold II (Belgique)

1967   Al Merito della Republica Italiana

1970   Commandeur de l'Ordre de Saint-Charles (Monaco)

TITLES AND SCIENTIFIC DISTINCTIONS

1958   Prix Berthault de l'Académie des Sciences

1961   Gold medal of the National Geographic Society, Washington

1963   Gold medal of the Royal Geographic Society, London

1965   Washburn Medal, Museum of Sciences, Boston

1968   Membre à titre étranger de Academy of Sciences of the United States

1970   Pott's medal, Franklin Institute
Doctor Honoris Causa, University of California at Berkeley and Brandeis University

1971   Grand prix d'océanographie Albert (gold medal)

1973   Grande médaille d'Or de la Société d'encouragement au progrès
Award of New England Aquarium
Prix de la Couronne d'or (Prix de la Couronne française)

1974   Manley Bendall prize (Acadèmie de Marine)
La Polena della Bravura, San Remo
Médaille d'or avec plaque "Arts-Sciences-Lettres"

1975   Membre correspondant de l'Institut hellénique d'archéologie marine

1976   International prize of the city of Cervia (Italy) pour la sauvegarde de l'environment et du territoire (environnement marin)

1977   International Environment prize, United Nations

1978   Honorary member of the Indian Academy of Sciences

1979   Honorary Doctor of Science degree, Rensselaer Polytechnic Institute and Harvard University

1980   Jean Sainteny prize
Kiwanis International Europe prize

1981   Prix "Firenze ecologia"
Prix Manley Bendall (médaille commémorative du Prince Albert Ier de Monaco)

1983   Grand Prix de vulgarisation scientifique remis par E.T.M.A. Cannes
Bruno H. Schubert Award, Frankfurt, West Germany
Doctor Honoris Causa en Science de l'environnement pres du Centre inter-facultaire of the University of Ghent (Belgium)

BIBLIOGRAPHICAL NOTES

That no autobiography has been written by Jacques-Yves Cousteau is no surprise. Cousteau has led a life so packed with adventure and achievements that any attempt to pick up the threads and arrange them into design and perspective has seemed absurd to him. Besides, he hates introspection, sentiments, looking back. Retrospection leads to oversentimentality, he maintains, to regrets and complacency. On the rare occasion when he has experienced a recurrence of past feelings – an emotion of his youth, a lost affection – he told Sara Davidson in 1972, he has felt like vomiting. What counts is this evening's setting sun, tomorrow's difficult dive. This moment, filling your lungs with this breath, is what heightens the sense of being alive.

Although Cousteau has always courted popularity and claims that sharing his explorer's adventures is the only justification for his books and films, both he and the official family try artfully to control image and projection. Of late, the sense of urgency that makes the remaining years so terribly precious to him has become another impediment.

That is, of course, the problem. There are always new projects, new concerns to which the legacy must take the back seat. Running yet another expedition has become a way of running away from the introspection that the accumulation of expeditions should foster. And finally, the family wants the transfer of power to the only surviving son to be "seamless" and, therefore, accomplished out of the limelight.

I first met Cousteau in Hollywood in 1967 when he received his third Oscar. The next meeting was in Paris when I was doing research for a book on one of Cousteau's heroes, André Malraux. As a fringe member of the Los Angeles French colony during the 1960's and 70's, I got to know Philippe. I believed a book on the world's most famous explorer would be appealing, especially if written at arm's length by someone who was an admirer but not of the Cousteau Society entourage.

If this book began with the distracted indifference of JYC himself, members of the next Cousteau generation became interested in its writing, family members who were squarely in the Cousteau history but not of it. Some of them spoke to me with candor and instead of diminishing Cousteau the man, their revelations heightened his stature as father, uncle, father-in-law, and lifelong friend.

The primary source of the factual material in this book is scores of hours of interviews, almost all tape-recorded, with over forty people. The sources and documentation supporting certain portions of the narratives are cited below:

INTRODUCTION. *TERRA AMATA.* Cousteau discussed marriage, philosophy, his aversion to introspection and the meaning of this life in his interview with Sara Davidson, *The New York Times Magazine,* Sept. 10, 1972.

1. ***SOCIÉTÉ ZIX.*** The author visited Saint-André-de-Cubzac in the fall of 1984. Figures and details of the region's winegrowing are from oenophile Svante Loefgren and the Syndicat d'initiatives. Details of the Cousteau family and Jacques-Yves and Pierre-Antoine's childhood are numerous and well-published, notably in PAC's *L'Amérique juive* (see Bibliography), *New York Times,*, Feb. 22, 1953; *Time,* March 28, 1960, and standard *Who's Who* entries. The author talked at length with Dr. Jean-Pierre Cousteau about his grandparents, Daniel and Elizabeth Cousteau, and the years with Eugene Higgins. Beth Myers, assistant archivist of Equitable furnished the data on James Hazen Hyde. *The New York Times,* July 30, 1948, carried the Eugene Higgins obituary. Clips from JYC's adolescent filmmaking were incorporated in the TBS tribute, *Cousteau; The First 75 Years,* broadcast June 23, 1985.

2. ***WILLPOWER.*** The author traced JYC's military career at the Etat-Major, Service historique of the Ministère de la Défense (Marine), Vincennes, and through the oral family history. Archivists at Air Liquide, Paris, furnished details of the Melchoir family. *Cousteau: The First 75 Years* included film clips of Jacques and Simone's first meeting and their wedding. PAC detailed his own journalistic career in several of his books. Details of his marriage and lifestyle were obtained from his

son, Dr. Cousteau. The history of the politicized Parisian press and *Je Suis Partout* is fully developed in William Shirer's *The Collapse of the Third Republic,* Herbert R. Lottman's *La Rive gauche,* and in the author's own *Malraux.*

3. **LOVE AND WAR.** Besides PAC's own prison commentaries on Paris under the Occupation, David Pryce-Jones's *Paris in the Third Reich* traces the ascent of De Brinon, Céline, PAC, as do *La Rive gauche* and Henry Coston's *Dictionnaire de la vie politique.* The archives of the Etat-Major, Service historique, Le Théâtre mediterranéen, tome ii, contains the history of the Toulon fleet from June 1940 to November 1942 in great detail including the June 13, 1940 sortie against Genoa.

4. **THE AQUALUNG.** JYC detailed the beginnings of the aqualung and his collaboration with Emile Gagnan in his first *National Geographic* article, complemented by Frédéric Dumas and Philippe Tailliez. Archivists at Air Liquide gave details of the patent and commercial agreements. The collapse of Nazi Paris and PAC's flight toward possible exile in Switzerland, arrest, and internment in Austria occupy the main part of his memoirs, *Les Lois de l'hospitalité.* James Dugan wrote of meeting JYC in wartime London in *The New York Times,* April 21, 1963.

5. **SANARY.** The author relied on Dr. Cousteau for the descriptions of the family life in Sanary in 1946 and for the details of his father's trial, conviction, and pardon. Abundant print documentation exists on the GERS minesweeping, Tailliez, JYC and the Fountain of Vaucluse

near-catastrophe, including Cousteau's *The Silent World*. PAC comments on his release and efforts to pick up his career in *Après le déluge*. Perry Miller told the author of meeting JYC and bringing his first short films to America. JYC has told of finding the *Calypso* on Malta on a number of occasions, including in his early *National Geographic* articles.

6. **"IL FAUT ALLER VOIR."** The author interviewed a number of early collaborators in Cannes and Nice, and Perry Miller in New York. Cousteau wrote about the first sea trials and expedition in *National Geographic,* in great detail in *Calypso.* Rachel Carson reviewed the book *The Silent World* in *The New York Times,* Feb. 8, 1953. Harold Edgerton wrote about his deep-sea photography work aboard the *Calypso* in *National Geographic,* April 1955.

7. **WORK AND WHALES.** The author interviewed Louis Malle in Mexico in 1966. The director has talked about his beginnings with JYC in a number of interviews, including *Film and Filming,* London, December 1975. JYC wrote on the Abu Dhabi oil expedition in *National Geographic.*

8. **FAME.** Dr. Cousteau furnhished the details of Fernande's death, his father's remarriage and last years. A number of participants were interviewed about the filming expedition of *The Silent World.* JYC and Luis Marden have published separate acounts in *National Geographic.* The film *The Silent World* was reviewed in *The New York Times,* Sept. 25, 1956, followed on Sept. 30 with a Sunday feature review, and by

Newsweek, Sept. 24, Oct. 9, 1956. The *Los Angeles Times* reported on JYC's warnings against skin-diving perils. Perry Miller gave the author the details of the post – *Silent World* business arrangements.

9. **THE GREAT DEPTHS.** The 1958 Monaco constitutional crisis was covered at length by *Nice-Matin*. Besides personal interviews in Monaco, including talks jwith André Portelatine and Raymond Vaissière and members of the Oceanographic Institute press office, the author consulted palace records and Steven Englund's *Grace of Monaco* for the history of the institute and Prince Albert. Cousteau's *Dolphins* and *Calypso* contain details of Albert Falco's dolphin hunting.

10. **THE BEGINNING OF A STRUGGLE.** Raymond Vaissière furnished the background for most of this chapter. The March 28, 1960, *Time* cover story on Cousteau described his U.S. visit that year and the new sports enthusiasm for scuba diving. JYC's first description of future undersea habitats was reported in the *Los Angeles Times,* Feb. 3, 1964.

11. **HOMO AQUATICUS.** *Newsweek* covered the October 1962 London World Congress on Underwater Activities, Oct. 29, 1962. James Dugan reported on the congress and JYC's ideas in the *New York Times Magazine,* April 21, 1963. Details of Conshelf I and II were published in *National Geographic,* New York *Daily News,* Dec. 17, 1964, Los Angeles *Herald-Examiner,* Dec. 20, 1964, and Encyclopaedia Britannica Yearbooks, 1962–66. Reviews of *World Without*

Sun appeared in Daily *Variety,* May 2, 1966, *The New Yorker,* Jan. 2, 1965. The controversial *New York Times* review of the film, JYC's answer, and Bosley Crowther's reply appeared Dec. 23, 1964, and Jan. 10, 1965. JYC brought it up again in *Sharks,* coauthored with Philippe.

12. **SHOWBIZ.** The author interviewed Bud Rifkin at length, David Wolper briefly, about the ABC-TV contract. Philippe provided details of the TV start-up. Weekly *Variety* reported the deal Feb. 22, 1967; *Nice-Matin* the *Calypso* sailing from Monaco Feb. 18, 1967. with Lawrence Schiller the author interviewed Philippe and Jan shortly after their wedding. *Good Housekeeping,* April 1974, and the *Los Angeles Times* June 26, 1977, published features on the couple. Cousteau reported on the difficulty of filming whales in *Whales.* Details of the *Calypso* crew's filmmaking techniques were culled from a number of sources, principally Philippe, Bernard Delemotte, Francis Bonfanti, and Colin Mounier.

13. **CONSCIOUSNESS.** Philippe talked to friends of his differences with his father. Rifkin told the author of both Philippe's and Jean-Michel's difficulties of striking out on their own and Dr. Cousteau of his two cousins' separate ways in Los Angeles. Philippe talked of his love of whales and growing ecological apprehensions in a lengthy interview with *Le Point,* Aug 8, 1977 and JYC about his new quest to preserve the oceans in a number of public appearances and interviews, notably *Time,* Sept. 28, 1970, *Christian Science Monitor,* Dec. 9, 1975, and in

a series of monthly letters he wrote, with the assistance of Susan Schiefelbein, in *Saturday Review* in 1976. *Nice-Matin* reported the Cousteaus' anniversary celebrations July 15, 1971. JYC's most revealing interview of the 1970's was with Sara Davidson, *New York Times Magazine*, Sept. 10, 1972. *TV Guide*, May 6, 1972, published a feature on the Cousteau expedition to Clipperton Island.

14. **DEFEATS.** The cancellation of the ABC series and JYC's switch to public television were covered by the Hollywood trade press. The author gained perspective on the cancellation in interviews with Michael Eisner and Rifkin, and in Paris, Antenne 2's Jacques Trebutat, and for the *Oasis in Space* series with Phyllis Geller in Los Angeles and Henri Colpi in Paris. Both JYC and Philippe commented on the Easter Island shooting in PBS publicity releases.

15. **BLUE PLANET.** Cousteau's evolving ideas about ecology and economics, "ecotech" and future trends were given wide exposure, including the Cousteau *Almanac* and interviews with *Westways*, September 1978, *Christian Science Monitor*, May 4, 1977, and Oct. 13, 1981. UPI from Monaco in May 1984, and *On Cable*, June 1985. Norfolk's luring of the Cousteau Society was reported in *The New York Times*, June 10, 1979. The two-part Nile programs were reviewed in the *Los Angeles Times*, Dec. 12, 1979, and Daily *Variety*, Dec. 10, 1979, after Philippe's death. The author interviewed Brice Lalonde in Paris in 1986.

16. **FATE.** Dr. Cousteau was the first family member to reach Lisbon following the PBY crash and descriptions of the wait while the body was located were largely his. Obituaries appeared in wire service dispatches and *The New York Times*, June 29, 1979. the funeral at sea was described in *Nice-Matin*, July 6, 1979. Susan Schiefelbein gave details of the months after Philippe's death in a conversation with the author and in "The Cousteau Clan" in *The Dial*, July 1982. National Film Board executives gave the Canadian reaction to the St. Lawrence series as did Delemotte and Jacques Leduc. JYC told of Delemotte's rescue of a baby whale to *Paris-Match*, Jan. 3, 1986. *Nice-Matin* covered the Oceanographic Institute's millionth visitor ceremony Dec. 22, 1983, and the Argyronète judgment, Dec. 8, 1984.

17. **WONDERMENT.** In an interview with the *Christian Science Monitor*, Oct. 13, 1981, Cousteau explained why he decided to associate with Ted Turner; *Variety* May 29, 1985 detailed the financial arrangements and payment per TV episode. The Amazon expedition received vast international coverage, beginning with a UPI dispatch from Brasylia, Jan. 9, 1982, and a *New York Times* correspondent's report from Belém on the start of the *Calypso* river voyage, May 14, 1983. Reuters, Los Angeles, interviewed JYC on the cocaine traffic, and Weekly *Variety* reviewed the *Snowstorm in the Jungle* segment Jan. 23, 1985. *Nice-Matin* reported the Pechiney-Cousteau covered by AFP, UPI, and AP: the floundering off the U.S. East Coast and

Atlantic crossing were covered by wire services. TBS Atlanta, and *Figaro Magazine,* Nov. 15, 1985. Cousteau's seventy-fifth birthday party in Washington and *Alcyone*'s New York docking were media events, covered by *The New York Times* and the Los Angeles *Times,* June 13, 1985; *Le Point,* June 17, 1985; *Time* and *People,* July 1, 1985; and *Calypso Log,* September 1985. The author interviewed Brice Lalonde, Dominique Martin, and Colin Mounier in Paris, John Boorman and Allen Pickhaver in London in January 1986.

18. ***SERENITY, NOT QUITE.*** *France-Soir* reported on the French seventy-fifth birthday celebrations and TF-1 broadcast, Dec. 30, 1985; *Tele 7-Jours,* Dec. 19, 1985; *Variety* outlined the WTBS-Cousteau accord, May 29, 1985. The author got details of the TBS release and syndication rights from TBS Atlanta and Cousteau benefactor George Montgomery, Atlanta. *Ocean Quest* was reviewed in *the New York Times* aug. 18, 1985, and *TV Guide* Aug 17, 1985. *Calypso*'s Haiti explorations were reported in *Calypso Dispatch,* October 1985, and *Calypso Log,* December 1985. New leaders for the U.S. environmentalist movement were the subject of a *New York Times* report, Nov. 29, 1985.

BIBLIOGRAPHY

Angel, Martin and Heather Angel, *Ocean Life.* London: Octopus Books, 1974.
Aron, Raymond, *Mémoires.* Paris: Julliard, 1983.

Behrman, Daniel, *The New World of the Oceans.* Boston: Little, Brown, 1969.

Burgess, Robert F., *Secret Language of the Sea.* New York: Dodd, Mead, 1981.

Clarke, Arthur and Mike Willson, *The Treasure of the Great Reef.* New York: Harper & Row, 1964.

Cousteau, Pierre-Antoine,

–, *L'Amérique juive.* Paris: France, 1942.

–, *Hugothérapie,* Paris: Ethéel, 1944.

–, *Mines de rien,* Ethéel, 1944.

–, *Après le déluge,* Paris: Librairie française, 1956.

–, *Les Lois de l'hospitalité,* Librairie française, 1959.

–, *En ce temps-là,* Librairie française, 1959.

de Gaulle, Charles, *The Complete War Memoirs.* New York, Simon & Schuster, 1964.

Dugan, James, *Man Under the Sea.* New York: Harper & Bros., 1956.

Englund, Steven, *Grace of Monaco: An Interpretative Biography.* Garden City, N.Y.: Doubleday, 1984.

Heller, Gerhard, *Un Allemand à Paris, 1940–44.* Paris: Seuil, 1981.

Idyll, C. P., ed., *Exploring the World Oceans.* New York: Simon & Schuster, 1964.

Iverson, Genie, *Jacques Cousteau.* New York: Putnam, 1976.

Marine Nationale, *Le Théâtre mediterranéen;* tome ii, 25 juin 1940–8 novembre 1942; Vincennes; Ministère de la Marine, Service historique, 1960.

Masson, Philippe, *Histoire de la Marine.* Paris, Limoges: Lavanzelle, 1983.

Pryce-Jones, David, *Paris in the Third Reich.* New York: Holt, Rinehart and Winston, 1980.

Shirer, William L., *The Collapse of the Third Republic.* New York: Simon & Schuster, 1969.

Simon, Kate, *Fifth Avenue, A Very Social History*. New York: Harcourt Brace Jovanovich, 1978.

Toffler, Alvin, *The Third Wave*. New York: William Morrow, 1980.